By MARGUERITE TJADER

MOTHER ELISABETH

The Resurgence of the Order of Saint Birgitta

HERDER AND HERDER
New York • St. Louis • San Francisco • Düsseldorf
London • Mexico • Sydney • Toronto

123456789BPBP798765432

Library of Congress Cataloging in Publication Data

Tjader, Marguerite.
    Mother Elisabeth; the resurgence of the Order of St. Birgitta.

    1. Hesselblad, Maria Elisabeth, 1870–1957.   2. Birgittines.
I. Title.
BX4705.H564T58   255'.979 [B]   72-3010
ISBN 0-07-073812-2

Contents

Preface

"YOU have promoted the glory of God by writing down this extraordinary vocation," wrote a famous Jesuit astronomer to Maria Elisabeth Hesselblad, better known as Mother Elisabeth. "This Ms. must remain a document in your Order, and its value will increase with time."

Father Hagen had asked Mother Elisabeth to make a record of her life and it is the core of this book. Sections from it have been set off to make it easily recognizable.

We are also indebted to Oskar Eklund, a devoted personal friend of Mother Elisabeth, for his contribution to the early part of this story, namely, his firsthand account in Swedish of Mother Elisabeth entitled *The Most Remarkable Woman in Rome.*

The title was taken from a remark of Cardinal Merry del Val concerning the simple Swedish woman who brought new life into the medieval Order of St. Birgitta, and restored Birgitta's House in Rome to Swedish hands.

Birgitta is to Sweden what Joan of Arc is to France, for it was she who first gave her own land world fame ("That little land so far North that further North it is impossible to dwell," according to an old chronicle). And it was her great double monasteries, spread throughout Europe, that brought Sweden into the ranks of culture-spreading nations, in the fourteenth and fifteenth centuries. She did not live to see her own Order flourish, but it was from this House in Rome that she prepared the way, nursed the sick, took in pilgrims from Scandinavian countries, and lived that intense, spiritual life which is reflected in her *Revelations* and in the records of the Swedish priests of her household, the distinguished scholars, Petrus Magnus and Petrus of Alvastra.

When she died in her House in Rome, she was already considered a saint, and her body was carried in procession back to Sweden. The House was first guarded by priests of her Order —but it had a strange history and was finally lost to any Northern influence.

It was only in 1931 that it was restored to the Daughters of St. Birgitta through the amazing perseverance of another Swedish woman—Mother Elisabeth.

"Behind this accomplishment lies a life so filled with courage, so brimming over with faith, with sacrifice, with adventure, that it is a wonder that no one has recorded it sooner." So wrote Oskar Eklund as he finished his own narrative some years ago.

It may seem incongruous to write about the Mother of a religious order in this day and age, when Sisters are abandoning traditional ways and habits, or fleeing like the proverbial rats from the rocking (though not sinking) ship of the Church.

But change is the law of nature, the rhythm of history; tumult, decline, resurgence, triumph, and decline again—the wheel of human life. Some Christians have made a symbol of the globe, surmounted by a small Cross: *Stat Crux dum volvitur orbis* (the Cross stands while the world revolves).

So the meaning of certain lives, like works of art or manifestations of truth, stands out, defying time. May it be so with Mother Elisabeth and the work she accomplished through her suffering and love.

Chapter I

Origins

MARIA Elisabeth Hesselblad was born in the village of Foglavik, province of Västergötland, on June 4, 1870.

It was the eve of Pentecost, a time of peace and expectancy after the long winter; Swedish spring, filled with the twitter of birds in the endless twilight; blossoms of fruit trees and wild-flowers alive in the eerie white night.

When Maria was grown, her mother told her of a strange incident:

> When I was born, the old nurse took me, quite naked, and placed me on the hearth-stone; my mother on seeing this, asked in astonishment: "Why do you lay my tender babe on the cold stone?" "This child needs to be hardened in time," replied the old nurse. "She will have to go through great trials in her life."

Indeed, her words proved prophetic.

Maria's parents were August Robert Hesselblad and Maria Daag. They were middle-class country people who had a hard time supporting the thirteen children who were born to them. Maria was their first daughter.

Before Maria was of school age, her father moved his family to Falun in Dalarne, in an attempt to better their condition. But his health failed and their life was increasingly difficult.

Maria was bright and quick, and eager to help. She had a readiness to talk and act, which is often said to be typical of those born in Västergötland, the first province to be touched by the beginnings of Christian culture coming from England and Denmark.

In Dalarne, she was influenced by that genuine Swedish quality, mystic and poetic, which lives in the region today. Here she acquired that singing cadence of speech and accent which she kept throughout her life. And while people who leave their native land often forget their own language, or speak it faultily, losing their original accent, Maria Elisabeth, who left Sweden at the age of sixteen, until she died at eighty-six, spoke a pure and genuine Swedish, without the slighest error, although she returned to Sweden only rarely.

Her family had moved because of financial difficulties. As Oskar Eklund has said: "They had never been rich in money, but they had the treasure of a happy and healthy family life of the old-fashioned sort; a love for their children so great that it inspired their love and respect in return. Maria had these marvelous gifts for her heritage; love of her family; love of home; love of her country; and besides these, a great courage and a very strong will."

Another trait, common to her family and to her time, was the strong strain of religious feeling which cannot be explained without an understanding of Sweden in those days.

Scandinavians in general, and particularly Swedes, seem to have a natural tendency towards psychic experience, or extrasensory perception. Almost every Swedish family has its ghost story to relate, or examples of premonition or mental telepathy. This proclivity also makes them sensitive to religious and mystical experience; and at the turn of the century, Sweden was caught up in a vast swirl of religious movements.

From the time of the Reformation until 1860, the Swedish State Church had reigned supreme in the field of religion. It was forbidden by law to hold any religious gatherings not connected with the Lutheran establishment, even in private homes. If one did not fulfull one's parish duties, one risked being escorted to church by the police. But after these restrictions were lifted, fires of religious activity broke out everywhere; it was much like the revivals in England at the time of John Wesley or George Fox.

Evangelists appeared and preached a free Gospel, converting

2

many and gathering their own followers into sects which varied in their teachings about salvation or communion; but all were marked by great fervor and a desire to follow Christ by lives of self-denial and service. Most of the "Free-Churches" active in Sweden today have their origins in those times.

Maria Elisabeth Hesselblad was then twelve years old; she must have known of these movements, since she was a naturally serious child and ready to listen to religious discussions among her elders.

She spoke of friends of her father's, or relatives, who sat around in their home for many hours discussing religious matters. Her family regularly attended the Lutheran Church, but felt quite free to question and explore all points of view.

Maria was drawn to supernatural thoughts. She loved to read the Bible, and formed the habit of reading it every day—another practice which never left her.

A profound experience of these early years was Maria's Confirmation and First Communion. She describes it in her *Notes* as follows:

I remember reading at that time St. John, Chapter VI, verses 51–52, believing in the Real Presence of Our Lord in the Sacred Host. With great earnestness for a whole year, I prepared myself carefully for my First Communion, and when the great day came, I certainly thought it was Our Lord I was going to receive. The graces vouchsafed to me were certainly wonderful; I felt so overcome, and such a great sinner, that I begged to be left alone the rest of the day, which I spent in praying and weeping before Our Lord. This was the only Communion I received in the Lutheran Church. Did Our Lord perform the miracle of giving Himself to His believing child? (I believe that He did.)

I had a great love for my studies at school, for learning and for art. And at the age of sixteen, I had dreams of an altogether different life from what God's Providence had destined me. Family adversities and what the world would call misfortunes became for me the stepping-stones to a life in closer union with Our Lord and made me, when only a child in years, look at life from a most earnest and serious point of view.

Because of her deep nature, and her proclivity toward mystical experience, Maria, from the very first, sought to know the

Truth, and there was no easy way for her to understand or dismiss such religious movements as were defying the State Church.

Many people—among them some of her school friends—went to a strange variety of chapels, mission halls, or prayer-meetings in private homes, wherever the new sects assembled. She had pondered over the words of Jesus: "Other sheep I have that are not of this flock, but even those I must bring; and they will hear my voice and there will be one flock and one shepherd."

In her *Notes,* Mother Elisabeth described her young dismay and confusion:

When quite a small child and going to school, seeing my schoolmates being taken to many different churches, I began to wonder which was the real, true fold because I had read in my New Testament that there should be "One Shepherd and One Fold." I often prayed to be guided to this one fold and remember especially on one occasion when walking under the big pine trees in my native land, how I looked up into the sky and said: "Dear Father in Heaven, show me where is the one true fold that you want us all to be in."

I felt a wonderful peace coming into my soul and there seemed to be a voice that answered: "Yes, my child, one day I will show you."

Maria Elisabeth's childhood was short and hard, for the family had kept on growing, and she had more and more duties to perform, which she tried to fulfill cheerfully. At home they called her "our wonderful Maria" and so they remembered her all their lives. She took care of her smaller sisters and brothers with great affection. "She was our little Mama," her sister wrote later. "We went to her with all our troubles, and she always had time for everything, and was always interested in everything and everyone."

Her father was ill and as his health continued to fail, it was hard for him to keep up the same standard of life. Maria suffered with her parents over this matter, and did everything to be useful at home. And all this preoccupation with her younger brothers and sisters was probably the cause of the sickness which ruined her own health for life.

She was hardly twelve years old when she had a serious ill-

4

ness which caused ulceration of the intestines. The condition progressed until she began to have internal hemorrhages. For a time the grave symptoms abated, but she was never again completely well. Many years later, Mother Elisabeth said to Oskar Eklund: "God gave me the grace very early to understand that all difficulties are sent to be overcome. With the aid of God, anything can be surmounted, but without His help, all strength is useless."

Certainly, from the start, she was endowed with a rare tendency to interpret life in spiritual terms. Speaking of her continuing physical pain she simply stated: "It helped me to subdue my naturally impatient nature."

Even at this early period, although Maria was surrounded by a religious atmosphere full of conflict, there seemed to be no doubt about the all-important issue: that one's life should be given to God. The great question was *how* best to serve Him and worship Him.

This was the real trial that Maria had to go through, for many years, of soul-searching and prayer. What was this *pure religion* which seemed to defy all organized Churches, all rituals and liturgies, particularly those of the Catholic Church, which was hardly considered seriously in Sweden of those days, except by a handful of foreigners in Stockholm?

How could one adore God in public, without the risk of being considered a Pharisee—the hypocrites that Christ Himself had denounced? If you went to church too often, it might look as if you just went to be seen. Christ had said: "But when thou prayest, enter into thy closet and when thou hast shut thy door, pray to thy Father which is in secret; and thy Father which seeth in secret, shall reward thee openly."

Did you really need to demonstrate your respect for God by attending formal, high-church services? There must have been doubt about it in Maria's soul, for even though she had experienced deep, mystical joy on the occasion of her First Communion she does not seem to have attended her own State Church thereafter.

Of course, Maria had heard of Birgitta, that remarkable

Swedish heroine who had had the courage—five hundred years before—to travel to Rome, and to stand forth and attack what was wrong in the Church of her day. This was the Catholic Church of which Maria had only a vague idea. She had heard that even before the Reformation, Swedish Christians had never followed the Popes as blindly as did the Catholics of Latin countries. Birgitta had even denounced the evils she saw within the Church, and actually predicted the Reformation. Many Swedish Lutherans were confused about this, and tried to call Birgitta a pre-reformer, like Jan Hus in Bohemia.

But such questions could hardly then have concerned Maria; she had read in school of Birgitta's pilgrimages and how she had renounced her position in Court as cousin of the Swedish King to follow God's leadings. Afterwards she had settled down in Rome and cared for the sick and needy, and had written her famous *Revelations*. Maria was full of admiration for her, and longed to travel to such distant places.

The schoolbooks of that day did not have illustrations. Everything in them was quite cut-and-dry, without fantasy. And so Maria could not have had any idea of what Birgitta's House in Rome might have looked like. Yet even at this early age she had a dream, or waking vision, of Birgitta's House. It was one of the many dreams or premonitions that she was to have throughout her life.

Perhaps Maria's experiences are common to many people who have vague intuitions about the future, or the feeling that something happens *that has happened before.* . . . But in her case, these instances were often clearly defined. She describes them in the *Notes* which she wrote down at the request of her spiritual director, years later. The first one recorded concerning Birgitta she relates as follows:

Again, when quite a child, I once saw myself in what I thought was a dream, standing in an open square where I saw the House in which St. Birgitta of Sweden had lived in Rome; especially one window on the left side attracted my attention. Next, I saw myself standing in that window and looking out—(twenty years later, a room with this very window was given to me for a cell to live in. . . .) When I was older

6

and studied the history of Sweden, this so-called dream made me feel a great interest for this place in Rome and a great desire to visit it.

What could this dream mean to Maria at that time—She had so many things to think about. She wanted to study and *become somebody;* but there was no money for this. Her father still looked for work when he could; her mother grew more and more exhausted. She pondered and prayed for a solution. Finally, a plan became clear.

These were the years when Sweden was gripped by the *fever for America.* Swedes were migrating by the hundreds; they wrote back chanting the praises of the U.S.A.—this was the land of promise; the country where anyone can make a living. Everyone said: "Go to America—you can get rich—even young girls can make lots of money."

So Maria, too, caught the fever. She could make money to send back to her father and mother and brothers and sisters— then all their dreams might become a reality.

In her *Notes,* she describes her departure quite simply:

At the age of seventeen, seeing the great difficulties my dear parents had in obtaining the necessary means for the education of my little brothers and sisters (we were ten children) I thought and thought what I could do to help them. Hearing what great opportunities there were in those days, for women in the United States, I decided, with the approval of my parents, to go there. I travelled over England to America with a party of friends of our family, and through them, got a good post.

Maria left her country only with the aim of helping others. She intended to come back soon; but it was the will of Destiny that she would never again settle down in Sweden during her long, dramatic life.

Chapter II

Out in the World

IT is hard to imagine what a voyage across the ocean meant to immigrants in Maria's time. Ships were small, overcrowded, with none of the comforts and securities of modern design. The rough seas must have been frightening to a girl of seventeen. But Maria felt safe and secure because she had always believed, from her early childhood, that God was with her and could help her with all things. In her *Notes,* she never dramatizes her own situation, and recorded only that, by the grace of God, the little band of Swedes arrived safely in the harbor of New York.

It was easy for Maria to find work through her traveling companions. She attracted the attention and good-will of all around her. She had grown quite beautiful with her regular features, sweet expression and manner. Her hair was thick and brown, swept up in a graceful knot, and her brown eyes were usually smiling and full of light.

Her first job was as a mother's helper. She worked long hours, and studied English at night, when she was barely able to stay awake. Her friends thought she was overtaxing her strength, but she was happy because she could soon begin to send modest sums home to her dear ones in Sweden.

The second summer of exhausting work in the heat of New York City was too much for her. She began to feel that her old illness was returning, yet she would not stop.

Later in life, Maria reproached herself for not being more careful. She should *not* have ruined her health in this way.

There was also pride involved; her desire to succeed and to send money home.

Finally, she could not even keep water in her stomach. As the rays of the sun fell pitilessly on the city, the thing which she feared came back: Intestinal hemorrhage; a jogging, horse-drawn ambulance rushed poor Maria to the big Roosevelt Hospital.

One of the primitive cures which was practiced in those days was the application of hot compresses. Maria came in on one of the hottest days of the summer, and was put to bed immediately in an immense ward. A hot compress was applied, early in the morning.

She lay there shaken with pain, alone and homesick, while the oppressing heat filtered through the windows into that bare dreary room, which smelled horribly of disinfectant. The hours passed slowly, and no one remembered her or the hot compress which had been placed on her abdomen. She lay forgotten, in a bath of sweat, without having the strength to move, in a heat that grew more and more suffocating. It seemed as if the strength that she had always had, completely disappeared; she was abandoned in a strange country, in this room, frightfully gray, full of pain, of fear, of sickness, and of death.

The hours passed, meals were served, but since fasting was part of her cure, no one approached her. Only near midnight, an old nurse passing by realized that this patient with an intestinal ulcer must have had a compress and that it should have been removed by now. She examined her and was surprised to find it was still there. The patient had said nothing. She was simply lying in her bath of perspiration, weak and pale, as if she were already dead.

"But you should have told them to remove it," said the nurse in a tone of reproof, and with a quick movement, she tore off the compress.

The plaster had been there too long; the skin of the abdomen was lacerated—a great, watery and bloody wound.

Left alone once more, Maria tried to hold the sheet up to

9

keep it from touching this new sore—how painful it was, this large skin wound, so deep! Maria cried with pain, but she cried out also, inside of herself, continually turning to God: It was not a lament, a cry of reproach or desperation, but a prayer: "O Lord, make me well, and if you do not want to make me entirely well, for reasons that I do not know, let me at least get well enough to take care of the weak and the sick, who need help. Lord, if you will give me the strength to stand all this, I promise to dedicate myself to the care of the suffering. Help me to help, help me so that I may be able to see that no one is abandoned, as I am now abandoned."

All night long, her prayer was raised toward God: "Lord, help me to help others." Patience and perseverance came back into her soul; she grew stronger.

The next morning, when doctors made their first rounds, they discovered that here was a serious condition. And many decades later, the daughters of Mother Elisabeth, as they took care of her in her last illness, could still see scars, the traces of this long summer night in the big hospital of New York.

Little by little her strength came back. For Maria one thing became clear—God had done what she had requested, therefore, it remained for her to do that which she had promised.

After six weeks, she was again on her feet; still weak and tired, but with her old, inflexible will. The two remaining weeks of her convalescence in the hospital gave her many opportunities to prove to herself whether she could keep her promise.

The nurses soon saw how ready she was to help in every way; so they began to make use of her in the care of their patients, and since Maria showed herself to be humble and eager to learn, she began to gain the confidence of all. The services she had to render were not always pleasant, but that only strengthened Maria's dedication and confirmed her conviction that this was the will of God for her: To serve Him in His children, the sick and the suffering.

Soon Maria was able to carry out her purpose, as she relates in her *Notes:*

10

After leaving the Roosevelt Hospital, I applied at once for entrance into the "Post Graduate Training School for Nurses" in New York. In so doing, I could combine my desire to help my little brothers and sisters and at the same time prepare myself to serve God in His sick, and I thanked Him for this providential leading. I was not yet nineteen years old.... With heart and soul, I entered upon this life which I considered like a sacred vocation, the responsibility of which I felt most deeply. My soul during these years since my first Communion, was full of uncertainties and doubts, I could not feel that I belonged to any church, but tried to look for God within my heart....

Maria's trust in God was limitless. Her faith in His closeness and guidance in human lives and destiny was firm and immovable. Of course, many of her friends advised her against this profession—"Think of your health," they said, "you can never make it!" But Maria stood fast. She was sure that this was God's will for her.

The big hospital was overcrowded. In the general wards where the young nurses were trained, cases of every sort streamed in, from sudden illnesses to injuries occurring at work or on the streets. Not far away from the hospital, the big Catholic cathedral of *Saint Patrick's* was being built, and almost every day, workers were brought in that had fallen from its scaffolds. Maria was ready to take on any case—old, broken men, or boys wild with fear and pain—but she could not help thinking, "*Why* did the Catholics have to build such a huge church?"

In her own *Notes,* Maria gives an account of some of her first cases, some very puzzling to the young Swedish girl with her Lutheran background:

On entering the Training School, it so happened that I was sent to the Roosevelt Hospital (which was at that time, served by nurses from the Post Graduate Hospital) and to the same ward (The Woman's Medical) where I had been a patient myself the year before. The Head Nurse was a big, strong Canadian woman of German extraction. I was given various little things to do, and shown around the hospital.

After we had taken lunch and returned to the ward, a stretcher was brought in by two orderlies. The Head Nurse pointed out to them the last bed in the corner of the ward, because the woman was very restless, suffering from *Delirium Tremens.*

She made a sign for me to come with her and we spread a rubber

11

sheet over the bed. Then the orderlies lifted the woman they had picked up in the street onto the bed and disappeared. When they were gone, the Head Nurse turned to me and said: "Now, young lady, these are the glories of our profession; you must clean her and wash her and cut off her hair; it is all tangled and full of mud from the street, you can see she has been rolling in the gutter."

I set to work with great joy in my heart. The first sick person God had sent me to take care of! I began by undressing her and in doing so, a string of beads fell to the ground. I picked it up and placed it on the little stand by the bed. When all was in order, the Head Nurse came back to see how our patient was. I held up the string of beads telling her that I left this behind when her clothes were taken to the fumigation room. "Oh yes," she answered, "it shows she is one of those drunken Irish Catholics—they use those for prayer,—better they stopped drinking!" I said nothing, but wondered: prayer—drinking—*delirium tremens,* how could they all fit together?

The next morning my first patient was a little better, and regained consciousness. While I was washing her face she opened her eyes in bewilderment and asked: "Child, where am I?" "You are in a hospital, but have courage, we hope you will soon be well again." She could hardly speak, but in a whisper she continued: "Might not be too many times like this—Child, call me a Priest—Did you see my beads?"

How glad I was to have kept her rosary, even though I did not know then what it was. I handed it to her and she closed her eyes, moving her lips in prayer. I told the Head Nurse of the sick woman's wish to speak to a Priest. One of the Paulist Fathers was sent for, their church being just opposite the hospital. After her confession and communion, she could hardly speak any more but a great calm came over her face, although its color was red and blue purple from so much drinking and it was swollen and bruised from having been knocked down in the street. When I made her comfortable for the night, she said "Thanks, Child, for all and for getting me the Priest—I have made my peace with God. He has been good to me, a sinner." When I returned to the ward the next morning, I found her bed empty. She had collapsed during the night after internal hemorrhages and her soul had gone to meet her God.

After three months in this Woman's Medical Ward, I was sent to the ·Men's Surgical Ward. There we often received poor workmen who had fallen down from the scaffolding of St. Patrick's Cathedral [as mentioned above]. One young Irishman, whose name was also Patrick, impressed me very much. He was one solid mass of plaster-of-Paris when he came back from the operating room. There was hardly one bone in his body that had not been broken. Only through a little space left open over his left ear, we could take his pulse. After days of unconsciousness,

12

he suddenly began to speak in his broad Irish accent, and asked for his mother. But when he looked around the ward, he understood that his mother was not here, but back in Ireland. During long nights when he could not sleep from pain, he often repeated the prayers his mother had taught him when a little boy—and he never complained.

Later, Maria related how confused she had been to hear his prayers as she passed or sat beside him:

"Mother, Mother, Holy Mary, Mother of God, Help me, Help Pat as you used to." It would seem as though he were really at home, in his humble cottage; at the same time, he seemed at home, here—here, with another mother. Had he *two?* How strange!

"Mary, Mother of God—Pray for us."

Maria pulled herself back—O, he shouldn't talk that way! It wasn't *Christian* . . . Catholics had such funny ways.

After four months, Pat was able to go about on crutches and became the pet of everybody—patients, nurses and doctors. All wanted to see and speak to brave Pat, who was like an innocent child in goodness and purity. He was doomed to walk with two crutches for the rest of his life, but he bore his cross with cheerful resignation.

So Maria went on, tirelessly nursing the sick, fulfilling her vocation. She spared herself no trouble. When a patient seemed near death and there was no one to send for a priest, she herself ran over to the nearby Catholic Church, in the night, in storm, in rain, and cold.

One night, when she had run out in a frightful storm to call a priest for a dying man who had really wandered far from the "narrow path," the old Father said to her, as he went back to his church: "God bless you, Dear little Sister. God reward you for your thoughtfulness, your warmth—you cannot yet understand, unfortunately, what a wonderful service you are doing, for so many, so many. . . . Some day, you will understand. . . . You will find the way. . . ." Maria smiled to herself She was only glad she had helped her patient and made the old man happy.

13

Toward the middle of the second year of hospital work, we were given four weeks' rest. One of my companions, a Norwegian, had a brother who was a sea-Captain. He invited his sister to take a trip on his boat going from Philadelphia to Cuba and Jamaica, and said she could bring a friend with her. I accepted the invitation gladly and the voyage proved very beneficial for us both. There was only room for six passengers on the little steamer—on this voyage, we were the only ones. We had one large cabin to ourselves, where we could read, study and rest.

We left Philadelphia in beautiful, summer weather; after rather rough sailing, we came into the tropical waters where the still air made one feel the heat very much. To relieve the thirst of the sailors, the Captain had a large bucket of cold water, with raw oatmeal mixed in, placed on deck and they made good use of it, drinking freely out of large, earthenware jugs, those sturdy, always respectful and clean Scandinavian men of the sea.

At Port Maria, Jamaica, cargo of various kinds was left and fruit, especially bananas, were taken on board by Negro men and women, who entered by one gangway and left by another, to save time. It was an interesting sight to see row after row of these black figures dressed only in a piece of material around the body, with multicolored handkerchiefs tied around their heads. They sang doleful, Baptist hymns as they strolled along, carrying the big bunches of bananas on their heads....

The owner of these vast plantations was a big and sturdy Negro, "Squire Johnston," a very cultivated man who had graduated from one of the English universities. He was enormously rich and had over one thousand Negroes working on his sugar-cane, banana, coconut and cocoa plantations. The Squire offered to take us and the Captain over his whole property. It took us almost a day and was most interesting. The Overseers, also Negroes who had formerly been slaves in the time of the Squire's father and grandfather, explained everything to us in a very intelligent manner....

After visiting several ports around Cuba and Jamaica, we sailed back to Philadelphia. When we were leaving, we found all the officers and sailors standing in a long row on the deck; they all wanted to thank us and we could not refuse the strong, friendly handshakes of these good sailors. The Captain asked if he could say a word to me; his sister stepped aside, and he began: "I want to thank you again for having come with my sister on this voyage. It is the first one in ten years on which I did not drink so much that my crew had to carry me on board in every port before we could sail."

I was astonished, for he looked so honest and good. I answered—not knowing quite what to say—"I am so sorry! But Captain, how can it be

14

that the presence of two weak human beings can have this influence? It is God who has helped you."

His sister heard sometime later that he had given up drinking and returned to his wife and children in Bergen, a changed man!

Perhaps this encounter with the sea captain was the nearest Maria had ever come to romance in her young life. There is no record of any love interest in her heart other than her passion for God. Certain souls seem born for vestal purity, a pure love which shines through them, helping others and keeping them, as it seemed to keep Maria, free even from temptation.

After this voyage Maria felt a new interest in Blacks, having seen them in this tropical setting and becoming acquainted with them, particularly with Squire Johnston.

She wrote:

Returning once more to the Roosevelt Hospital, I was given charge of the children's department. I loved them all, but what impressed me most was the quiet suffering of the little black babies; they looked at me with wonderment in their expressions and they rarely screamed in passion, as the majority of white babies do. There were babies of all nations and all colors! What a nice meditation on human brotherhood and love! If I could love them so much that no sacrifice seemed too great, how infinitely more great must God's love be for all His human creatures—that Love which flows from His Sacred Heart? That Heart that wants His own burning Love to be kindled in the hearts of all men, to burn away all that is mean and unworthy of a being *created in His image*.

In the Waiting Room of Death—This was the title given to the remarkable incident told to Oskar Eklund and recorded by him at greater length in his original manuscript: At the hospital, one of the doctors or nurses had celebrated a birthday, and Maria was included in a gay party which lasted late into the evening.

As is sometimes the case when people are relaxing from very serious work or grave responsibilities, they suddenly feel the need of doing something completely shocking or ridiculous. Now one of the young doctors suggested that they should go down and visit the hospital morgue at the ghostly hour of midnight.

The idea met with some opposition, especially from the student nurses, who were not enthusiastic about going down into the cold, vaulted cellar of the dead. But the doctors teased them and told them that it was especially good, just for them, to get used to such things!

Maria did her best to dampen their zeal for this morbid and —she felt—rather tasteless expedition, and she was about to say in strong language that she, for her part, did not want to go and take part in any such nonsense. However, the words seemed to stick in her throat. She was one of the senior nurses, and perhaps it was best for her to go along, to see that the younger girls did not get too frightened.

Finally, the party broke up; some excused themselves, and it was a rather small and nervous band that started down into the basement of the hospital. There was some confusion as to what door led to the morgue, and whether or not it was locked. This is the most probable explanation for what happened; as they wandered along the low corridors, suddenly a door swung open, and they found themselves in the *waiting-room of death*.

The hospital had been unusually crowded. The vault where the dead were kept was as cold as possible. (It was before the time of refrigeration.) The sight there was almost overpowering. The long, vaulted room was nearly full of dead bodies, half-concealed under skimpy sheets. An eerie night-light was the only illumination.

Maria was surely the one least shaken by this macabre scene. For her, death was a natural ending to a work-filled life. Certainly a serious matter that should arouse meditation and self-examination, but nothing to cause the unreasonable fear that grips many at the sight of a dead human body.

Silently, Maria began praying for the dead, and also that the living should have time to finish the work that God had for them, before they lay cold and still. The young student nurses were whispering and giggling to mask their fear. Maria moved farther away from the little group that stayed near the door. Suddenly, the room was empty. They had done the only sensible

16

thing to do—they had left. But in their uneasiness and haste, they had forgotten Maria.

Maria was glad that they had gone. But what now? There was a click. The heavy insulated door had swung closed, locked from the outside. There stood Maria alone, among the dead. She was not afraid, but she began to wonder how many hours it would be before she would be released—unless someone might die in the night. She began to make a little plan for herself. In order to keep warm and to give some meaning to this forced vigil for the dead, she decided to go from bier to bier, and pray for each one who had passed on.

Her prayer filled her with warmth and light, in the freezing stillness. Stillness? Maria suddenly became aware that it was not altogether still down here. She could hear her own steps resounding under the vaulted ceiling, but there was something else, too . . .

Maria was gripped by the thought that if she had heard something, it was the sound of breathing—a frightening thought, since she was alone and could not get help. She went as quietly as possible from one body to another, holding her own breath, until it was painful. Yes, it *was* the sound of breathing!

It must be here—a young man—wasn't he warmer than most of the bodies? She pressed her ear to his chest, but heard nothing. She began to rub his hands and feet, and tried all kinds of massage to stimulate his heart. She tried artificial breathing. On his ticket, it said he had died of a heart attack. Maria worked hour after hour. At last, she heard renewed sounds of breathing.

Was this the reason that she had been closed in? Maria called out to God for help and guidance. She took off all she could of her own clothing, to warm the body that she was working over. Its temperature had gone up a few points, but was far under normal.

When she was about to give up, the man gasped. In her uniform pocket, she had a tiny flask of brandy, and pressed a few drops to his lips. Again she worked, praying for strength to hold out.

When morning came at last, they found an exhausted, and far from conventionally clad nurse, sitting by a bier in the mortuary chamber. But on the bier, warmed by the woolen cloth of her uniform, there was a young man, brought back to life.

There was no record of this incident in the *Notes,* which Mother Elisabeth later wrote down at the request of her confessor. She seems to have thought that the story had little significance, or was she too humble to record it? But a few lines on a piece of separate paper were found among other writing of hers, concerning this ghastly night.

When Oskar Eklund expressed a desire to write about her life, she talked at length with him when in Lugano, in 1926 and 1927, and then again in Rome, at the end of the 1940s and beginning of the 1950s. During these times, she related many things which are in this account and also, the story of the hospital morgue. But, as Mother Elisabeth expressed it: "Don't ask how it happened. I don't know. God did it! I was only a simple tool!"

Her period of training was complete; Maria was a full-fledged nurse, but she did not intend to stop there. With her superior mind and memory, she began to ready herself to take preparatory doctor's examinations. She also took private cases in homes where it was usually easier to study than during the hard days of work in the hospital. However, at times it turned out to be the opposite. Sometimes she went to the homes of the rich; sometimes to the less fortunate. To quote another incident from her own *Notes:*

I was called to a poor widow living alone with her only son, who was fourteen years old. She underwent a very serious operation and all hope was given up. The surgeon had visited her for the last time and informed the family that he could do nothing more for her; the family doctor repeated the surgeon's words to me, but he added: "I leave her to you now. You can do whatever you think will comfort her and make her last moments easier."

Her poor son stood outside waiting with tearful eyes to know his mother's condition. A great sorrow filled my soul, and I prayed, "Dear Jesus, Thou who raised the widow's son from the dead and gave him back to his mother, help me to save this mother and give her back to her son."

The woman had been unconscious for many days and the temperature of her body was fearfully high. What could I do—what did God want me to do? Suddenly, the thought came to me to go all over her body. I did so, and discovered near the wound left by the operation a cavity which was burning hot. I prepared the solution the Doctor had ordered for cleansing the wound and, with a syringe, washed out the cavity. To my great surprise, almost a litre of matter and black stagnant blood came out. Two hours later, the poor woman's respiration was easier, her colour had become better and her temperature went down. At 7 o'clock in the morning, she became conscious, opened her eyes and asked for something to drink. God had saved her. He was giving the mother back to the son.

The doctor came in about nine o'clock to comfort the boy; turning to some relatives who had arrived, he said:

"The Nurse has saved her life—she is a woman in a thousand." Now I repeat this to show the Grace our Dear Lord gave me. But at the time, a terrible repugnance came over me at the thought of this praise and I wished that I could have hidden under the bed of the poor woman. After this experience, I used constantly to pray the Good God to grant me the Grace of humility.

Chapter III

The Search

DURING the years that Maria had worked in the big New York hospital, she had come in contact with people of every background and religion. She was still searching for the *ideal faith* —some form of basic, pure community which really practiced the principles of Christ—*His own Flock,* to which He had promised to lead her, long ago, in the Swedish forest.

Her search led her to many churches and meeting halls. Some were costly and ornate, with great works of art. Others, bare of anything which might distract the mind or seem to foster worldly pride in possessions; yet such places were often noisy and conflicting ideas were argued or expressed. Nowhere did she feel completely at home.

She liked the stillness in Catholic churches. But why did people move around here and there, kneeling and getting up and making the *Sign of the Cross.* Was it necessary to "show off" one's faith? No, it should be kept secret, holy. She said in her *Notes:*

I often visited all kinds of places of worship, including the Jewish Synagogue and the lecture-hall of the great infidel, Robert Ingersoll. But nothing satisfied that interior life of my soul which was awaiting the fulfillment of a promise.

The *Seventh Day Adventists* attracted me very much because they strove to copy Our Lord's own life in their devotion to the poor and sick. For a short time, I joined in their works of charity in the slums of New York.

But by the bed-side of dying Catholics, I always felt it a sacred duty to send for their own priests and to prepare a little altar for them.

Many priests, seeing these things, tried to speak to me, but I carefully avoided them all. But on one occasion, when I had sent to the Jesuit Church on sixteenth street for a priest to hear the confession of a Spanish patient, Father Cardella came, and as I had to show him the way out, he turned to me and said these words: "You will not only become a Catholic, but you will die a nun."

Some days later, I was invited by a Catholic friend to spend some days of rest away from the city, at a Dominican Convent, in Saratoga Springs, New York. While there, I went through great battles of the soul. I had for some years been reading both Protestant and Catholic history and an intense fear, like a death agony, came over me at the thought that the Roman Catholic Church might be the true one. I tried harder than ever to avoid religious conversations, but Providence made use of a circumstance that made a great change in my life and was a turning point.

I noticed that one of the Sisters had a stiff arm. I felt sorry for her because it made it impossible for her to accomplish the work necessary in the house. I said to her, "Sister, this arm can be cured, but it will take six weeks' treatment. This I will return to give you, if your Mother Superior permits. I can return in two weeks, if you write me what you decide."

In a week, I was called back to the Convent. As the arm only required two or three hours a day, I had much time at my disposal. I made good use of the Convent library and spent hours in prayer in the little Chapel. A friend happened to be staying at the Convent at the same time, a niece of the celebrated infidel, Ingersoll. But she, unlike her uncle, had a warm belief in God and loved and spoke in favor of many Catholic customs. Her remarks helped to open the door for me, although she remained outside herself.

One day, when in the library, my eyes fell upon Cardinal Wiseman's Lectures on the Real Presence of Our Divine Lord in the Most Blessed Sacrament, and on reading his comments on St. John, Chapter VI, I said to myself, *"Why, this I have believed since I was a child!"* Still, I was full of doubts and perplexities.

One of the things that bothered Maria was the Catholic attitude to Mary, God's Mother, and all the many saints who inspired devotion and almost worship.

Her *Notes* reflect how she reasoned with her forthright, original mind:

How could I believe in the power of the intercession of the Blessed Virgin Mary and the Saints? Would it not lower the merits of Christ's

Passion and Death? Would it not take away the honor and glory due to God Alone? Would it not be idolatry, placing them before God?

On the other hand, how could I explain the Communion of Saints if holy men and women, on leaving this earthly pilgrimage, lost all their interest in us? Was it natural that Christ, who was to us the Model of all virtue and perfection, should put his mother, from whom He had taken human flesh, entirely aside? And would it be natural that his Mother, the model of all womanhood, would cease to interest herself in her Son's great Mission, because He had died before she did? If man's earthly existence is to be followed by a still more perfect state in the next life, why should holy men and women have no power. God gave them the grace to help others on earth, was it consistent to believe that this was no longer granted to them, when they were in a spiritual world still closer to Him?

One day, I was sitting and pondering over these things and light was dawning more and more in my soul; suddenly, I lost my train of thought and became, as it were, transported to a distant land.

I was sitting at a table where there were only men dressed like Catholic Priests speaking very earnestly on a grave matter, when presently the door flung open and in came the Lutheran minister who had prepared me for my First Communion. I rose to my feet, for the respect that I bore him, knowing he had given all he had of God to me. To my astonishment, he did not stop to greet me, but walked rapidly around the table where we were, and when in front of me, I saw his face becoming gray like clay and his whole body the same, and with a tremendous noise, the clay form before me fell in pieces at my feet. I opened my eyes—

What had taken place, I do not know. I came back to my senses. Cardinal Wiseman's Lectures were still in my hands, I rose to my feet and then fell on my knees, whispering my first appeal to a saint: *Birgitta, Ignatius, pray for me.*

There was a picture of St. Ignatius in the room and I was no longer afraid of addressing him. I tried to forget and blot this experience out of my memory. But it was brought back to me many years later in Rome, when I found myself sitting in the same fashion, by a table at the grating in the parlor of St. Birgitta's House, speaking to some Catholic Priests regarding the grave matter of the restoration of the Fathers of our Order. (There were present, among others, Rev. Fr. Hagen, S.J., and Rev. Fr. Benedict Williamson, later a son of St. Birgitta.) Until that time I had believed the incident to be a foolish dream which should not be considered, and now, when in humble obedience I write it down, I leave the judgment of it to those who are capable of understanding, because I am not.

In the guests' dining-room of the Convent at Saratoga Springs was a statue of Our Lady of Lourdes, which always attracted my attention when entering. I was not of a superstitious mind; in fact, I was considered very matter-of-fact, but I must confess that the eyes of this statue seemed to follow me with a look of deep sadness. I had not yet learned to call Mary "my Mother," but as my Savior's Mother I respected her. One morning, entering the dining-room alone and earlier than usual, I went up to the statue and, looking up into her face, I saw dust and fly-marks on it. I went back to my room and brought some soft medical cotton and a little water and washed her face. Then I went into the garden, to find something to put in her hand. It being late in the autumn, I found only a green branch, but this I carried to my Savior's Mother and put it in her hand. The Sisters noticed the change in the statue and were pleased; they also saw the little green branch and they began to pray still more for me.

I relate this because the branch in Our Lady's hand remained fresh and green for several months, which according to nature, would have been impossible as the statue stood near a radiator from which a constant dry heat was flowing. Months after I had returned to New York, the Sisters wrote to me: "Think of our distress—the branch that Our Lady kept green for you so long, was swept away by one of the cleaning women today, but we are happy to have seen it, all of us, including our Mother Superior who came last week to visit us from Albany. We all consider it a miracle and a sign of Our Lady's good will toward you!

My belief in Our Blessed Lady's help as a true Mother was yet feeble, still I often pictured her to myself, at the foot of the cross where my Savior was dying for us. But a circumstance made her my friend, my Mother for time and Eternity.

During a month's absence of one of the superintendents, I was called to the Hospital to take charge. One evening when we were making all the sick comfortable for the night, a telegram was handed to me and I knew it brought me news of my Father's death far away in my native land. Oh! The pain and regret and the struggle to bow in resignation to the wish that had not been granted—that of being by the death-bed of my own father, and to close his eyes, as I had done for so many other fathers and mothers. But duty and will made me strong. I did not open the telegram. I put it near my heart, in my Nursing uniform and, swallowing the tears that wanted to force themselves out, I continued for two hours more going from bed to bed, changing bandages, giving medicines and trying to cheer the down-hearted. At seven o'clock the night superintendent came to take my place; I could now retire to my room, be alone with God and give free flow to my tears.

But as I closed the door, a wonderful sweetness filled my soul and, kneeling down, I held up my hands to someone whom I knew was there with me and said: "Mary, my Mother, I give him to you. Take him, O Mother and make him happy." It was my first prayer to Mary, who suddenly became near and dear to me: "Now I know your value, dearest Mother, nothing in life or death shall ever divide us. I am your child, Mary, my Mother!"

As I look back upon the many long years since that memorable day, I can only say: "Oh, what a wonderful Mother you have been to me!"

Maria had come a long way in her religious development and still it would be some time before she could come to any practical step. Her new relationship to God's Mother and her friendship with His saints, well, this was something which must remain hidden—certainly nothing to "show off."

Maria had begun to feel herself restless, rootless. God had given her many little "pointers," but she could not follow them, not yet. During this time, she began to throw herself into medical studies with an almost fanatical zeal. The first examination which would open the way to her becoming a doctor was just ahead of her. Her studies began to seem easier. But then she began to feel that perhaps her old illness was coming back again. What was this? Why did no certain path lie before her?

The warm, inner faith of her childhood was her only refuge. Yet even to pray with all her soul did not satisfy a new longing which had grown in her heart those last years—to be united with some spiritual community, to realize the presence of God, not only in her own soul, but with others, or in a church. She had accepted the phenomenon of the Blessed Sacrament as it is explained in Catholic churches, but she felt comfortable only when she was there in silence. Ritual and pomp, and many people, confused and troubled her. Where was the *little Flock* to which God had promised to lead her when she was a girl, in the pine forest of her native land?

One night, when she was alone in her small room, she heard a knock at the door. It was her best friends, young sisters of a wealthy South American family of Spanish descent. Maria had nursed their mother through a lingering illness, and they had become devoted to her because of her strong, loving nature. They had come to beg her to travel to Europe with them, as they were fearful of going alone, and also wanted to give her this vacation: "We need you," they said, "and we know you need the rest." And so it was that Maria was persuaded to leave for Europe with the Cisneros sisters, who were to play an important part in her life.

THE FEAST OF CORPUS DOMINI

The three young women arrived in Brussels, Belgium, for the famed procession of *Corpus Domini* at the St. Gudule Cathedral. The Cisneros, who were ardent Catholics, insisted that Maria attend the ceremony, somewhat against her will. She describes the scene in her *Notes:*

I did not know that anything was carried by the Bishop, but looked at the procession merely as I would at an interesting military pageant, and seeing my two friends and most of the people go down on their knees, I slipped behind the big door of the cathedral so as not to offend those around me and standing there I said: "Before you, my God, I kneel, but not here."

By this time, the Bishop carrying the Monstrance had reached the door; my soul, so full of pain and struggle, was instantly filled with sweetness, and a gentle voice which seemed to come both from without and from within my heart said: *"I am He Whom thou seekest."* I fell on my knees! The air was full of a sweet odor like the fragrance of a meadow covered with spring flowers. Was it the melting of the ice and the budding forth of spring-time in my soul? There, behind the Church door, I made my first adoration of Our Divine Lord's Presence in the Blessed Sacrament.

The procession had reached the altar: I rose to my feet and went out to my friends, saying to them: "I went behind the door so as not to offend you, but as the procession passed, something wonderful also passed and I have been on my knees." My friends understood and opened their arms to me and we all three embraced on the Church steps. (Of these two friends, one became a nun and the other led the life of an Apostle of Charity in the world.)

From then on, Maria's search through still more doubts and interior struggles can best be followed in her own account, which leads to the decisive step of her entering the Catholic Church. The *Notes* continue:

My soul during the following months was plunged in an ocean of darkness. I had to rise at night from my bed, and on my knees plead

25

Our Lord for Mercy. I could not pray, only weep and repeat the words of the Psalms: "In Thee, O Lord, have I hoped and I shall not be confounded." Holy Ghost, guide me and enlighten me!

After a year and a half spent in the different countries: England, Germany, Belgium and France, we returned to the United States. The impression of what had happened on the Cathedral steps at Brussels never left me, and the effect of the Presence of the Blessed Sacrament was such that whenever I passed a Church where the Blessed Sacrament was kept, I was forced by something like a magnet, drawing me, to go in and right up to the altar rail, to kneel. I went frequently to the Catholic Church for Mass and Benediction; in fact I had not entered any other church for some years—still I could not see my way clear to make the final step.

A new circumstance made me hesitate. My dearest friend—one of the two that had stood beside me on the Cathedral steps that memorable Feast of Corpus Domini—was to enter a Convent. My human affection, so full of self-love, would not bow to the sacrifice of losing a friend. I thought to myself, "How is it possible that a religion which asks such heart-rending sacrifices can be the true one?"

I accompanied my friend to Washington, when she entered the Visitation Convent there. Still in my darkness, I hoped that she might change her mind and return with her sister and myself to New York, and in this hope I went so far as to go to the Jesuit University nearby to beg the Fathers to persuade my friend to return home with us. The good Fathers were amused and tried to comfort me, but we had to return to New York alone.

What did it mean to live in a convent? Maria could not understand. Wasn't it only an escape, cowardly and selfish, a way to try to reach holiness in the easiest manner possible? Her dear friend Emma had just begun to lead a life of true unselfishness, dedicating herself to charitable work for others. Then why should she try to run away from the world?

The Jesuit father had tried to explain convent life to her: He had said that no one goes into a convent to escape work or the problems of the world. Some few may have come to a convent to escape personal problems or temptations, but they are the exceptions. Those who seek convent life without a *calling* or a *vocation* of almost supernatural origin are never happy and seldom remain. "As far as our mutual friend is concerned, she can

26

always change her mind and leave—" The kind Jesuit had reasoned long and patiently with Maria. It was the first time she had talked openly with a priest. She went back to New York, deeply disappointed over losing her friend. But now her own doubts were still more troubling. What if she were hiding herself away from the light? Seeking her own will, clinging to her own opinions, and unwilling to see what might be the *will of God?*

For another winter, Maria worked among the poor of New York City, with various religious organizations. She was still tormented by introspection and still searching for that *pure, little Flock.*

Then gradually, it seemed to become plain to her that she must decide on something that *already existed in this world.* There is no such thing as a perfect religion, a pure Communion of Saints on this earth. How could she expect the Catholic Church, or any other, to be foolproof, spotless, here below?

Holy Birgitta, who had been so dear to her from childhood, was a true daughter of the Catholic Church, yet she had attacked the wrongs and injustices of many prelates and even of the popes who lived in luxury at Avignon and would not return to Rome!

How could there be such a thing as an assembly of holy people excluding all who are weak or guilty, in this world?

Even Christ Himself had not been able to create a *perfect Flock* out of his own followers. Judas betrayed Him. Peter denied Him. His disciples slept, tired, without effort to support their Master in his hour of anguish in the Garden of Gethsemane. Then, when the soldiers came to seize Jesus, the disciples ran away, trying to save themselves.

And Maria had expected to find a *fold* of pure, perfect souls, down on this earth. . . . How could she have been blind so long!

From this point on in her thinking, Maria began to approach the idea of becoming a Catholic from a new angle. For the first time, she felt that this Church could offer her that religious haven, that spiritual companionship that she had been looking for. Suddenly, for her, it represented the Truth, the *Fold* that Christ had Himself created, and every day away from it, from now on, would be a loss.

This was the passion for truth that had always guided Maria, and had filled her being with a spiritual purpose, ever since she was a child and had sacrificed herself to her family. She had felt guided, and she was guided, through many strange circumstances all through her life, to fulfill a completely unpredictable destiny. At this particular time, she had arrived at a turning point from which there was no return; in her matter-of-fact, and at the same mystically sensitive, character, there was never any spirit of compromise. She wrote to her friend Emma Cisneros, postulant in the Visitation: "Now I see everything clearly. I am coming to Washington."

Another outward circumstance had hastened her decision, for Maria had been urged by Marie Cisneros to take another trip to Europe. This time, they had planned that Marie should stay in London while Maria visited her own beloved family in Sweden. She had worked hard and long, and she was afraid that her old ulcers might return if she did not take a rest. But before she left, she wanted everything settled in her religious life.

It was on the twelfth of August, 1902, that Maria Elisabeth Hesselblad came to Washington and went to Georgetown Uni versity to look for the Jesuit father to whom she had talked a few months before. Again, her own *Notes* convey the extraordinary *directness* of her mind and soul, as she took this final step:

"Father, do you remember my coming here ten months ago to beg you to persuade my friend, Miss Cisneros, to return with me to New York? I come on quite a different errand this time—I humbly ask to be received into the Catholic Church."

The good Priest looked pleased: "How happy I am to hear this," he said. "How I should love to help you myself, but you see my bag here; I must be off to give a Mission to a Church some hours away, but I will bring you one of our Fathers, a very spiritual man who will help you with everything."

A few minutes later, the Rev. J. G. Hagen, S.J., entered, at that time Director of the Georgetown Observatory. Looking up at his graying

28

head and deeply spiritual face, I felt in my soul an assurance that "This is the man of God for me!"

Little did these two, Maria and Father Hagen, dream that at that hour the foundation stone was laid for a long and remarkable, spiritual relationship.

Without hesitation I said: "Rev. Father, I must leave for New York in a few days and then sail for Europe, please be so kind as to receive me into the Church at once!"

The good Father looked surprised and said: "My dear child, how can I? I do not know you, nor if you have been instructed well. It is impossible."

"O no, Rev. Father, pardon me, but it cannot be impossible. For almost 20 years I have struggled in darkness, for many, many years I have studied the Catholic Religion and prayed for a strong faith, a faith so strong that if the Pope in Rome and all the Priests left the Church, I would still stand firm! This faith I have now and I am ready to be examined on every point referring to our Faith."

"Oh, is it possible?" said the good Father, looking still more surprised. "Have you such a faith? If it is so, let me see what we can do."

And now a very long conference and questioning began, at the end of which the Venerable Father said: "I see no reason why I should not receive you into the Church. Today is the 12th, and on the fifteenth is the Feast of Our Blessed Lady's Assumption. I will say Mass over in the Convent Chapel that day and receive you into the Church. Next Sunday, the 17th, you can receive Holy Communion. The days now left you can spend in retreat at the Convent and come to me for two instructions a day."

Oh, what days of Grace! I could not describe what happened in my soul. The good nuns of the Convent showed me every kindness and sent nice meals to my room, but it was often impossible to touch food, so overwhelming were God's gifts.

At one of the last conferences, my good Father said: "Do you clearly understand everything? Have you no doubts about anything?" "No, no, Father, I believe everything and shall never question or doubt because I am now a follower of Christ; I have ceased to be the searching student: There is only one thing that makes me feel a little strange, it's corporal discipline."

"And why?" asked the good Father. "Because I am a human being, Father, and that would make me feel like a dog." "And human beings," remarked the Father, "who offend God, are they not more deserving of chastisement than animals that have no understanding and cannot offend Him?

"You have read the Bible so much—have you never thought of the words of St. Paul, *I fill up those things that are wanting of the sufferings of Christ in my flesh, for His body which is the Church.* (Col. I:24) It does not mean that the Passion of Christ was not complete, but it shows us that His Passion continues in the members of His Church, His *Mystical Body*."

Father Hagen must have spoken to her earlier of those ascetical practices which have often been part of convent life and are also used by many followers of Christ who seek after spiritual perfection.

It is common knowledge that penances of various sorts, such as fasting, the wearing of chains, hair shirts, as well as corporal discipline, have been found to increase the fervor of religious temperaments, and through the years, souls have found deep emotional and spiritual satisfaction in believing that their penances can unite them to the Christ who suffered and sacrificed Himself for them.

In the same way, pain or sickness that comes unwanted to the individual can be offered up in prayer and so *united* to the sacrifice of Christ—can perhaps even become part of the power of *Redemption*.

Father Hagen must have sensed that Maria would have need of this mystical interpretation of suffering, even so early in her Catholic experience. For she had already passed through the school of much physical pain and was ready for the highest teaching in the field of spiritual knowledge. (Indeed, this sublimation of suffering was perhaps the very key to her spirituality as it developed in the years to come.)

Maria says in her *Notes* that Father Hagen left her with a realization of what the meaning of pain and penance could be:

How clearly I saw at once the truth and beauty of it; and a secret longing crept into my soul to be permitted to be with my Dear Lord in His Passion. How different from modern concepts which seek to avoid all suffering.

The conference was over and I returned to the Convent Chapel meditating on St. Paul's words, and as I knelt there before Our Lord in the Most Blessed Sacrament, I offered myself to Him with that secret longing in my soul, and I whispered to the Tabernacle, "Only then I can say with St. Paul: *I live now, not I, but Christ liveth in me."*

... The three who had stood on the Cathedral steps in Brussels met again in the Convent Chapel on the morning of August 15th....

I was Baptized into the Catholic Church on the steps of the Sanctuary, my two god-mothers standing by my side, one on the right, one on the left, with lighted candles in their hands.

I had had the Baptismal Water poured over my head, I had been anointed with the Holy Oil, the consecrated hand had been placed on my head, and I had listened to the beautiful prayer of the Church: "I supplicate Thy Eternal Goodness, O Holy Lord, in behalf of this Thy servant that Thou wouldst vouchsafe to enlighten her, cleanse her and sanctify her, give unto her true knowledge ... "

I went back to the priedieu and the whole world seemed to have vanished. It would be impossible to describe the experience. It was as if I saw my whole past life in the *twinkling of an eye;* all the beautiful scenes of nature I had witnessed in my journeys, through the mountains of Sweden, Norway, the Alps ... and other scenes on land and sea; all the art I had seen in many art galleries; and all that I had desired of the good and beautiful things of this world. All was placed on an immense table and a strong hand, with one sweep, brought it all down on the ground. The only thing I saw, I felt, was God. My only desire was to do His Holy Will at any cost. This does not mean that I could not afterwards see God in His Creation, but it was an interior grace which showed me Himself, as I firmly believe, in a higher form; He was to me a fullness, as never before, something *All in All:* I desired nothing else.

In an instant God's Love was poured out over me. I understood that this love could only be answered by sacrifice, by a love ready to suffer for His Glory. Without hesitation I offered my life, my will to follow Him on the way of the Cross.

Chapter IV

Over the Sea—Fridhem

BACK in New York, Maria was preparing for her second trip to Europe. She was full of joy and eagerness; Fr. Hagen's brief but revealing instructions had opened a whole new world of spiritual thought to her.

It was indeed fortunate that she had found this exceptional Father. Already a noted astronomer in his fifties, his passion was tracing variable stars. He was tall with handsome features and far-seeing eyes. His lofty mind was constantly raised to contemplate the wonders of the universe; yet, from the first, he must have felt that there was something unusual about this young Swedish woman who had approached him with such directness. He had recognized her integrity, her loneliness, and without hesitation, he had adopted her as his spiritual child. (This was all the more remarkable because later, when Maria sent other friends to him for advice, he remarked that his work was scientific and not apostolic, yet he had never refused her his time.)

When Maria left Washington, Father Hagen had made her promise to write to him whenever she had problems or questions to ask. From New York she wrote him, asking if she might practice some penance to commemorate the crucifixion during the Holy Hour of the *First Friday* of the month, when she hoped to be already on shipboard.

Father Hagen's first letter to her—one of many to follow—reached her as she was leaving on the S.S. *Celtic,* September 3, 1902:

My Dear Child in Christ:

In Christ I have begotten you, said St. Paul to his own Christians. Why should I not say the same to you? Your words of gratitude and heavenly joy were very eloquent and sounded like an echo from the soul I know so well.... I am also well pleased to read that your big *I*, which Paul calls the Old Man or the first Adam, has become "small"; but I add, it is not yet small enough. A "branch" is no plant and a "member" is not a person. Thus, the truth is that you are nobody.

Your proposition to commemorate Our Lord's Passion on Fridays, is very good and finds my approval. Only I would give you more freedom of time, and expand it from Thursday evening to Friday evening. It is quite general to celebrate Holy Hour on Thursday night. At 3 o'clock, you may not always be free. You can offer all your good works, especially your holy communions, for your beloved Sweden.

I hope this letter will reach you on the Celtic. Do not miss seeing the planet Jupiter in the South East, and a little to the right of it, Saturn (the nearest bright star to the right of J.). A good field glass should show you Jupiter's four satellites and perhaps Saturn's ring. They will give you my greetings every evening from the Observatory. Send yours back to me by them.

With the love of Christ and kindest regards to Marie and yourself, I remain,

> your father,
> J. G. Hagen, S.J.

Georgetown College Observatory
West Washington, D.C.

Once more, Maria, with her dear friend Marie Cisneros, was traveling toward Europe. The voyage began with great promise. The weather was beautiful. Maria's heart was overflowing with gratitude and deepest awe for God's Power as it was manifest in the greatness of the ocean.

In her *Notes,* she pours out her emotion; but then she also tells the story of her new trial: On the very day of her resolve to *commemorate her Lord's Passion,* the pains and anguish of her old illness came over her!

On the morning of the First Friday, we had reached mid-ocean and we were sitting writing letters, when suddenly I began to feel very ill. ... I had barely got inside my cabin when I had a very severe hemorrhage from the old gastric ulcers which had again opened themselves.... The hemorrhage continued for three days and I grew very weak in body,

33

but my soul had the most beautiful peace and I was happy to have something to suffer in union with Our dear Lord's Passion.

After seven more days, we arrived in Liverpool, and had to cross England to London. My friend had telegraphed a doctor to meet us on our arrival at the Assumption College, on Kensington Square. When he heard that I had crossed England in this condition, he said, "Bring me a rope and we will tie her to the bed.... I am surprised you have not bled to death."

FRIDHEM

Finally, Maria was well enough to plan her second return to her beloved Sweden. All the years since her first departure as a girl of seventeen, she had kept in close touch with her family, writing frequently to each one and sending contributions to help with their education and training. The youngest sister, Eva, kept and treasured all Maria's letters, and later had them privately printed, in a handsome little book which reflects Maria's continuous devotion and concern for her parents, brothers, sisters, and even grandparents. It is in this book of letters that she describes a long visit to Sweden in 1899–1900, when she first went to Europe with the Cisneros daughters, Emma and Marie.

Earlier than this, Maria had written colorful letters from Barranquilla, Colombia, showing how her friendship with the fabulous Cisneros family had developed. They had originally come from Cuba, but Mr. Cisneros was a financier who played a large part in the development of Colombia. Like many wealthy South American families, they had visited Europe and sent their daughters to schools in France and England. Maria had been called to nurse the ailing Mrs. Cisneros in New York. Since she wished to die in her own home at Barranquilla, they had embarked upon a small steamer which passed through a heavy storm. The day after they arrived in port, Mrs. Cisneros breathed her last. She had left a letter begging Maria to remain with her own daughters and husband, who was also in poor health. Mr. Cisneros was a leading figure in Colombia, and took them all on a tour of inspection into the interior, and also to the capital, Bogota. Ever after, the three girls were like sisters, and Maria would

34

never have been obliged to return to nursing, had it not been for her independent spirit and desire to serve others. It was after she had worked again for over a year in a New York hospital that Emma and Marie had persuaded her to accompany them to Europe.

In her *Notes,* Maria described only her experience on the steps of the Cathedral of St. Gudule in Belgium. But actually, the three young women had first come to Skara, where the Hesselblad family was living, in August, 1899. In the *Letters,* Maria speaks of long stays in a health resort outside of Stockholm. They visited Norway, after celebrating a typical Swedish Christmas with the Hesselblads. She writes proudly about her youngest brother, Sten Ture, who had begun to rise in his career as a seaman officer.

The year before Maria came to Sweden in 1903, her family had purchased a little home, which Maria's money made possible. It was in her native Västergötland. She had seen a photograph of it, but now she had come to it for the first time. Her *Notes* reveal the joy, but also the stress that this visit was to cause her:

The following December, I was sufficiently recovered to cross the North Sea, to Gothenburg, to visit my dear mother and my brothers and sisters in Sweden.

The year before, I had bought a beautiful, little villa in the Swedish country-side where I intended to spend the rest of my life together with my dear mother and where we arranged to have the family meet on holidays and in vacation time. I had spent long years in the care of the sick, my health had become very poor and I longed for a quiet, retired life in my native land. So I wrote to my mother, "We shall call our little place *Fridhem* (Home of Peace) and we shall be so happy there."

Now I was returning home for the first time, a Catholic! As the steamer came in sight of land and I saw the solemn gray rocks of my native shore, a tremendous battle rose up within me; it was as if thousands of demons were whispering around me and saying: "You fool—how can you appear before your good and upright people? How can you face that mother who nursed you at her bosom, and whose heart you have broken? What will you say when they pray in the manner of your childhood?" My blood ran cold within me and such was the battle, that I could only walk up and down the deck with wild speed....

35

One of my brothers met me at Gothenburg where I was able to hear Mass and receive Holy Communion in the small church in charge of Jesuit Missionaries. At noon, I continued my journey with my brother, to my little place in the country, the *Fridhem* of my dreams.

The comfortably heated train rushed onwards, revealing one beautiful landscape after the other, little frozen lakes, gray rocks. How sweet my native land looked, covered with a mantle of pure white, the majestic pines and fir-trees partly covered with the soft, newly fallen snow, which glittered in the sunlight.

After some hours of traveling by rail, we left the train at Borås and, at the station, found a sleigh with fur-lined rugs waiting to take us through the beautiful pine-forest, where my little *Fridhem* stood. It was a very pleasant ride; the bells on the harness of the horse joyfully ringing and the air so pure and invigorating.

Soon we found ourselves by the gate of our home of so many hopes and dreams of earthly joy and comfort. The doors were thrown open and out came my dear mother and sisters to welcome with open arms the daughter and sister for whom they had waited so long with affectionate hearts, and whom they now hoped to keep, always.

But I had to explain that I could then only stay to spend the Christmas holidays with them, as I was obliged to return to England as soon as possible. At mid-day, my two youngest sisters, who were studying in High School, came home full of joy and affection.

Nobody knew the step I had taken, but when we were all standing around the dinner table, and grace was being said, I signed myself with the sign of the Cross—that wonderful "sign that unites us all, children of the Church...."

All eyes were fixed on me at once. I looked up and said: "My dear ones, why do you all look so frightened and astonished?" And I made a second sign of the Cross, saying the words out loud: "In the Name of the Father, and of the Son and of the Holy Ghost," adding, "Is it not beautiful to begin and end all our actions in the name of the Holy Trinity and to openly confess that we are followers of Him who died on the Cross for us?"

"Yes, it is nice," said one of my sisters, "but isn't this just as nice, and enough?" And while saying her *grace,* she joined her hands together, as pious Protestants sometimes do.

We all felt the need of changing the subject of the conversation during dinner.

Later on, when alone with my mother, she begged me to keep secret this strange thing I had done, in becoming a Catholic, so as not to scandalize the family and others. My sisters, who happened to enter the room as we were speaking, remarked: "What can you find, dear sister, in that strange religion which attracts you? Such impossible things, for instance, as the celibacy of the pastors of the church, and the nuns. Our Lord never forbade any one to marry!"

"Ah, my dear ones, now you have touched on the very subject that first attracted me to the Catholic Church, namely the firm belief that God can give human beings strength and power to live angelic lives in human flesh. To doubt this, we would doubt God's omnipotence; and even in the ordinary nature of things, all are not called to the married state. Why, it is easy to see how a loving Providence and a Christian institution are joining hands, as it were. Now you refer everything to the Bible, have you ever considered these words in Matthew XIX:21: *He who can take it, let him take it.*

"St. Paul says in his first Epistle to the Corinthians: 'He that is without a wife is solicitous for the things that belong to the Lord; how he may please God,' and he continues later, 'The unmarried woman thinketh on the things of God, but she that is married thinketh on the things of the world, how she may please her husband'."

In the pine forest not far from our house was a grotto made by Nature herself, at the foot of a small crag, and the deep snow that covered the forest did not come near this cave under the rocks. Here I used to go and pray alone, and plead with God to show me His Holy Will. I felt that God wanted something of me, that I could not continue my life as before.

Then came Christmas, a happy time for Maria and her family. The high point of Christmas Eve was when they gathered around to hear the Gospel story of the Savior's birth, which her mother read out of the old family Bible.

The next morning, they all attended the traditional *Jul-Ottan*, celebrated in all Swedish churches, with candles burning in the hour before sunrise—corresponding exactly to the Catholic Mass-at-Dawn.

Maria felt very close to her beloved family at this time, and yet something was driving her on. Didn't God want her to stay here where she could at least witness to her relatives that her new Catholic experience had not separated them?

No, there was some other task waiting for her, although she was far from sure as to what it was.

She must break away from her dear ones at *Fridhem*. In London her traveling companion was waiting for her. She went back to Gothenburg, to take passage for England.

Maria was glad to get back to London again. Marie Cisneros had many acquaintances old and new—and these young ladies often took Maria out with them, to the theater, to concerts, or on excursions to the surrounding countryside.

But Maria seemed to have reached a different level of living: she rejoiced only in the fact that she could go to daily Mass and Communion once more, and her soul seemed caught up in a sense of God's presence. She says in her *Notes:*

> I cannot remember to have lost His Presence no matter how occupied I was. In the midst of the turmoil of London—very often driving with friends through crowded streets like Piccadilly—I would become so absorbed in the attributes of God, or the mysteries of our Holy Faith, that I lost all sense of place and time.
>
> Again, my friends would take me to the theatre; the play would be half over and I had not heard or seen anything. I only knew that God was with me and I was with Him.... My friends could not understand the change my soul had undergone and reproved me often for not showing the right interest in things, thinking it was from rudeness or lack of appreciation.
>
> And then something happened which in God's Providence was the means of turning my life into a different channel. My friend (whose mother I had nursed through a long illness) was now going to visit the Eternal City and invited me to go with her. My heart went up to God in gratitude and joy, and I exclaimed to myself: "Now I shall see the House of St. Birgitta!"
>
> And I saw myself again, as I had done as a child, standing in a big square, looking at a window in one corner of it. I had not as yet heard or read anything about the appearance of this House, nor did I know where it was in Rome.

Maria had also described the House as having two columns in front of it; was this the entrance, or a little church in itself? She was never sure. But now she would know whether her dream was just an illusion, or how near it had come to reality.

Chapter V

The House of St. Birgitta of Vadstena

WHEN the two friends arrived in Rome, it was late on a spring afternoon. They took a cab to a *pensione,* which had been recommended to them because it was run by Sisters, near the Fountain of Trevi.

They soon ventured out to see the famous fountain. Streams of water rose and fell, dark-eyed youths strolled about or strummed on guitars, singing romantic melodies. Couples crowded around the broad basin, and children sought to reach the lacelike foam. Elegant ladies and gentlemen passed by in private carriages.

Was this Rome? It looked like any big, worldly city.

Her first night in Rome—Maria could hardly sleep. She thought of the House of St. Birgitta—the strange little church between two columns, that she had seen in her dream. Would she ever find it? She had heard that it was a convent now, but Italian convents lay behind walls with big gardens. She had seen nothing but a row of yellow-gray houses on a little square—but no green anywhere.

Early the next morning, Maria slipped out to Mass. When she got back to the *pensione,* her friend suggested that they drive at once to St. Peter's. Maria agreed; if she had said what she herself wanted, it would have been to look for the House of St. Birgitta *first.* But after all, she was only a lucky companion, a guest of her kind friend.

They jogged along the Corso, and then the driver said: "Would you like to go through the Campo di Fiori?" "Yes, alright," said Maria's friend, not knowing just what he meant, "But don't let's take any long detours."

Now they were on a smaller street and soon came out on a wide marketplace, filled with flowers, vegetables, meats, and even old clothes and knickknacks of all kinds. A lively chatter filled the air. They could not help laughing at the gay scene. This was really the south!

They passed through the color-mad array. The little street continued only another block. In front of it was a magnificent Renaissance Palace, standing on a somewhat smaller square, and here a fountain played.

The cabbie stood up and turned to explain that the Palazzo Farnese was a masterpiece of Michelangelo and Sangallo.

But the words stuck in his mouth. He had seen many strange tourists, but this one must be crazy. She was standing bolt upright—white as a sheet—and staring across the right side of the square:

"The House"—she cried—"The House of St. Birgitta!"

Yes, that was the House—just as she had always seen it— The small church between two enormous columns. Without any explanation, Maria jumped out of the cab and went into the church.

Her friend paid the cabbie, and followed her. But Maria was lost in prayer.

She said afterwards that she remembered how cool and dark it was inside the little church, and that she got an impression of good balance and proportion. The high altar was lit by a ray of sun coming through a round window. On the altar were many candles and a monstrance.

The choir was closed off from the nave by a high grille. But from it floated out the clear tones of Gregorian chant. Nuns were singing their Office.

Maria saw and heard everything as though through a fog. As soon as she had come in, she had sunk down on the nearest prayer bench. An indescribable feeling of *being home* came over her, and again, as previously in her prayer hours, she seemed to hear actual words, coming to her from some mystic Source. As she related in her *Notes:*

> While I was kneeling there, pouring out my heart's thanksgiving for all the graces I had received, I heard a voice saying *"It is here I wish you to serve me."* Half an hour passed and when my friend touched me, saying we must go, I thought we had only just arrived. I had profoundly realized the Presence of God, but when I rose to my feet, a great fear came over me that it was an illusion and I pleaded with Our Lord to guard me and not permit me to be led astray by foolish imaginings. But the more I prayed, the stronger grew the impression of those moments passed before Our Lord in the Most Blessed Sacrament, in the Church of St. Birgitta. Ever after, during our five weeks stay in Rome, I felt something like a magnet drawing me to that little Church on the Piazza Farnese.

> One Sunday afternoon, I planned to spend an hour alone in the room from where St. Birgitta's soul had taken its flight into Heaven. I was seeking my way through the streets with a guide-book in my hand, when suddenly a respectably dressed woman came up to me and saying *"Oh! you Church-running foreigner"*—spit in my face! I felt, for a second, pained and confused, but then I put my hand on my heart and said to Our Dear Lord, "I am not worthy to have had done to me, what was done to you." Then with a feeling of gratitude toward the woman who had been instrumental in my being permitted to take this part in My Lord's Passion, I continued my way through the streets to the Piazza Farnese.

Maria washed her face in the fountain, and went inside her beloved church. But now she was determined to find out more about the situation here.

High up under the ceiling vault there was a fresco showing a white figure, surrounded by happy and unhappy souls. Was it not Holy Birgitta?

There were two side altars, one to the left, with a painting of Saint Birgitta, dressed in the habit of her Order, and beside her stood another woman saint—was it St. Teresa of Avila, the great Saint of the Carmelites? She must talk to the nuns about this.

But soon Maria found out that she could not visit with the Sisters in this House. They were indeed Carmelites living under papal enclosure. There were no Brigittines left in the world—at

41

least none here! That was the message she received from the convent porter.

She now felt she must turn to the Jesuits, to Father Brandi, to whom Father Hagen had recommended her. Here she was to find another Jesuit who played a guiding role in her life.

Father Brandi was a very busy man, prominent in the Vatican, but he gave Maria freely of his time. At once he was interested in her case:

Of course, I shall arrange for you to meet the Carmelite Sisters in their Parlatorium. That is the only way possible. Concerning Brigittine Sisters, that is more difficult. I am not an expert on Scandinavian Orders. To tell the truth, there are so many women's Orders that it is hard to keep track of their histories. But the Brigittines, Double-Convents—yes, there *were* originally double Convents of Brigittine Priests and of Sisters. But now the Priests do not exist any more—I have no time just now, but I'll find out about it. In the meantime, there is something quite different that I would suggest to you.

In the middle of March, Bishop Albert Bitter, who represents the Catholic communities in Sweden, is coming to Rome. Father Hagen and I thought we could arrange to have you confirmed by Bishop Bitter. A daughter of Sweden should be confirmed by a Swedish Bishop...

Maria was eager to comply. A young Jesuit was sent to prepare her for Confirmation. She wrote in her *Notes:*

The day of my Confirmation was another day of grace. It became clearer and clearer to me that my life should be dedicated to the service of St. Birgitta's and my own, beloved country.

I had the great privilege of receiving a special Blessing from Pope Leo XIII for my Confirmation, but as it arrived just as the ceremony was over and the Bishop had gone from the altar, he told us that he would give it to us from the altar after Benediction in our Holy Mother St. Birgitta's House on the Feast of the Annunciation, March 25th.

This was indeed a fortunate circumstance. The kind Bishop Bitter now saw his chance of helping Maria to meet the Carmelite Superior and to enter the rooms associated with holy Birgitta and her daughter Catherine. He also wished to visit them and talk with the Carmelites. In his company, they would be obliged to receive her as well. And so it was.

42

They first visited the room of St. Birgitta, going up through the entrance on Via Monserrato. Maria would have liked to stay for hours in this room where the holy woman had died. She kissed the glass that covered the top of the wooden table on which the Saint wrote down the Latin text of her Revelations; the table on which she had also breathed out her last sigh. She had wanted to die on wood, as her Lord, on the wood of the Cross.

After Benediction, followed the solemn papal blessing. Then the guests assembled in the Parlatorium. To Maria it felt very strange to come inside of those well-protected walls, for the first time.

A table was set right up against the grille of the cloister and there, on the other side, sat the Mother Superior and two other Sisters.

The conversation went on, partly in German. The usual, conventional questions were asked and answered. It was almost time to break up. Then Maria, who had been introduced, at last had the chance of asking the question for which she had indeed come. Were there any Birgitta Sisters, and where?

"My dear—unprepared as I am, I cannot answer" said the Superior. "In Spain there are some Sisters of the Order you mean. . . . You might write to them—that is a thing that might have value for Sweden. . . . There are *some* other Convents, I would think, small, poor, may God in His Goodness prevent them from dying out. But where? How many? Possibly we have some notes about them in our archives."

The visit was over. The kind Bishop wished Maria well and hoped that he would see her again in Sweden.

Father Brandi, as a parting gift, handed Maria a ticket to an audience with the Holy Father (Leo XIII).

Her time in Rome was getting short. Maria visited St. Birgitta's Church as often as possible. One day, when she was deep in prayer, that soundless Voice came back again: *It is here that you must work. You, daughter of Saint Birgitta, must work for God, and Birgitta herself will help you.*

Dear Lord—how can I work for God. Where? How? and again the voice seemed to say: *You are St. Birgitta's daughter; you shall work for God. Isn't that clear enough?*

Maria says in her *Notes:*

The last morning in Rome my friend and I went to receive Holy Communion in Our Holy Mother St. Birgitta's Church. I felt the same, incomprehensible *drawing* and could hardly tear myself away. I thought the voice I had heard in that Church on my first visit was imagination and that it was my duty to do all that I could to forget it. But as the train was taking us away from the Eternal City, my soul seemed to be left behind with St. Birgitta.

On the way back to London, we stayed in Genoa and visited the famous cemetery, the Hospital of St. Catherine of Genoa and some Churches, but whenever I went where the Blessed Sacrament was, I heard the same voice saying: *Return to Rome, to the House of St. Birgitta.*

We visited Paray-le-Monial, and while there, I prayed earnestly to the Sacred Heart and Its great Apostle, St. Marguerite-Marie, to be delivered from any illusion I might be suffering under. I became very disturbed in soul as I had no one to whom I could confide this matter.

And so Maria prayed to be delivered from *illusions*. Back in London, her confessors there, who did not really know her, also warned her against them. Yet her *Notes* relate a fresh experience:

One evening after supper in the Convent where we were staying, I went as usual to visit the Most Blessed Sacrament before going to my room and again I heard distinctly the same voice—"*Return to Rome, to St. Birgitta's House*"—

My soul was so full of pain and distress, that as soon as I reached my room I sank down again on my knees and continued to pray to be delivered from illusion. While I was praying, I seemed to lose my thoughts and I saw myself dressed in a gray habit behind the window of St. Birgitta's House in Rome. Two delicate, beautiful, wounded hands were holding a cross and offering it to me. For a moment, I hesitated in strange fear, but something within me suddenly grew stronger and I held out my arms to receive the cross saying, *Thy Will be done: it is all I seek.* I came back to my thoughts, rose to my feet, and found that it was four o'clock in the morning. My body, though it was wintertime, was covered with perspiration, the struggle in my soul had been so intense; But interiorly, I was again at peace and full of confidence.

Last Visit to Fridhem

It was in May, 1903, that Maria left London once more, for her home in Sweden. She stayed over in Gothenburg on the way, with the Elisabeth Sisters, who worked among the sick. They had access to the Jesuit church, mentioned before, which lay on an old street in a poor section of the city. It was only open on Sundays for Mass, but they had lent Maria a key so that she could visit the Blessed Sacrament, so neglected here. One day, she was going in, when a band of ruffians came by, and as she unlocked the door, pushed her rudely inside, and stamped and rampaged around, until she thought she was going to be killed. Finally, they rushed out again, and she was able to lock the door; she writes in her *Notes:*

> When alone with my dearest Lord, I begged Him to forgive my presumption, in fearing I would meet a martyr's death, and before Him, in the sanctuary of His Love, the only thing I heard was *"Return to Rome, to St. Birgitta's House—"*
>
> I spoke several times with the Jesuit Father in charge of the little Church. He had been a friend of Fr. Hagen. . . . I also told him how I had met the Bishop of Sweden in Rome and how I felt drawn to the House of St. Birgitta. But he did not give me any direct advice; he only said: "If you have plenty of money, visit the Mother-House of the Elisabeth Sisters who nurse the sick." Plenty of money, I did not have, and no interior drawing to that Order. I had loved my life in the Hospital and it was my joy and consolation to labour for the sick-poor, but after my visit to St. Birgitta's House in Rome, I felt that God wanted something else."

Later, on her way back through Gothenburg, Maria met Bishop Bitter, and again, asked his advice: "Dearest daughter," he had said, "One can serve God in so many, countless, ways. Just now, we cannot consider any more Catholic institutions in Sweden. Sisters in Rome? In Birgitta's House? A beautiful dream. . . . Go back to America. You have good connections in New York. My advice is to leave and start a work for Sweden, *there.*"

The bishop had spoken. But had God spoken? From Father Hagen, Maria had learned the highest respect for the Churches' bishops and priests. But at the same time, their saintly Jesuit

Father in Gothenburg had said, "No one can advise you really well, except your own Confessor, who knows you in and out."

Yes, she felt that it was Father Hagen who could give her the right counsel. In the meantime, she had been to Fridhem. Let her tell in her own words of her last visit there.

At my home, the sweet and, at that time, so dear *Fridhem*, I was received with greater affection than ever. The best room and the most comfortable bed had been prepared for my arrival. I had seen *Fridhem* in its winter dress of pure, white snow; it was beautiful then, but still more so now in the fresh, young green of May. The flag of our country was hoisted high on the big flagstaff in the middle of the garden, as I walked up the steps with one of my brothers who had met me at the station. I heard the voices of my younger sisters welcoming me home with music and singing and on the door-step stood my dear mother with open arms. All was so sweet and beautiful, the hope and desire of many years, of being able to give a home to my dear mother, was fulfilled.

But when my elder brother spoke to me with praise about this and of the gratitude which the whole family wished to express to me, my soul was profoundly saddened by the foreboding of a fierce inner struggle to come. Evening came and I retired to my room, and remained long in prayer before going to bed.

I did everything to drive away the thought of St. Birgitta's House in Rome, tried in every way to interest myself in our home and the beautiful country-side around, and I prayed continually to know and do God's Holy Will alone. The battle within my soul was so great that I could never have endured it, but for the many graces my dearest Lord granted me. The Rosary was my companion and I used to go out in the woods and into the little grotto, praying for hours.

It became clearer and clearer to me that I had to follow Our Lord's invitation: *"Go sell all you have and give to the poor and come, follow Me."* One day, when I had been in my home about six weeks, I felt that I had to tell my dear mother sisters and brothers, that I could not remain many days longer. Oh, how very, very hard it was.... We all loved the sweet, little home, our *Fridhem*.

The wind blew through the trees, just as in her childhood days. But no beautiful promise came to her now. The wordless Voice carried a note of reproach as if Maria was not sufficiently filled with confidence: slowly, very slowly, but with deadly seriousness, it went like a sharp sword into her soul:

Sell what you have—and then come, follow Me—

Sell what you have—but it would be the others who would suffer most—that could not be right. It was she who should make a sacrifice, but not the others.

Then one day her sister Agnes came and said: "Maria, I believe you have entirely different tasks that await you. You have done enough for us. I can take care of Mother, it would be wonderful to have her with me, you'll see—everthing can be arranged. Let us sell Fridhem!

After some days of inner struggle, Maria agreed. The family seemed to take it more as a matter of course, than she. "*We have had only the loan of it,*" they said.

Maria thanked God for this solution. The others were glad to be able to do her a favor, after all she had done for them. But for her, it was hard to ask them to give back a present that she had so willingly given. She felt as if she were robbing them; it was one of the worst trials that had been given her.

It was in July, 1903, that Maria left Europe, to sail for America once more. The future lay unknown and insecure before her. She knew nothing of what might be ahead, but she counted on help—God's help, through Father Hagen's good counsel.

As always, on her way over the ocean, Maria was seized by the thought of God's mighty Spirit, "brooding over the waters," by God's endlessness, and man's insignificance. She often stayed up on deck late at night to pray under the twinkling stars:

> Ave Maris Stella
> Dei Mater Alma
> Atque semper Virgo
> Felix Coeli Porta

She prayed, as the steamer was taking her farther and farther away, from her beloved Sweden, from Rome; but it was also taking her to her saintly Jesuit Father, whom she trusted that God had sent to help and guide her. Yes, Father Hagen was indeed Maria's last hope as far as human counsel could go, in the difficult choice ahead.

Chapter VI

New York—Sten Ture

BACK in New York once more, Maria seemed determined to counteract her mental uncertainty and restlessness by settling down to a demanding, practical task. Strange that she did not seek at once to speak with Father Hagen. She wrote to him for an appointment during the following month, but in the meantime, contacted the *Guilds* for whom she had worked before. Perhaps she was testing herself once again. She describes this next period in her *Notes:*

> During the next four months I plunged myself into more active charity work than ever, visiting the sick-poor for one of the Catholic Guilds, visiting as many as thirty or more poor families in one day, many of them living on the 6th, 7th or 8th floor of the most terrible tenements. During these months, I was absent a few days in August to assist at my friend's profession in the Visitation Convent in Washington, and to consult with my dear spiritual Father Pater Hagen, S.J. regarding the state of my soul.

The letter he had written to welcome her shows how clearly he believed in her vocation.

Georgetown College Observatory
West Washington, D.C.   August 1903
My Dear Child in Christ:
   My absence for a few days must be my excuse for not answering your question sooner. You will find me on the 12th and 13th at any hour you may please. On the 14th in the afternoon I shall be out. I shall be very glad to see you again, especially about your vocation. Your last letter was a genuine "manifestation of conscience"; it speaks loudly

and clearly that you are called by Providence to lead a higher life in a religious Order. You may regard this question as settled. To what place you are called does not seem clear yet and will be the subject of our conversation and prayer.

Thanking you for your good wishes and congratulating you on the light God has given you, I remain,

In the love of Christ, your Father,
J. G. Hagen, S.J.

At last, Maria had several conferences with Father Hagen. She made clear to him that she did not feel any true satisfaction in her work in New York. She told him, in every detail, about her feeling of being *drawn* to St. Birgitta's House, and her longing for it.

With Father Hagen's permission, Maria wrote to the Carmelite Superior in Rome. Maria told of her great love for St. Birgitta. She described how she had had visions of the House and seen herself there, both as a child and again, when older. Also, that she truly felt herself to be a daughter of St. Birgitta—not only because she was Swedish, but because of these experiences.

Maria went back to her charity work in New York, her hard work of love. She allowed herself no rest. And still, whenever she prayed for help and guidance, there came the answer: *Go back to St. Birgitta's House.*

October came; the fall was cold and raw. But a ray of light pierced the gloom. The Carmelites had answered her, saying that she was welcome to come to St. Birgitta's House, to unite with them in work for the convent so dear to them both.

With Father Hagen's consent, she then wrote to them, accepting the invitation. . . . But in the meantime, her old illness began to come back. Hemorrhages set in. Her old friend, Marie Cisneros, came back into the picture; she was furious that Maria had been so careless about her health, and insisted on taking her to a private hospital.

Maria wrote again to the Carmelites that she wanted very much to come to Rome, but that she was temporarily sick. That nothing could be decided for the moment.

Maria was not happy in the luxurious, private hospital. She

49

found everything too expensive and fussy. Worst of all, they didn't seem to like having a priest come to give her Holy Communion. They warned her against long prayers and meditation. Her friend was sure that it was Father Hagen who had put her up to all this exaggerated piety and life of sacrifice. One night, Maria woke up suddenly from a dream—it seemed as though someone wanted to steal Father Hagen away from her!

What should she do? She wrote to Father Hagen of her "dream." What would he answer? Fortunately, we have his letter here:

Georgetown College Observatory
West Washington, D.C.   Nov. 15, 1903
My Dear Child in Christ:

Your *dream* was a reality. I have received two letters, but by one answer, I have discouraged further correspondence, because it is calculated to undermine your confidence. The letters are mainly on your state of health and the fear of losing you.

You question me about writing to Rome. I fully approve. Let them decide; and then you will have one more sign from Providence. In your case, I see more and more that it is safest to watch the Hand of Divine Providence and see where it leads you, by circumstances, by health, by needy souls thrown into your way and such signs. Like Daniel, I shall follow these signs with greatest interest.

Maria's condition grew worse. Specialists were called in and they were far from optimistic. But they wanted to do what they could for this "friend of the poor." They agreed that she might be removed to Bellevue Hospital, where she had a small, bare room, with iron bed and chair. Here, she had to remain from November, 1903, until February, 1904. But she was content. She could live in that simplicity that pleased her Franciscan spirit. Almost all hope had been given up for her recovery, but she had not given up, as she relates in her *Notes:*

I said to Our Dear Lord, "If it is Your voice that bids me go, give me only sufficient strength to rise from this bed and I will go there to die for You and my country...."

With Fr. Hagen's permission, I had written to the Superior in Our Holy Mother's House in Rome, asking her to give me a little corner

50

outside the Enclosure where I could die, because the best physicians had told me I had not long to live. To this request, I received the following letter:

"Our Rev. Prioress wants me to tell you that the place for the sick child is in her Mother's House."

At these words, and on Fr. Hagen's assurance that I was *carried by Grace,* as he expressed it, peace, strength and confidence filled my soul (the letter continued):

"Our Mother-Superior awaits your announcement of when you are able to undertake the journey here, and would like to know in good time, the day of your arrival...."

They were awaiting her in St. Birgitta's House. They were waiting for her to come home! When would she dare to risk the departure?

In her *Notes,* Maria relates how she finally found the strength to leave the hospital for a convent where she prepared to undertake the long voyage to Rome.

Her health was somewhat better, and she received a final permission and advice from Father Hagen, to leave before more obstacles arose in her path. (The attempts of her friend to retain her, extended even to sending a telegram to the captain of the steamship on which she intended to sail, warning him that his passenger would die on the boat.) She had already obtained a ticket for a crossing to Italy, via the Mediterranean. And she had the additional encouragement of a traveling companion— her youngest brother whom she had helped to educate and who was an officer on a ship in the Pacific Ocean. She had written asking him to help her, and as she said:

Providence arranged it so that my letter reached him as his ship came in to San Francisco. He obtained two months leave and arrived at the Convent one afternoon. He had dressed himself smartly as a man of the world, and brought a beautiful bunch of flowers for his sick sister. But when he saw the place I was in, the crucifix on the wall, he exclaimed: "My dear sister, what has happened to you?" "Dear Boy," I answered, "your sister has found faith, peace and joy in Our Lord. May He grant you the same!"

"Oh no!" he replied, "I have other things to think about. I must make a man of myself." So we said no more about it at that time. The next day he went to the Steamship Company and obtained a ticket for himself...on my boat. The Convent was on 142nd Street, New York, and as I was so ill and had promised Fr. Hagen to be as prudent as I could, I drove with my dear brother to a house opposite the Church of St. Francis Xavier on 16th Street to spend the night there and divide the journey to the docks in Hoboken into two parts. After I had heard Mass and received Holy Communion early the next morning (The Feast of St. Francis Xavier) we drove in a cab to the steamer. My body was so full of pain that I could hardly sit up in the carriage and my brother had to help me on board. But the moment we put our feet on the deck of the ship, a wonderful feeling of confidence and peace came over me, which upheld me during the whole voyage.

So Maria had left New York once more; had seen the Statue of Liberty disappear. For eighteen years, the United States had been her homeland. The place where she had worked, where she had developed her profession. Now she had left everything which represented any kind of security in this world, and against the advice of many, started directly out to follow God into the pathless desert of an uncertain future.

In her *Notes* she describes her voyage:

It was the month of March, the month of storms, but the ocean was like a clear mirror all the time. My dear brother was like a little nurse, helping me up on deck every day and when he put the travelling rugs under his arm for me, I put the Catechism book under my arm for him, and so we marched daily to our little corner on the deck where we could speak undisturbed about God and the Holy Faith. When we talked of the seriousness of life, he said:

"Do you know, Maria, I could never do anything that I know you wouldn't like. When I hear something bad or when the Captain or friends try to take me with them on drinking sprees, or things like that, I can just see you in front of me, and hear a voice in my heart, saying *What would* Maria think of *that?*—and then the temptation is gone."

When we had only a few days more on board, my brother was walking very thoughtfully up and down the deck where I was sitting and suddenly he stopped before me and said: "Do you know, my dear sister, that I fear before we part in Rome, you will see me kneeling down before the Altar to be received into the Catholic Church."

It was indeed a happy Maria who landed with her brother at Naples on the evening of the twenty-fourth of March. They went together to an early Mass and then took the train to Rome.

Rome: The Carmelite Community

Maria and her brother arrived in Rome on the eve of the Annunciation, just one year from the day that the bishop of Sweden had given Maria the special Benediction from Pope Leo XIII, from the altar of St. Birgitta. She was deeply moved to be back once more, and Sten Ture was impressed with this fine building; it was not merely a small church between two large columns, but a square palazzo, not to be compared with the magnificent Palazzo Farnese across the square, yet still a handsome structure which had been built around the old House and Chapel of Birgitta, incorporating and protecting them, as has often happened with historic monuments in Italy.

Across the lintel of the little church was written: *Domus sancta Birgitte Vastenensis.* And above the facade, two white stone statues: St. Birgitta and St. Catherine. The tall, brown walls stretched out on either side with ample windows opening on the square, and another lengthy facade lay along the adjacent Via Monserrato.

They rang the bell at the heavy door to the right of the iron church gate, and it was opened by an out-Sister who seemed to be expecting them. They were shown up to the small parlatorium where Maria had been with Bishop Bitter. Somewhat timidly, they took chairs facing an iron grille. Soon a curtain was drawn back, and there appeared two figures in brown habits and black veils. From one of them came a friendly voice:

"Welcome to the House of St. Birgitta, you are very welcome, Miss Maria. I am Mother Hedwig...." Maria, in her deep voice, expressed her gratitude.

Sten Ture was speechless. He had never seen anything like these wax figures, who sat motionless, their faces hidden. He was used to the warm, quick gestures of southern lands—and those iron bars! He would never let his sister stay in a place like this!

But then the gentle voice continued: "Your brother is welcome, too. We have found him a room nearby. Perhaps you would like a little refreshment after your trip from Naples."

The out-Sister brought in a small tray with two glasses of wine and a few cakes—"So this was convent life, too," thought Sten Ture, more and more puzzled. It made him feel strange to eat his cakes, with the Sisters watching him through the bars. He felt as if *he* were an animal in a cage!

The interview was over. Maria was to be shown into the convent, and Sten Ture to his room nearby. It had all happened so quickly. Maria did not realize she was to be accepted so soon. Mother Hedwig had said they could meet the next day, and Maria would be free to come and go as long as her brother was in Rome.

The following morning, Sten Ture begged his sister to leave the convent. He could not stand the thought that she was to be enclosed like this, behind bars. She tried to explain to him the beauty and meaning of a cloistered life—but what had she really experienced of it, herself? She did not argue with her dear brother. She was happy enough that he had found God in his own way. She arranged to have Father Brandi give him instruction, so that he could soon enter the Church.

(But perhaps this was one of the reasons that Maria Elisabeth, later, Mother Elisabeth, was always against a strict enclosure. It had given her brother and many others a false idea of what the religious life really was—as if there was some secret magic or *hokus-pokus* about the cloister. Why should there be a reason to hide so much that was rich and beautiful in the daily life of an Order? Maria herself was a natural contemplative who enjoyed the *clausura*—but she never overestimated its value. As we shall see later, the developing Mother Elisabeth weighed the advantages and the disadvantages of it, with clear discernment.)

That first night, when Maria went to her room, it was not long before Mother Hedwig appeared. She was no longer the wax figure behind the grille, but a delicate, warm, gentle person who radiated love and interest. She had been deeply impressed with Maria's letters and she said that it was a joy to have with them, a soul who was so plainly a child of St. Birgitta. She was happy to see her brother, too, and she had already said that

Maria was free to leave the convent as she wished; "You must only be careful not to overstrain yourself; you have been very sick. But be confident, my Child, God's almighty Providence will surely continue to lead us."

Alone in her room, Maria was calm. Surely, God would lead all for the best. Wasn't she already in St. Birgitta's House? Only that was proof that God, in a special way, had helped her. . . .

The night was calm. Maria slept. . . . It was early, early morning when she awoke. She had a feeling that she should get dressed, though it was much too early to go to Mass. Should she write letters? Yes, she must tell Father Hagen how happy she was that she had really reached St. Birgitta's House. But where was she really? There had been so many steps, so many turns when she came in, tired, the night before.

She must look out of the window. It was hard to get the heavy blinds open. (Later, Maria understood that they were not supposed to be opened; she had broken one of the Carmelites' rules on that early morning of the twenty-sixth of March, 1904.) Finally, she succeeded in opening them wide and leaned out.

She looked out; she leaned out of the window—the fountains splashed and played, but it was as though she heard a sound still louder, a song of some miraculous origin, coming out of the past. . . . She sank back. Why, why was this so amazing?

She began to orient her thoughts; she had been standing and leaning out, almost in the same position and *in the same window* in which she had seen "the little Maria" standing when she had first had her dream or vision of the square and of St. Birgitta's House. The "little Maria" had stood in a window of St. Birgitta's House long before the grown-up Maria had seen it with her own eyes.

Now, just now, the grown-up Maria, tired and weak, was standing inside that window. She had never mentioned anything about a window in her letters to the Sisters in Rome, nor had she ever described that window to Father Hagen, when she had told him about her dream of the House. But she herself had always known exactly what window it was. And now she was there . . . leaning on that very sill.

Did she need to doubt any longer? Could there be any possible doubt that God had lead her there? Her soul was overflowing with joy.

The days went by. The Carmelite Sisters did everything to help Maria and her brother, as long as he was still in Rome. Maria spent much time with him, and she followed along with Father Brandi as he explained to Sten Ture the great mysteries of Easter into which they were just entering. Sten Ture must go back to his work on the sea, so it was arranged that he should be taken into the Church during Holy Week.

The Carmelite Sisters had arranged everything beautifully in the chapel. Early in the morning, Father Brandi came, bringing with him a friend, who was to be Sten Ture's Godfather. This friend was the Swedish Count Klaes Lagergren, a colorful character and a convert who later wrote his memoirs. In them, he gives a description of Sten Ture, and the ceremony, saying that he was deeply moved by both brother and sister:

"Young Hesselblad, who was a seaman in the American commercial fleet, had a handsome and manly appearance. His sister was a young woman of about thirty with a peculiarly attractive expression in her face, and her eyes radiated mildness. Something indefinable issued from her personality. She had a wonderful smile when she told me that she had come to Rome to become a nun. Words fail me to describe the deep impression she made upon me."

In the High Mass that followed soon afterwards, in St. Birgitta's Church, Sten Ture received his first Holy Communion; Maria kneeling beside him, offered her communion for her brother's welfare and happiness, this dear brother who was even nearer to her now. Little did she think, at that time, that his life would be shorter than her's!

In 1915, after the first World War had started, she had a prophetic dream about him. She relates it in her *Notes,* after she described his departure from Rome:

56

A few days later my dear brother returned alone to America, crossing the ocean from Naples to New York and then across the United States to San Francisco to take up his post as second in command on the S/S Pacific, which was ready to leave for the Philippines.

The following years he wrote regularly and was leading the life of a good Catholic Officer. But when the (first) World War broke out, all news from him was stopped. I redoubled my prayer for this dear brother who had also been "my son."

One day in 1915, when praying for him, I was, in spirit, transported far away and saw before me a large stretch of water; a terrible storm was raging and on the black waves, two vessels were struggling, one large and one small. The larger one was almost under water, and no sign of life could be seen. The smaller boat was sinking rapidly, only the upper part of the bridge could be seen. On it, stood a beautiful figure holding out her arms to them all, and someone was kneeling at her feet. The light emanating from her was wonderful and threw a bright, heavenly light over the dark water. The kneeling figure turned his face and I recognized my young brother, peaceful and calm, looking up to her as a small boy looks at his mother. There were young faces and old, and storm-worn faces in the water; all were turned toward their young Captain and to the figure on the bridge of the sinking ship. And then all of a sudden, burst forth the melody of the well-known hymn so dear to my heart: *Ave Maris Stella.*

After the war was over, in 1920, I received from the Philippines, the news that my dear brother had offered to go out from Manila with his boat and eleven men to try to save the crew of a torpedoed warship, but a terrific storm made every effort useless and all the brave men were lost.

Chapter VII

Rome: The Carmelite Community

EASTER was over—Rome had had its big Feast. Now Maria was ready to go through an even greater ceremony—that of leaving the outside world entirely, for the stricter, higher life of the Carmelite Convent.

No one knew of her determination except her brother and Father Hagen, who had felt so sure of her vocation. Mother Hedwig, too, seemed to be convinced that she should accept this unusual girl with her great love for Birgitta, into the House of the Swedish Saint; but just how this would work out, she, the Superior herself, did not know.

Of course, the Carmelite Sisters did expect to receive her as one of their own. But Mother Hedwig was afraid she was too weak to follow the rule of the Order. The Sisters' day began at five-thirty and ended at eleven-thirty at night. Maria must rest more; she could eat little enough as it was. She must not fast. When Maria said she wanted to be considered like the others, Mother Hedwig said, with her soft, winning smile: "My Dear, to obey is better than to sacrifice—I will see how much you are able to stand. It is much better to begin slowly."

There were several young girls who were postulants at the time—but Maria's position was quite different. She could take part in the Sister's life and live in the House, but she was not entirely one of them. Her seat in the choir was nearest the door —she was glad to have this humble, anonymous place—for she felt her old malady returning.

But how could she thank God enough for letting her come

here, even if it were only to die under the roof of Holy Birgitta of Vadstena.

In this House the great Swedish prophetess lived for more than twenty years—in the deepest humility and sacrifice; here she wrote her forthright warnings and letters to the powerful of her world, without fear of man (or public opinion); here she worked over the Latin version of her *Revelations* which should come to be of such great significance for many inside and outside the Church.

In her *Notes,* Maria speaks of these days:

My health was about the same (which meant, very bad!) for the following five years in Our Holy Mother's House. I had only been there a week, when I begged the Rev. Mother Superior's permission to order from an Art printing house in Sweden some thousands of small and larger pictures of St. Birgitta of Sweden and St. Catherine of Sweden. These I used to send all over the world—to Sweden, to Spain and to the U.S.—to Churches, Priests and schools; so great was my desire, that my Heavenly Patron and Mother would again become better known. And during recreation with the nuns, the subject I always spoke of was my two dear Saints and their virtues and my hope of their help for the spiritual revival of my countrymen.

I used to spend the greater part of my time in prayer in the room where our Holy Mother St. Birgitta died, sitting on a low stool or on the floor. When I was able, I used to follow the Community exercises in Choir, etc. And I considered this a great privilege for which I should show gratitude.

While often so ill that I could only go to the Choir for Mass and Benediction and then back to bed, I had much time to read, and so I continued to study Church History, especially the Swedish and I learnt about how some Brigittine Fathers who had been in this very House, had fallen away from the Faith. A great sorrow filled my soul and I pleaded with My Lord to take my life in reparation and grant that the Brigittine Fathers might be again restored.

Indeed, this House of St. Birgitta had had a strange history, ever since the first chapel was built, probably between 1433 and 1435, by the Vadstena monks who were first appointed to live there and maintain the House as a hospice for Swedish pilgrims.

In 1513, Petrus Magni—called Månson in Swedish—built the larger church, of the same size and location as the present one, but with a simple, wooden roof. After being Rector of St. Birgitta's House for many years, he returned to Sweden and became the last Catholic bishop of Västerås. The history of the Reformation shows that he was a link between the old and the new Swedish Churches through the apostolic succession. Whether this is accepted or not, the fact remains that the builder of St. Birgitta's Church in Rome eventually had a strong impact on the history of the Church in Sweden.

In 1523, the last Brigittine monk of Vadstena in Rome (Lars Bengtsson) was buried in St. Birgitta's Church. His epitaph is well preserved in the gray marble floor. From 1560 to 1589, the Magdalene Sisters took up residence in the House at Piazza Farnese. After this, the House was supposed to serve as a seminary for young men wishing to become priests. In June, 1673, the famous Queen Christina, who abdicated the Swedish throne in order to become a Catholic, was nominated Administrator of Birgitta's House. In these capacities, she is presumed to have visited it, but there is no record of her staying there. We only know that she resided for some time on the opposite side of the square at the beautiful Palazzo Farnese.

In 1692, Brigittine Monks of Altomünster obtained the right to settle in St. Birgitta's House, to take care of the church and the rooms of the two saints, Birgitta and Catherine, which had been left undisturbed, though apartments had been constructed around them. At this time, the church underwent another renovation. On one side of the entrance, is the ornate, marble tomb of Count Niels Bielke, a Swedish nobleman who left his country to retain his Catholic faith, became a Roman senator, and remained so until he died in 1765.

When the Altomünster monks were obliged to leave, at the time of Napoleon, the House was vacant. No monks nor member of St. Birgitta's Order claimed this historic place. In 1828, Pope Leo XII, who had been a canon of Santa Maria in Trastevere, gave the House, the church, and all its possessions to the Chapter in that ancient basilica. No one showed any interest in the House of Santa Birgitta. It fell into a miserable state of neglect. Finally, in 1855, the French Holy Cross Fathers obtained the right to inhabit the house, provided they would undertake the necessary restorations. They used a few rooms themselves; the rest of the House was rented out to various persons. The present sacristy was turned into a coffee shop or bar. We must give the Holy Cross Fathers credit for having taken good care of St. Birgitta's room. Its present condition and paintings were ordered by them. A French painter created the frescoes and a large canvas of St. Birgitta on her deathbed. Thus, the room acquired its rich, baroque appearance, but lost its original simplicity.

In 1889, the Holy Cross Fathers left; it was at this time that Polish Carmelite nuns were looking for a place to make a new Foundation. Here hides another strange story. Mother Hedwig had unjustly been forced to leave a convent which she had formerly headed in Poland, and sought this means of re-establishing her Community. She was a member of the Polish Aristocracy and also a strong character who had suffered much and that is probably why she had so much understanding for Sister Maria Elisabeth. Mother Hedwig was able to obtain the House on a very long lease from the Chapter at Santa Maria in Trastevere. It was never fully hers. But at least she felt settled for her own lifetime.

When Mother Hedwig acquired sudden wealth, through the death of an uncle, the House and church received another renovation in 1892–1894. The rich orange-toned marble of the church and altar, and much of the gilt decoration, date from this time. A large scene of St. Birgitta with St. Teresa, was painted above the side altar; (this Mother Elizabeth later painted over, transforming St. Teresa into St. Catherine!) The room of St. Catherine was adorned by two large paintings of scenes from her life.

A heavy grille divided the chapel from the choir, but up in a small tribune, under the round window of the church, was a lighter grille through which it was easier to see the altar and to look down into the church. It was in this little tribune, ten years later, that Maria was allowed to sit when she was too weak to go to the choir.

We have few details of Sister Elisabeth's first months as a postulant, but fortunately, we have letters which she wrote to her family at this time. She never complained and when she wrote, it was to reassure them that she was happy here. Always faithful to her correspondence with her mother and sisters, she told them in simple language of her new life, and of Mother Hedwig.

12/5/1904, to Agnes. Day of the Ascension:...
You ask me if I can ever come to Sweden? That lies in God's Hands. Humanly speaking, it is impossible. But for God nothing is impossible. My health, thanks be to God, and to the good Mother here in the House, and to the love and care of the Sisters, is much better than I had hoped it would be. To tell you the truth, I had hoped only to get here, so that I might die in this House....

Our Mother Hedwig belongs to the family of an old Polish King. All her large inheritance she has spent, restoring this House and this Church to the honor and memory of St. Birgitta. She is the same loving Mother to the simplest country-girl that comes to live the Convent life, as to a young lady of high rank. She is now nearly 70 years old, but never spares herself....

8/25, to Anna:
...The last weeks, I have been worse again. Writing you from my bed. The Sisters are very kind and do everything they can for me. They have some hens down here in the court-yard and let me have all the fresh eggs. The little capital that I have left would never be enough to live anywhere, except in a place like this, where what one does for the sick is not measured by its worth in money, but is done for Love of God.

The weeks went by. Maria's condition seemed a little better; but doctors were of a different opinion. They had told Mother Hedwig that Maria would probably not live long. But for Maria herself, it was hard to believe that her situation was any more desperate than it had been before. In spite of all her medical experience, she could not accept the fact that her life might end before she had accomplished more of what she felt that God wanted her to do.

One evening, the convent confessor called on Maria, so that she might rid her soul of any troubling thoughts and receive the balm of forgiveness after confession.

About an hour later, there was a knock at the door, and the warm, gentle voice of Mother Hedwig said: "My daughter, are you ready to let the Lord come in?"

Then she entered, with two other Sisters, carrying the little altar that Maria knew so well from her hospital experiences by the bed of the dying. So they really thought this was the end for her—she hesitated a moment and then replied in her calm, deep voice: "Yes, Mother, I am unworthy, but if it is God's will, I am ready—"

Then Mother Hedwig began to recite those short prayers which the Church has gathered for the consolation of the suffering and to prepare the soul for its release from the prison of its body.

"Look mercifully upon thy servant who labors under sickness of the body, and refresh the soul which Thou hast made; so that at the hour of its going hence, it may be found worthy to be borne to Thee, its maker, free from all stain of sin, by the hands of the holy Angels—"

Through the door could be heard the delicate ringing of the little bell which the Sisters carried to accompany the Blessed Sacrament, coming nearer and nearer, in the hands of the priest. Then he crossed over the threshold, and Maria made a great effort to raise herself up.

The Sisters stood around her, helping her to make the responses and blending their prayers with hers, in faith and love.

It seemed to Maria that she was surrounded by a light, an unending light, where the Good Shepherd was waiting for her— but then she felt as if a warm, cleansing fire, or a current was passing through her body—

Per istam sanctam unctionem—she heard the words of the priest—*through this anointing with the consecrated ointment*— and she felt how the priest's finger touched her body with the holy oil, to cleanse, to sanctify, perhaps to heal.

After the priest had gone out, a few of the Sisters stayed to watch with her. An extreme weakness had overcome her. But slowly, after some hours, she came to herself.

What were Maria's thoughts in those hours? Is it presumptuous to think that she had perhaps felt the same longing that St. Birgitta had had in this very House, five days before her death?

It was on that day that Birgitta had been seized by the desire to be clad in the habit of her own Order which did not yet exist, but for which she felt that Christ Himself had given her instructions, even to the exact habit that her Sisters were to wear. In her *Revelations,* (the Rule, Chapter 4.) she describes it in detail; the gray habit and the white crown with five red dots for the wounds of *The Most Holy Savior.* (Birgitta had had such a garment made for herself and is supposed to have worn it on her deathbed—or at least so it has been pictured.)

But Maria had been told that she must wear the brown habit of the Carmelites. It was only later that she began to express her overpowering desire to wear the gray habit of a Brigittine.

Perhaps she would have been allowed to wear it, if she had come still closer to death. But now she seemed to gain new strength through her anointing—it would be two years before she would finally be professed as a Carmelite or as a Brigittine.

This entry from a personal diary—not from the *Notes*—reveals that her mood was sometimes darker than she would admit; the struggles in her soul were not yet over.

Extract from a "*Diary of our Venerable and Beloved Mother Elisabeth* Feast of St. Elisabeth, November 19, 1904

"*The Chalice which my Father has given me, shall I not drink it?*"

These Thy own words, Dear Lord, give me courage and strength. If You hide Yourself from my soul and offer me the Chalice of darkness, the cup of anguish and bitterness, still let me always say, *Thy Will be done*—

My heart is ready, O Lord, My heart is ready to do whatever pleases Thee, and whatever Thou ordainest. Into Thy loving, Fatherly Hands do I commit my future days, if they be few or many.

Chapter VIII

The Carmelite Noviciate, 1904–1908
The Gray Habit

THE following four years of Sister Maria Elisabeth's life were hidden in the strict *clausura* of the Carmelite noviciate. She was in the House of St. Birgitta, which was almost sacred to her, but the House itself at that time was an austere place in which to live.

The high, narrow cells had tall windows darkened by heavy shutters, affording no view. In the hot, Roman summer they were cool but not airy, and in winter, icy. There was no heat of any kind, and a minimum of cold running water for washing or cooking.

The Community room on the top floor, however, was spacious and pleasant, particularly in summer. It was tiled in gray marble and opened out on a loggia; a circular iron stair led up to the broad, red-tiled roof. Here the Sisters could go for recreation, see the sky and look off at the tops of other buildings, the tawny-red walls and plant-rich terraces of Rome.

The wall around their terrace was too high to permit them to see down directly into the piazza, but the noise of the fountain and the life of the square made a cheerful murmur. The heads of the huge statues of St. Birgitta and St. Catherine above the church entrance could be seen in profile above the wall, their whitish stone pockmarked with age. To the right the huge, ornamental cornice of the Palazzo Farnese loomed higher than their own roof. Off to the north, several large church domes could be seen and toward the southwest farther away, the great dome of St. Peter's.

Besides plants and flowers on their own roof, the Sisters had a small courtyard, with a vegetable plot and even a few chickens, for Sister Maria Elisabeth had said in one of her letters that the Carmelites gave her fresh eggs at times when she could eat little else.

Indeed, she had many setbacks as far as her health was concerned, and only because Mother Hedwig watched over her and tempered the rule for her delicate novice, she was able to continue her training.

Interesting sidelights on Sister Elisabeth's noviciate are furnished by a book entitled *A Danish Carmelite,* the story of a certain Sister Birgitta, who was in Rome at this period. The book is made up of her letters, written to her son, with his narrative in between. As such, it is a warm, human document, a moving and beautiful picture of convent life and of Mother Hedwig, whom Sister Birgitta loved dearly.

This Danish Sister was older than Sister Elisabeth; she had been left a widow with two young sons, and became a Catholic in 1893. Two years later, she came to Rome, and entered Carmel at the age of forty.

She speaks of the extreme cold in the convent with its marble floors; the masses of roses on the roof terrace; her exultation over the beauty of the Office—"more beautiful than all classic literature"—

She relates that all are taught to feel admiration for St. Birgitta and her House; that many people come, twice a year to visit her rooms.

Unfortunately, the book says little of Sister Maria Elisabeth, but merely refers to her once: "An outsider of another kind is a Swedish Birgittine Sister who was in Rome to prepare the foundation of a House for Brigittines. There were many in Sweden who interest themselves in the House of St. Birgitta, as the old national Shrine it once had been...." Sister Birgitta asks her son to pray that she may be helpful in her many contacts with Swedish visitors

In 1906, Mother Hedwig was studying the possibilities of making two new foundations, as the north of Italy was overrun with French Sisters, obliged to leave France, because of the new antireligious laws. Her Community in Rome was far above the prescribed twenty-one members common to Carmelite Houses. Consequently, she founded a small community in the mountains north of Tivoli, and later a convent in a former Capuchin monastery on the Italian Riviera, at Porto Maurizio. Sister Birgitta was then made Mother Superior of this new House on the sea, and writes to her son of how glad she is to hear the song of the ocean which she has loved from childhood.

This extension of her work, had caused great strain to Mother Hedwig, both physical and financial. It is all the more remarkable, then, that her attitude toward Sister Elisabeth was so patient and loving.

Again, it was through Sister Maria Elisabeth's letters to her family that we are able to glimpse certain details of her life, first, as she describes her emotion upon becoming *a bride of Christ.*

Nov. 15, 1904, to her Mother and Anna:
I got a letter...saying that Gustav's wedding has been postponed til November 24.

On that same day, if I am a little better, I will be taken into the Sisters' Community here and be wedded to my heavenly bridegroom, a bridegroom who grows more beautiful and more beloved, with every day. If my step is hard for you to understand, my dear ones, it must nevertheless be a joy to you that I am happier in my soul, than any Queen on earth. Yes, if nothing unforeseen happens, after the 24th of November I will become Sister Maria Elisabeth of St. Birgitta....

I hope that you all, especially Mamma, will not feel any disappointment over the step that I am taking. All my dear ones there at home, know that I have never sought any money or gain for myself in what I have done in my past life. So much less, now. Let us look beyond this worldly life, Dear Little Mama—to eternity!

Jan. 15, 1905, to Family
Marie Cisneros was here, and went from here to Nice, to visit an old Aunt, and is now in London. If you want to write, you can say on the envelope: Sister Maria Elisabeth Hesselblad. Many change their

names, but I said that the name my father and mother gave me, I want to keep. I always will remain your Maria.

May 5, 1905 to the family

I am distressed to hear that Agnes has been in the hospital. I hope she is well again.

I was quite sick during February, March and April, so bad that we thought of sending after one of you (Eva or Agnes) but at Easter time, I was better again. Half the time lying on my back, and some of the time sitting up, I was able to make a little wood-carving. It is a little stand to put the Chalice on, when the sick take communion....

May 20, 1905 to Agnes

That was a great honor that the Rector gave you when he got you a position as teacher in Borås. It is a great joy for me, when I hear of your successes, because, all these years, since the day when I stood ready to sail for America and at the hour of farewell, patted my sleeping baby-sister's little head, I have felt as though I were your second mother.

I send the enclosed letter to grandmother, perhaps she will not be able to receive many more letters from us. Do send her a little box of candy and cakes that she likes, from me. You remember when little grandma put camphor balls in her mouth!

Eva comments:

In these letters there isn't much that shows Maria's humor, but she had a good sense of humor, that both warmed and teased. For instance, when I complained that it made me sad to sell *Fridhem*, she said: "Alright, marry the man who is buying it. Then you can live there all your life!" I answered: "No, he's too dirty!" Whereupon she said: "Well, then you'll have to wash him up!"—and her eyes danced with fun.

June 6, 1905, to Eva

Our good Mother Hedwig has moved me into a bigger room for the summer, where there is more air and shade. Outside is a little balcony, where I can sit and work....

August 23, 1905, to her mother

Dear Mamma, you want me to be in Sweden; Sten Ture would like me to live with him in California; Miss Cisneros would like me, sick or well, to live with her. But God wants me to be here—whom shall I obey?

The saddest thing to me is that I do not hear from the boys in America, whom I love so much. You could hardly believe how I suffer over it, but I bear it with patience. I know that the seed which is sown in love, must one day bear fruit, even if it does not do so on this earth, then under the sun of eternity.

It was in April of 1906 that Sister Maria Elisabeth wrote to Agnes that Father Hagen was coming to Rome. Her noviciate was nearing its end and this was a momentous time for her, but she writes with typical understatement:

"An old gentleman priest and outstanding astronomer, whom I knew very well in Washington, has come here to take charge of the Vatican Observatory."

Toward the end of the book of her sister's letters, Agnes tells of a visit with Father Hagen in 1921, and concludes, "I think it was Father Hagen that instructed Maria when she went over to Catholicism, but she never said so. People used to remark: 'Do you know that your sister is a Saint?'

" 'Yes, we know it better than anyone else,' we would answer. And then Agnes quotes the noted Lutheran Bishop, Nathan Söderblom: *'Saints are people who in word and deed demonstrate the fact that God lives.'* "

The intimate tone of Maria's family letters does not reflect the tremendous conflict going on in her soul as she neared the day of her Profession. It was indeed fortunate that Father Hagen had been called from his post in Washington to take charge of the Vatican Observatory at this very time, and that she could have his help to encourage her in the daring, lonely climb toward what she felt God was impelling her to do. He had always believed in her vocation—What vocation?

True, she was safe in the House of St. Birgitta, but she could not feel content to stay there, peacefully praying the rest of her life as a member of the Carmelite Community. She wanted to die—or live—as a child of St. Birgitta, to wear her habit, and then go on, she did not know exactly how, to bring her Order back to Rome, to this House, although this seemed at the time, the most impossible dream.

She could only see the next step—the gray habit.

From her *Notes* as originally recorded at this period, it is hard to ascertain the exact sequence of events. Some were written on odd scraps of paper, and in pencil, tucked into books or old envelopes. Some were from a diary; secret confessions to herself. But the pages that follow are spiritual documents, leading up to the time when she was finally *Professed* by Father Hagen, in the gray Brigittine habit, with the white crown, and its five crimson dots.

Father Hagen and Father Brandi had both worked to obtain special permission from the Vatican for Sister Maria Elisabeth to be able to wear this habit of St. Birgitta at her profession in a Carmelite convent. But it was the inspired generosity and foresight of Mother Hedwig that had responded to some inner prompting of destiny. For the actual turning point at which Sister Maria Elisabeth, an obscure novice in the Carmelite Order, was allowed to become a Brigittine can only be understood as a psychic or spiritual phenomenon best described by her own *Notes:*

Having now, for almost a year, prayed that I might be buried in the Brigittine habit, as ever since I came into the House I had felt that St. Birgitta was constantly by my side and that I belonged to her, it was a very difficult and painful position that I was in. I felt as if there was not a square foot of ground on which I could stand: The House was my Mother's, but there was no place for me. What gave me strength was the saying of Our Lord: *"The birds of the air have their nests, and the foxes their holes, but the Son of Man has nowhere to lay His head."* And the assurance in my soul that I was there according to God's will and that He in His time would arrange all for His greater Glory.

One day, when I was walking along the hall leading up to the terrace, I saw before me five nuns dressed in the Brigittine habit, I walking at the back of them. The impression that this made on me was so great that the tears came streaming down my face. Again I prayed my Dear Lord, not to be lead by illusions.

(Nine years later, on the 8th of September, 1915, the very Reverend Fr. Hattais blessed the four black veils, with the white bands worn by the Brigittines on the head, symbolical of our Lord's Crown of Thorns, for my first four companions. As I followed them in procession back to the Chapel, when their veils had been put on, I saw again this same scene.)

One of the first days of June my Carmelite Mother called me and asked what my intentions were for the future. I answered that the only thing I thought of was to pray for the Scandinavian people and that

I felt that St. Birgitta was always by my side, prompting me to do this, also St. Catherine of Sweden and Blessed Richard Reynolds, the English Brigittine Martyr. I also told her what had happened in my childhood regarding St. Birgitta's House in Rome. She remarked, "It is very wonderful, dear child, God must have some design with it all."

A few days later, she called me again, but this time speaking very gravely and severely—(perhaps to test me, as I have since thought, but I did not understand this at that time)—She asked me how I could expect to remain in that house if I did not wish to become a Carmelite. She added that I had not been prevented from spreading the devotion to my Saint and Country-woman, and that in no (other) Convent would they accept anyone in my state of health.

"Woman, what dress will you wear? What shall we do with you?" This and many other things were said by the Mistress of Novices who was sitting by her side. A tremendous battle arose in my soul. It was as if I stood between two fires devouring me, but I kept the eye of my soul fixed on my Dear Lord Jesus, whose spouse I so much longed to be, and left all in His Hands. Strength came, and I spoke, saying:

"My dear Mother, forgive me all the trouble I am giving you. I cannot leave this house. Put me in the cellar or in the Tower, and dress me as you please, even in this—" and so saying, I touched the little piece of gray rag-carpet under her feet.

At that instant, a most wonderful, clear and pure light filled the whole room. Everything (else) disappeared. The only thing I saw was a most minute speck like the smallest atom. I looked and looked at that small speck, a nothing, much smaller than the particles of dust one sees when sunbeams penetrate a dark room. But the light was far stronger than the light of a sunbeam, and the same voice that bid me come across the sea said: "*It is you*"—As suddenly as it came, the light disappeared. [*Note within note added by a Sister:* "Our dear Mother considers this the greatest grace she ever received."]

I rose and kissing the Mother's hand, returned to my cell. There alone, I knelt down at the foot of the Crucifix and a beautiful strengthening peace filled my soul.

While I was praying there, the door was softly opened and in came the Mistress of Novices, saying, "Our Mother wishes you to go to her cell." I went at once, and the good Mother made signs for me to follow her into St. Catherine's Chapel where the oil painting represents her in the Holy Habit of Our Order. My Carmelite Mother pointed to the painting, saying: "Is this what you want?" I knelt down and embraced her feet, answering "Yes, my dear Mother, I have prayed long that God might make known that such is His Will and my desire."

I then asked permission to write to Fr. Brandi, S.J. who was at that time my Director. We told him all that had taken place, and we both

71

begged him to ask the special permission for me to be clothed in the habit of the Brigittine Order on the approaching Feast of the Sacred Heart. This permission was obtained from the Pope himself, Pius X...

Deeply personal papers found among the *Notes,* but not a part of them, express struggles still going on in the heart of Maria Elisabeth. But then she resumes her *Notes,* on the strong tone of her practical nature. The words of Mother Hedwig put a seal on the day of Maria's profession; they seem to summarize Maria Elisabeth's passage through the Carmelite Order as a phenomenon of spiritual guidance.

The very Rev. Father Hagen having about this time arrived in Rome from Washington, was asked to come and say the Mass and bless the habit in the room where Our Holy Mother St. Birgitta had lived and died.

Present at the Mass and Clothing were two Carmelite nuns, The Rev. Mother Prioress and one of the Sisters.

Just before the Clothing, I knelt down to ask my Carmelite Mother's blessing. She gave it to me and embraced me saying: *"I give you back to St. Birgitta and St. Catherine, who, I thought, had given you to me!"*

I felt most unworthy of being called the property of any Saints, but pleaded that my Dear Lord and Spouse of my soul, would fulfill Himself all that was wanting in me and to grant me the grace to die always more and more to self.

A few days later, I made my vows as a daughter of St. Birgitta of Sweden, and I had the consolation of doing this just before receiving Holy Communion. My Spiritual Father, very Rev. J. G. Hagen S.J. held the Sacred Host before me, and when I had pronounced the vows, he gave me my Lord.

AFTER PROFESSION, SEARCH FOR A COMMUNITY

But this was not the end of the story; it was only the beginning. After her profession, it became increasingly clear to Sister Elisabeth that she must fulfill her destiny as a Brigittine. She must reach out to the other convents of St. Birgitta, to urge them to send Sisters to Rome, to honor the House of their Holy Mother, and in some way, renew the strength of the old Order. She had sent for books from the convents still existing, to learn more about the rule, and Brigittine life.

72

Since she had been very sick with her recurrent ulcers, that autumn, she had suggested that her sister Agnes come to see her in Rome, when she was free from her school duties as a teacher, during the Christmas holidays. Agnes arrived late in December. Sister Elisabeth had arranged for a good friend to show her around the great city. This was a remarkable soul named Agnes Lincoln who had come to Rome as a rich young woman and lived there almost as a pilgrim, doing works of charity under the guidance of a Jesuit Father. She was very helpful and kind to Agnes, as she was also devoted to Sister Elisabeth—and a valuable friend in the years to come.

The high point of Agnes' visit was an audience with the Pope, Pius X. This had been arranged by Father Brandi and Sister Elisabeth had long been anticipating it. She describes it in her *Notes:*

In the early part of January, 1907, I had the great consolation of a private audience with H.H. Pope Pius X, together with my youngest sister, Agnes, who had come down to Rome to spend her Christmas holidays. Being unable to walk up the many flights of stairs, my spiritual Director had kindly obtained for me the permission to go up in the lift to the apartments where the Holy Father received. We were taken through several of the large rooms, also the Throne-room, and after having waited half-an-hour in the room next to the private study of His Holiness, we were taken in to the Holy Father, who received us with fatherly kindness and asked us to sit down. The Rev. Fr. Brandi who was with us, introduced us and told His Holiness that I was that child of St. Birgitta of Sweden for whom H.H. had granted the special permission (to wear the Brigittine habit) and that I was the only Brigittine in Rome. The Holy Father, on hearing this, turned to me and said: "*Povera figlia di Santa Brigida, tutta sola in Roma nelle Casa di Santa Brigida*"—

Then I thought—now is my opportunity—and I answered, "Yes, Your Holiness, but praying that St. Birgitta's children may again return to Rome and to our Holy Mother's House. And now I must humbly beg Your Holiness to help that this may be possible, for God's greater Glory." I also told H.H. what an historical place our Holy Mother's House was for our Scandinavian people, and how they always visited her shrine with great veneration. He placed his hand on my head and answered that he would see what could be done for St. Birgitta's honor. But he added—(as if he knew that he had not many years to live—)

"The life of a Pope is sometimes not long enough to see all desires fulfilled."

We then asked and obtained his blessing for all our relatives and friends, and for all our countrymen, for my sister to take back to Sweden. We had brought with us a carved frame, with Our Holy Mother Birgitta's [photograph] picture. He seemed pleased, and showed much interest in both the picture and the work on the frame [by M. Elisabeth] and thanked us so sweetly for this simple gift.

Again, Sister Elisabeth held to her firm purpose of reviving a House to the Honor of St. Birgitta, here in Rome, to which she might then belong. With the permission of her kind and understanding Carmelite Mother (Hedwig) and that of Father Hagen and Father Brandi, she had the courage to plan a visit to all the Brigittine convents of which she had knowledge, through the Vatican and other sources. Most heartening of all, was the consent of the Holy Father she had visited and who had not forgotten her:

Notes:

On the 12th of February, 1908, I asked someone who was very near the Holy Father to speak to him again for Holy Mother's honor and to ask his blessing for my journey to visit the Brigittine Convents in England, Spain, Holland and Bavaria. He sent me back his blessing and these words, written with his own hand: *"Deus sit tibi propitius et clemens."* And now when he has gone to Our Lord, may he continue his prayer for St. Birgitta's humble children in Rome. Surely those three great and holy men Pius X, Cardinal Vives y Tuto, and Fr. Brandi S.J. who on earth believed that our humble desires were inspired by God will help us from Heaven and obtain for us some corner in Rome, sanctified by our Holy Mother St. Birgitta's life.

Omnia pro Te, Cor Jesu!

Father Hagen, Sister Elisabeth's extraordinary confessor, now becomes a leading figure once more, in the drama of her life.

What joy it must have been to her to have him to talk to once more, to know he was always nearby for consultation and encouragement. For as firmly as he had believed in her vocation, so he was now convinced that Providence had a special purpose for this vocation, as a daughter of St. Birgitta. It was certainly providential as well that he was transferred from the Georgetown College Observatory at this time. Had he possibly

74

requested this himself, in order to watch over his *Child in Christ,* as he always called her?

Now he was there to stand by her side when she refused once more, to form part of the Carmelite Community, but planned and awaited the possibility of taking a further step in the direction of calling into being a Community of Brigittines in Rome.

The tall, almost gaunt, distinguished astronomer who looked something like the Abbé Liszt could be seen striding toward the Piazza Farnese, or later, alighting from a carriage, as he was not too strong, and already in his seventies. When he could not visit Sister Elisabeth, he wrote to her:

"My Dear Child in Christ: Your second letter reached me this morning. . . . This afternoon, I took my cloak and hat and went out as far as the garden gate, which needed quite a resolution. But there, something held me back so strongly, that I stopped and prayed. It was like a fear that came over me. . . ."

He explained his weakness, and added: "Do not feel neglected, my dearest; with Our Lord whom alone we love, we have all we need."

The stars are frequently mentioned in their correspondence, as if it were natural for him to share his love for them with her:

"You must help me to thank God for a great gift. Do you remember the experiments about *the earth,* from the large tower? They have succeeded perfectly and a new proof is established in honor of the Vatican and the Holy Father. It remains now to make the instrument finer and to make numerical measurements. Until that is completed, we keep the matter secret.

"The other day just an hour before Mercury passed the sun's disk, the Swedish lady came to see me. . . . I was taken by surprise while preparing the transit of Mercury."

Another time, he reproached her mildly for sending him visitors in her zeal to help them: "Apostolic work is not my lot. My last years belong to the Holy Father's Observatory. . . . But please do not feel discouraged in writing to me, when *you* wish me to come."

Again, when she was gravely ill, he wrote: "You are in company with Our Savior. Do not forget now, dear child, to be a *good branch* letting Our Redeemer continue His own suffering in you, as in his own member. The greatest thing that ever happened was the sacrifice on Calvary, and your suffering is a continuation of it."

A letter of later date (Ascension, 1910), expresses his esteem:

"Dear Child in Christ. You will always be the child of the father who has begotten you in Christ. And being thus linked to the great work of sanctification of self and others which God is evidently doing in you, has always been considered by me a special grace for which I am very grateful to God."

These extracts from letters, chosen out of many, reflect the simple affection and beautiful spiritual bond between the venerable Father Hagen and his child Elisabeth. It is necessary to understand the depth of this relationship which, like a pillar, driven far into the earth, gave her the strength and support to start off on her search for a Community which could eventually be established in Rome. Both Father Hagen and Father Brandi, who was the younger and more practical of the two, encouraged her in every way to pursue her idea.

She had first written to all the convents of St. Birgitta of which she had knowledge. Through her friends at the Vatican she had finally secured the addresses. Father Hagen had backed her up in this effort, writing himself to recommend her to their Superiors.

From Syon Abbey in England, Altomünster in Bavaria, Germany; Valladolid in Spain, she had received answers expressing interest and vague desires to help with the founding of a House in Rome. In each case, she was invited to visit these convents, to explain her concept. Alas, it was indeed still somewhat vague in her own mind. But she felt sure it was not uncertain in the mind of Divine Providence. She felt impelled as before, to take another step and trust that the way would open before her. Her next objective was to visit these Brigittine convents, to learn their life, and to find the fellowship of her own Sisters of St. Birgitta.

The following terse statement was written by Sister Elisabeth at the beginning of her account of the three long journeys she now undertook. It was as if she wanted to sum up what she had already

76

done to become a Brigittine. It was the beginning of another series of unbelievable efforts of this young woman, sick and alone in her purpose, driven by that sense of Divine Destiny in which she blindly believed.

From March 1904 to May 1908, I lived in our Holy Mother St. Birgitta's House without ever going out.

In 1906, I received from Altomünster Abbey a copy of our Breviary and from that time I was able to unite my prayer in a special way with all the Birgittine Sisters wherever they still existed.

I also received the original Rule from Vadstena through an antiquarian Bookseller in Stockholm and many other books in old Swedish relating to our Order.

From Syon Abbey—England—I also obtained the Rule and Constitutions, also from Holland and Spain and I corresponded with all the Houses of our Order.

From all I received expressions of appreciation and sympathy and the offer to help, to revive St. Birgitta's honour in Rome.

I strove always to lead the life of the true Birgittine as much as it was possible for one to do alone.

Chapter IX

Learning the Brigittine Life: Syon Abbey

WHEN Sister Elisabeth finally started off to visit the convents of St. Birgitta which she had been able to contact, her first objective was the great Syon Abbey. It was one of the nine Communities that had survived from Medieval times; there was Altomünster in Germany; two convents in Holland, five in Spain, and this unique institution which had had a marked place in English history.

The first Syon Abbey was an impressive monastery at Isleworth, on the Thames River, not far from London. It was a center of culture and learning, as were most of the double monasteries of St. Birgitta.

"Such was the fervor of their lives and the quality of their recruits that they made a tremendous impact on the spiritual life of many countries in northern Europe during the century before the Reformation. Such was certainly the case with Syon Abbey." This quotation from the English historian, F. R. Johnston, M.A., gives the background of his story of the Brigittine priest Richard Reynolds, whose fate was linked with that of Syon.

"Syon was founded from Vadstena in 1415, under Henry V. It consisted of some sixty nuns, strictly enclosed, and a separate community of thirteen priests and eight lay brothers. Each had separate choirs in a common church. . . .

"Syon became one of the richest monasteries, with many of the nuns coming from aristocratic families, and the brethren from the universities. Yet despite their wealth and prestige, the community remained faithful to their austere rule. . . . The life of a Brother of Syon was especially suited for a man who wanted a life of study and prayer. In the older Orders, a graduate Monk would be called upon to fill administrative posts, whilst the friars were occupied with an active apostolate in the towns. In a Brigittine Abbey, administration was the responsibility of the Abbess. The brethren were to act as chaplains to the nuns and confessors to the pilgrims who came to worship at St. Birgitta's shrine. They were to devote themselves to prayer and study and were specially charged to expound the Gospel on Sundays. Such was the life upon which Reynolds entered in 1513, and was to enjoy for twenty years."

Then came the dreadful crisis in the English Church, when Henry wished to have his marriage annulled by the Church so that he might espouse Anne Boleyn. He claimed Royal Supremacy over the Church, and this made the English Reformation take on an especially worldly and brutal character.

Richard Reynolds was one of those distinguished scholars and churchmen whose cooperation the King most anxiously desired. As Johnston says: "The government set great store on securing the submission of Syon." But Blessed Richard, like St. Thomas More, and the three others martyrs who suffered with him, held out against the ruthless Henry. In 1535, he was imprisoned, and a few months later, was cruelly put to death.

Syon Abbey was thereafter oppressed and intimidated, until the house was officially closed in 1539. The Community of nuns were forced to disband, but managed to flee, intact, to Flanders, where they set up a temporary convent. Then they were offered a more secure haven in Rouen, on the Seine River; a large House and stone enough to build a chapel. However, after several years they were forced to flee again, this time to Lisbon in Portugal. Here they were able to maintain themselves for over a hundred years. Many young women secretly left England to join them, so that the Community preserved its English character. Finally, at the end of the nineteenth century, they made their way back to England again (1861).

The story of their *Wanderings* was written up in a book by that name. All through those years of exile, they had treasured the memory of their Blessed Martyr Richard Reynolds. And they had transported with them a precious relic of his suffering. This was a richly carved Gothic capital, stained with his blood.

For after he was hanged, according to the barbarous custom of those days, he was "quartered" and his mangled remains fixed to a post or doorway, as a warning to others. So tradition has it that this capital was originally part of the gateway of the old Syon Abbey, to which he was attached.

Somehow, the nuns had been able to obtain the capital and even though it was very cumbersome and heavy, they took it in a barrel, when they were forced to flee from England. All through their wanderings, when they could not transport it by boat or cart, they *rolled* it in its barrel—until they returned to England once more. It is now the treasure of the new Syon Abbey, in South Brent, Devonshire, near Plymouth.

By the time they had returned to England, there were no Brigittine Brethren left in any country. The Sisters settled near the famed Buckfast Abbey, where they found help from the Brothers of St. Benedict, and soon established their own apostolate of prayer for the *"Poor Souls"* in purgatory. For many years, they have published a small magazine, *The Poor Souls' Friend,* which is widely circulated in England.

When Sister Elisabeth arrived in England, she first visited the site of the old Syon Abbey.

Her *Notes* begin as she left Rome and traveled northward:

One of the first days of June, 1908, I left Rome in company with a "Mary Ward" Sister (?) and a young Italian lady. . . . Due to my illness, we broke the trip in Turin, staying with German Franciscan Sisters, and stayed over Sunday in Paris, at the Convent of Our Lady of Sion. . . . In London, I was met by my friend, Marie Cisneros, who took me to the Convent of the Blessed Sacrament in Brompton Square. . . . The next day, we were taken to Isleworth, where the old Syon Abbey used to stand. We were very kindly received by Father Green, the Rector, who showed us his new church. He said he would very much like me to begin the work entrusted to me by Our Lord, in Isleworth.

A few days later, Miss Cisneros took me to Tyburn Convent, which is built on the very spot where so many holy men were martyred for the Faith, among whom our dear brother (Brigittine Brother) Blessed Richard Reynolds. . . . On this spot, I poured forth my whole soul and implored the intercession of Blessed Richard for the restoration of the Fathers of our Order, and for all St. Birgitta's children.

After four or five days in London, I went down to Syon Abbey in Devonshire, to my dear Brigittine Sisters.

Note within note: (Our beloved Mother often told us what a profound impression it made on her to find herself for the first time, among St. Birgitta's children after so many years of suffering and struggles of all kinds.)

It was evening when I arrived. The door was opened to me by Sister Patrick ... and I was told to go around to the door of the enclosure, at which door I was received by the Lady Abbess, accompanied by the Mother Assistant, Mother Teresa, who both welcomed me with sisterly love. I fell on my knees and kissed the venerable Mother's feet. She was Mother Ignatius the last surviving member of the exiled community, returned from Lisbon.

My dear Sisters had prepared the Infirmary for me and also a cell, so that I might choose. I chose the cell, where I could be alone with "Him whom my soul loves."

Next morning I went to the choir to hear Mass and receive Holy Communion with the Syon Community, and I was afterwards introduced to all my dear Sisters. On the Feast of the Sacred Heart I had the great happiness of renewing my vows before the Lady Abbess, Rev. Mother Ignatius, and the whole Community.

After she had been in Syon Abbey only a few weeks, Sister Maria Elisabeth of St. Birgitta received a letter from Mother Hedwig whom she had left in Rome. This remarkable woman had been her Superior for almost four years, and had shown great concern and love for this strange, Swedish Sister whom, she felt, had been confided to her care, through some Divine plan—how else explain the generosity and understanding of her heart—and now it was as if she must show a further token of her supernatural intuition.

Perhaps other Sisters, or persons less charitable than herself, had told her that Sister Elisabeth was hoping to take the House of St. Birgitta away from her and indeed, in an indirect way, Elisabeth seemed to believe that somehow she *was impelled* to work for this end.

In any case, Mother Hedwig's letter reflects a small reproach, and a very big vision of what the Divine Will might be in this exceptional circumstance:

Rome, St. Birgitta
23 June, 1908

Dearest Daughter of St. Birgitta, of St. Teresa and also of mine:

Today, I write you in answer to your dear letter from Syon.... It seems really like a dream come true, to know that you are among Brigittines, dressed in their habit, which you received from the daughters of St. Teresa and in the very house where St. Birgitta lived and died.

All this seems to me so Providential, that I ask myself if Our Lord will stop there, or if He has perhaps some other plan [design] which has not yet been revealed to us? ...

Considering all this, at the Feet of our Sacramental Lord, I feel moved to say to you, Dearest Daughter, that even though I would be very displeased to think that you might be trying to combine some project as regards the House of St. Birgitta, and hiding it from me, nevertheless, I ask myself, in prayer, what my feelings would be as a daughter of St. Teresa, if the Monastery of Avila or of Albo in Spain, where my Holy Mother lived and where she died, were in the hands of Brigittine Nuns, and these would not cede it to us, the daughters of St. Teresa, in the event that we had the possibility of reacquiring it? And my eyes, filling with tears, gave me the answer: "Yes, according to human justice, I would have a right to keep it, but not according to the charity of Jesus Christ—

Therefore, my daughter, if Our Lord Jesus might only have chosen us, daughters of St. Teresa, to bring back to the light and to pious care this dear Sanctuary and if then it was in His Divine Will that the Order of St. Birgitta should take it back, and we had thus worked for the greater Glory of God, I would say: "So be it, Lord, because what You do, will always be the best!" There, my dearest Sister Elisabeth—this is what I have on my conscience to tell you; the rest is in the Hands of God.

Hardly had Sister Elisabeth settled into her new-found Community before the Superior of Syon Abbey turned to her, for help. She must have recognized the shrewd, practical mind that Sister Elisabeth had acquired from her years of nursing. She reports the incident in her *Notes:*

About the 7th of July, I had to go up to London to settle a very important matter for the Syon Community and it kept me in town for two weeks, during which time I stayed at a Convent.

I was ill for some of the time I spent at dear Syon Abbey, but I was able to go to the Choir and take part in the Community exercises which were always a great joy to me.

A happier event was Sister Elisabeth's renewed contact with Benedict Williamson, a young London architect who had abandoned his career to study for the priesthood. He had come to Rome in 1904 to study at the Beda College for delayed vocations, which was then on the Via Monserrato near the Carmelite convent.

It had been suggested to him by a friend of Syon Abbey that he seek to revive the Brothers of St. Birgitta, and this idea had appealed to him immediately; when he heard that there was a Brigittine Sister living alone with the Carmelites in the House of St. Birgitta in Rome, he had asked to see her. Sister Elisabeth had been allowed to meet him, and they eagerly discussed their mutual desire to see the Order of St. Birgitta take on new life. Later Sister Elisabeth began to sew Church linens and vestments for his future foundation near London, where he had been promised a parish when his studies were completed. His bishop had also given him permission to seek young postulants for a renewal of the Brothers of St. Birgitta in his parish house. He was in England for a brief visit, while Sister Maria Elisabeth was at Syon Abbey. They met at the Abbey, and talked over their aspirations with the Lady Abbess, who heartily concurred in their ideas. Benedict Williamson was to be ordained in Rome the following spring.

At the same time he planned to make his vows as a brother of the Order of the Most Holy Savior.

It was an integral part of Birgitta's plan for her Order that it was to consist of nuns and brothers (fratres), who should be the priests and counselors of the Sisters. This had proved to be a sound concept, and was no doubt one of the reasons that the Order spread and developed so successfully during the Middle Ages. Of the twenty-seven convents of that time, all were balanced by the presence of brothers, who shared large churches with the cloistered Sisters. The Sisters usually had a choir high up in the apse of the church, while the brothers, who were also for the most part, priests, officiated and sang close to the altar. Once a day choirs chanted the verses of the *Ave Maris Stella* back and forth together, making a marvelous music, in the vast, stone buildings.

Anyone as artistic as Father Benedict must have relished this thought and dreamt of a day when such communities might be revived.

Dr. Tore Nyberg, whose recent (1956) treatise on the Brigittine monasteries of Middle Ages is already a classic on the subject, has also made a special study of the Brigittine men's Order. He explains that Birgitta had conceived the idea of having a supplementary Order of brothers, or *fratres,* because she was familiar with the Cistercian Order of nuns in Sweden of those days and saw the difficulties they often had in obtaining spiritual direction from outside priests who had no knowledge of their rule. On the other hand, she did not wish to create simply a *"Double Order"* of nuns and monks, as the O.SS.S. was sometimes called.

She wished the priests to be attracted to the Order because of its intellectual possibilities, and besides their duties as priests and confessors to the nuns, they were to be scholars and preachers; to minister to pilgrims, and maintain contact with the outside world. She had envisioned a balance of thirteen priests and eight lay brothers to a community of some sixty nuns. It is probable that Birgitta felt that symbolically, the priests were to represent the thirteen Apostles; the nuns, lay brothers, and deacons numbering about seventy-two in all, represented the seventy-two early Christian disciples. The Abbess symbolized Mary, the guiding light of the early Church.

Birgitta herself had relied very heavily on intellectual priests; Prior Petrus, Cistercian of Alvastra, was her director at the time that she received her first *Revelations* about the Order, and gave her wise counsel and support. He and Birgitta both knew of the double Order of Fontevrault in France, made up of more or less equal numbers of monks and nuns. But they seemed to have agreed that in the Order of Our Most Holy Savior, vocations were different; the Sisters were called to a strictly contemplative life and the friars were to mingle with the pilgrims and townspeople who were welcomed in their large churches.

84

This was one of the features of the great Brigittine Monasteries so widespread throughout the north in the century before the Reformation. It was one of the things that gave them the special quality for which they were noted. For though different scholars have slightly varying ideas about the Order in its heyday, all agree that it had a distinctive character and unique influence.

It was true of Syon Abbey, with its *Saint,* long referred to as Blessed Richard Reynolds, but sainted by Pope Paul in October, 1970; certainly, this influence was felt at Altomünster and at Vadstena.

The Fathers of Vadstena have their record in the *Vadstena Diary,* published in Latin in 1721, later translated into Swedish. Among them were outstanding men of learning, interpreters of the Scriptures and of the *Revelations of St. Birgitta.* One of these was Johannes Hildebrandi, theologian and a man who made contacts between all European Brigittines at the time of the Council of Konstanz.

Thomas Ritter of Maihingen in Bavaria, copied a complete German translation of the *Revelations,* and Jörg Knöringer of the same Abbey, former secretary to Emperor Maximilian, after his conversion to the monastic life, got his royal master's support in having the *Revelations* printed in Nürnberg.

Fathers of the Abbeys of northern Holland went on recruiting novices long after Calvinism had been introduced. Here we find a remarkable priest, Father Christoph Langen, a German by birth. He restored the monastery of Marienbaum in the Rhineland, reestablished the life of the Fathers in Marienwater, and even managed to found a new monastery in a neighboring town, all in the seventeenth century.

At that time, a group of priests decided to move away from the nuns and establish convents only for themselves. This independent branch of the Order was called *Novissimi Birgittini* and existed in Holland and northern France until the Napoleonic Wars; However, the new branch evoked opposition in Bavaria and inspired Fr. Simon Hörman in Altomünster to call another general Chapter, which was held in Cologne in 1675. The Chapter established once more that the Brigittine priests should remain at the service of the nuns and pilgrims who came to the Abbey churches used in common by the nuns and brothers.

Father Hörman was certainly one of the most influential priests in the history of the Order. He secured permission for his Brigittine Fathers to establish themselves in Rome, in the House of St. Birgitta, where, as we have seen, they remained until the Order of priests died out in the times of Napoleon. The last Brigittine priest in Altomünster died hardly a hundred years ago.

Nuns of saintly reputation, such as Juliana van Thulden in Belgium and the two Brigittine martyrs in northern France, give indirect witness to the value of the spiritual direction of the Fathers of St. Birgitta.

Sister Elisabeth left Syon Abbey in September, as she felt she must return to Rome and then continue to Spain. She had learned much about the Brigittine life at Syon Abbey, and established a deep relationship with her spiritual Sisters. Yet she was disappointed that the Abbess did not feel she could take on the responsibility of working for a house in Rome.

She had left, driven by her inner conviction that God wanted her to forge still wider links between Brigittines wherever they existed. Yet she had created a lasting affection between herself and the Community at Syon which led to a second visit the following year, after her trip to Spain. The close tie now established is shown by the letter from Syon which followed her to Rome. The Sisters had been impressed by her personality and dedication. The symbolic gesture of the mantle she had brought them from Rome went straight to the heart of the Abbess Teresa, who wrote:

"I had a little struggle to put on your mantle; it seemed too sacred for me to wear, after having received the Holy Father's blessing and being in Holy Mother's House. . . . However, I thought of Elia's gift to Eliseus, and put it on with the prayer that the courage of its former wearer might be mine. . . . I shall always look back on your visit as one that has brought many blessings to us. . . . There will always be a corner in Syon for you, should you care to come."

Second Visit to Syon Abbey

A year and a half later, after a long stay in Spain (which is the subject of the next chapter), Sister Elisabeth returned to Syon Abbey, directly from the Spanish border. Here we have her *Notes* showing that she was always in touch with her spiritual director, Father Hagen, and made no moves without his counsel:

I had obtained permission to spend some months more in Syon Abbey, England, as I was desirous to stay there especially during Holy Week, in order to see the old customs and ceremonies.

The journey from Spain to England, via Bordeaux and Paris, to London was without any incident, except for (my joy at) hearing my native tongue spoken by travellers at the station in Paris.

I arrived at Syon Abbey for Holy Week. It was a great privilege to join in all the beautiful services and customs of this Holy season.

In England again, Sister Elisabeth was in touch with Fr. Benedict Williamson, who was now a full-fledged priest, and also a Brother of St. Birgitta. He wore a gray cloak, with the Brigittine Cross on his sleeve just below the shoulder, as was shown in paintings of St. Richard Reynolds. He was established in his parish of Earlsfield, London, and had been joined by Fr. Charles Murphy who had been ordained with him in Rome and had also taken vows as a Birgitta Brother. Besides, they had several young-men postulants who studied and lived with them in the rectory.

The Abbess of Syon followed their work with enthusiasm, and she was delighted to have Sister Maria Elisabeth again in the convent. When she had been there only a month, the Abbess entrusted her with another delicate mission. This time, she was to go to Ireland and bring back a young Sister of Syon, who had returned to her family, because of illness, but now begged to be "rescued" from a home in which she found herself very unhappy.

Both Father Benedict and the Abbess had asked Sister Elisabeth to look for postulants for them while traveling through Ireland, that land of many vocations, and she carried a letter of introduction to the Bishop of Cork.

She tells the story of this mission in her *Notes:*

In the month of May, I went over to Ireland, to bring back to the Abbey one of the young Sisters who had been sent to Ireland by the doctors for the good of her health.

On this journey we passed through Cork, Queenstown, Limerick and Dublin and down the coast again to Crosslair; from where we took the steamer back to Fishguard. Our Sister had a brother at Mount Mellory, the Cistercian Abbey, and as our journey took us in the neighborhood of this famous Abbey, we spent a few days there in prayer for our Order, also trying to interest the good Fathers in our need of members for Syon and our Roman Foundation. To travel about like this for anyone who had such a love for the solitude of the cloister was a real penance.

At the end of May we returned to England and Syon. The change to her native air not having brought about any change in our Sister's condition of health, Our Dear Lord evidently wanted her to be resigned to the Cross He permitted her to carry and which He himself could not fail to make light.

How often have I not experienced this myself! How useless all natural means are for preventing that which God makes use of, to lead us to a supernatural life, a life of special dependence on Him. By this I do not mean to say that I have not always tried to use reasonable means to obtain physical health, but that it never disturbed me when the looked-for result was not obtained.

At this very time, Sister Elisabeth had written to her mother that she was glad to be back in England again because of her weak condition. She said: "Doctors advise an operation, but I do not think this is wise for me. There is too great a risk. Not that I am afraid. I am well-trained in the school of suffering. But I feel that it is best to try to serve God the way I am. . . .

The Lady Abbess wrote to Sister Elisabeth after she arrived in Cork, saying: "I hope your visit will bear fruit for Fr. Benedict's work and the Order in general. For this you have my fervent prayers."

Father Benedict also wrote to her while she was in Cork, showing how deeply he felt involved in her work, as part of his own. He was thinking not only of his own need for vocations, but of her own future plan. He heads his letter with their common Brigittine slogan:

Amor Meus Crucifixus Est   St. Gregory's, Garratt Lane
                                                    Earlsfield S.W. London
                                                    June 19, 1910

Rev., and Dear Sister Elisabeth:

I was so glad to know that you had safely arrived in Cork—I cannot tell you how entirely my heart and prayers go out to you on your journey. Your letters, so sweet and generous, help me very much. . . . Let me have frequent news of you. I follow each step of your work with my poor prayers. I am ready to do anything you wish and think would be useful. . . . How I pray Our Lord to raise up for you, two or three loyal, devoted Sisters to help you with your first Foundation wherever it may be. I am sure Our Dear Lord is preparing them and that when the time comes, He will bring them to you. . . .

                                                    Benedict of Our Savior

Later, that same year, Father Benedict wrote Sister Elisabeth another remarkable letter, as she was leaving England and facing an uncertain future. He, too, had had his difficulties with his prospective foundation and experienced a lack of understanding on the part of his bishop, which he expresses here. He also shows his humility by putting her work on a par with his own, indeed he was already determined to help her and believed in her destiny:

I know how generously you have sacrificed yourself for Holy Mother's Order, and your strong courage has often nerved and helped me when all things went badly. . . . I am confident that our Lord will bring all right and arrange everything for His greater Glory. I know how alone you are. How hard it is to find that abandonment of local interest. This explains the Bishop's attitude to me. For the work I am doing for the Diocese he is glad but the larger view of the restoration of the Fathers to benefit the whole Church, with this he has no sympathy. . . . I know the width and sympathy of your heart, wide as the Church of God. If only I could become a woman, I would come and share the humblest work with you. . . .

Two happy memories of that summer in Syon Abbey were recorded in Sister Elisabeth's *Notes:*

For the second time, I spent a Feast of the Sacred Heart at Syon Abbey and had the consolation of celebrating the fourth anniversary of my profession, and little notes of congratulation from the Sisters were put under my door.

In July, I had a visitor from Sweden, in the person of my own dear sister Eva, who come to spend some weeks in England, together with two nieces of our Lady Abbess, in a house near the Abbey.

Eva herself says in her book of family letters, that she was in England in July, and had a wonderful time. She spent several days sightseeing in London and then came down to Syon. She wrote: "I lived nearby in a lady's house, but had my meals every day at the Convent with a young monk, their Chaplain. Every day, I could talk with Maria in a little room where she was restoring an old painting which belonged to the Convent. As usual, she couldn't be without work of some sort!"

After Eva left, Maria wrote her several affectionate letters; showing how close they felt to each other, after this visit:

30/8. I am so happy that you have such beautiful memories of your visit here. May God bless you richly! The days after you left, I was quite sick, but I am better now and planning to leave here, September 5th, by way of London to Holland. Pray for me, as I pray for you....

13/9. From *Convent of St. Birgitta, Weert,* Holland. The trip across was quite hard and often I thought, O, if I had only had a visible Guardian Angel, like little Eva, by my side. . . . It seemed strange to go out among strangers once again, but I must go where I am called. I am glad to see from your letter that you still treasure your memories of your visit. Yes, those were precious hours for us both in our little corner back of the Sanctuary.

Indeed, Maria Elisabeth *did* see her sister Eva many times in the following years. But although she corresponded with Syon Abbey she was not able to travel there again, in her full and difficult life. However, the Abbey with its great tradition, always held a special place in her heart. Her two visits to Syon were unforgettably a part of her development as a Brigittine.

Chapter X

Spain

SINCE her profession in 1906, Sister Elisabeth of St. Birgitta had been writing to the monasteries in Spain. One of her early letters, kept in the archives of Valladolid, explains that she had sent a number of medals of St. Birgitta, or Brigida, as the Spanish call her, to the Spanish Houses. She had also received a letter of thanks and a booklet, in return. She wrote:

> I am a Swedish convert, unworthy compatriot of our Holy Mother Sta. Brigida. Her House is occupied by a Carmelite Community. I came to this Holy House 3½ years ago, very ill, wishing to die under the Blessed roof of St. Brigida. But our Holy Mother prolonged my life and after having spent a noviciate in the Carmelite habit, God showed us that it was His Holy Will that I should serve Him here as a daughter of Sta. Brigida. A few months ago, I was permitted to make my vows to Sta. Brigida and wear a habit from Syon Abbey, England, through special dispensation. Being in very poor health, most of the time confined to the cell, I have tried to do a little good by spreading the devotion to Our Holy Mother.
>
> My humble prayers in the little Chapel where our Holy Mother died will often be for your House. I am greatly interested in Venerable Marina de Escobar and was very pleased to receive the little book about her.... My great desire is to make St. Brigida more known in the world and loved.
>
> With cordial greetings from my very dear Carmelite Mother, to which I join my humble and loving respects to you, Rev. Mother and all your dear daughters, In the Sacred Heart of Jesus,
>
> Your humble servant and Sister....
>
> Sr. M. Elisabeth of St. Brigida

It was almost two years later, in 1909, that Sister Elisabeth could undertake her long trip to Spain. She had had plenty of time to study the little book about Marina de Escobar, the re-markable Spanish mystic, who lived from 1554 to 1633.

Born of an aristocratic and pious family in Valladolid, then the capital of Spain, Marina was drawn to a life of prayer—even as Birgitta—in her childhood. But instead of entering a convent, which was a common thing for a young girl of her day, she spent hours praying in her room, like Catherine of Siena.

When asked why she did not join the Carmelite Order of her friend Teresa, who was only some thirty years older than she, her reply was that Our Lord had appeared to her, accompanied by His Mother and St. Birgitta, and had asked her to bring His Order of Our Most Holy Savior to Spain. This was at the time of the Order's greatest expansion in the north, as well as in France and Italy. Birgitta's *Revelations* were being circulated throughout Europe. Teresa of Avila had only just started to write of her mystical experiences and to reform the Carmelite Order. Marina herself never became a nun, but she organized a foundation of St. Birgitta's Order in a small palacio which was given to her for this purpose, in Valladolid. She was able to re-cruit Sisters already professed in other Orders to make this possi-ble. The first Prioress was Mother Inez, a very saintly soul. From Valladolid, four other Communities were eventually founded. They were in Paredes de Nava, Vitoria, Lasarte, and Azcoitia, all north of the former capital. From Vitoria, a convent of St. Birgitta had been founded in Mexico.

None of these Spanish convents had any connection with Rome, Sweden, or any other Communities of their Order. So they had been surprised and delighted to hear from Sister Elisa-beth. Her own account of her departure from Rome introduces the joys and also difficulties that awaited her:

Notes:

I left Rome on the 23rd of April, 1909. I had broken the trip at Porto Maurizo—(Mother Hedwig's new foundation on the sea near Genoa). On awakening the first morning, I saw myself as in a dream, arriving at a Brigittine Monastery, but the doors were closed against me...

92

At San Sebastián, I was met by the Resinis, who escorted me to the Convent of Lasarte, a suburb of the city. The Chaplain of the Community said he regretted that the Bishop had not given me permission to enter the Community. (False rumors had travelled to Spain more quickly than I.)

Sister Elisabeth retreated to the home of the Resinis, but a few days later, she had an overpowering desire to visit the convent, for it was the Feast of St. Richard Reynolds. She was received by the Superior, as she relates:

Dear Mother Margherita came to the grating and when she saw this child of St. Birgitta from Rome, tears came to the eyes of both of us. *Bien Venuta, Caridissima nuestra Hermana Isabel,* she exclaimed, and insisted on my remaining with them in the guest-house, even though the Bishop would not allow me to be with them inside the enclosure. The whole Community was called in and those who were sick were carried down in the arms of the strong and placed by the grating, to greet the pilgrim from Rome. It was a most touching scene. . . . We all spoke together about the Holy Order, and all wanted to know what the House of Our Holy Mother looked like.

When evening came, I was assigned to a small room next to that of the Chaplain's old mother. It must have been closed a long time, and the bedding was very damp. I awoke in the morning with high fever, and was unable to rise. The old Spanish lady asked me if I wanted *caldo,* which means broth in their language, but I thought of the Italian *caldo,* meaning hot. As I was burning with fever, I said no. She thought I did not want any food, and so I was left without any, until the third day, when I managed to crawl out of bed and get to the Chapel. On the way, I met the good Chaplain and he put his hand to his mouth, like a person drinking and said *Caldo, Caldo?* I then guessed that *caldo* meant some kind of food, and I said *"Si, grazie."*

Valladolid:
The next day, on the ninth of May, after bidding an affectionate farewell to the dear Sisters and Mother Margherita, I left by train for our Convent in Valladolid, where the Superior and Sisters had long begged me to visit them. At the station I was met by one of the out-Sisters and a friend, Senora Concha, who had come in a carriage to drive me back to the Convent.

On my arrival there, the Mother Abbess, Madre Josefa, greeted me most kindly, but with tears of regret; The Bishop had not granted permission for me to enter the enclosure.

The whole community came to see me and there was another scene even more touching than that at Lasarte, my dear Sisters inside the grating and I outside, looking at them.

The Arch-Bishop's Coadjutor came shortly after my arrival and with true Spanish gallantry, wished me welcome to Spain, at the same time expressing the Arch-Bishop's regret that he was not able to come. Several other Priests were present, friends of the Community. We were seated at a table, Donna Concha and I opposite to the Coadjutor and other Priests, outside the grating. The Bishop explained that the Community had papal enclosure and only the Holy Father could give me permission to enter. The Mother and Sisters present behind the grating, urged the Bishop to telegraph at once to the Cardinal Secretary of State, Cardinal Merry del Val, to obtain this permission from the Holy Father. He consented, and while writing the telegram he turned to one of the Priests saying in rather a sarcastic tone, and low, as if I did not understand Spanish: "She has come here to reform our Monasteries! ..." On hearing this, I answered: "Pardon, my Lord, this humble child of St. Birgitta has come not to reform, but to learn."

As it was nearing the time of the Great Silence, one of the out-Sisters took me to a little room near where they slept. The shaking of the train and the fatigue of the day had irritated my old infirmities and I spent the night in great physical pain, being unable to rise until noon the following day. At 12 o'clock the Arch-Bishop's secretary came to announce that the Arch-Bishop would come to visit at 3 o'clock.

The Mother Abbess received His Grace with me. He spoke in a very kind and fatherly way, saying: "You must not consider me an important prelate, but a father who is willing to help you in all that he can." He said that he greatly regretted that the permission had not yet come from Rome, but he hoped it would come the next morning. He added that if he opened the enclosure it would mean excommunication for him, as it was Papal enclosure. Then, looking at the Spanish dictionary in my hand, he said: "I am an old man and a man of experience; some books I can read without opening them, and so it is with Sister Elisabeth, for her I do not need any recommendation."

He then permitted the big, iron grille of the enclosure to be opened just to allow the dear Sisters to embrace me, and to kiss his ring, after which the heavy locks of the gate were again turned and the Arch-Bishop left.

I went to the beautiful Convent Church which is closed all day, except for the early morning Mass. There, before Our dear Lord in His Tabernacle, I spent some precious hours.... Before the end of the day, the Papal permission for me to enter the enclosure had arrived from Rome. I found the Sisters waiting along the broad cloister to receive me with sisterly embraces.

I spent several months in this handsome old Monastery, full of holy memories. It was the first-founded Spanish Monastery of our Order. Six years after the death of venerable Marina de Escobar, King Philip II himself gave one of his castles for the Monastery. The beautiful Church contains statues and ornaments of great artistic value, also paintings.

.... On the Feast of the Holy Trinity, we received the joyful news from Rome that Father Benedict and Father Charles were to be ordained priests in the Basilica of St. John Lateran on this great feast-day. We all offered Holy Communion for them and prayed fervently that God would bless their future lives and labours in His vineyard. (At this time, they were also taking vows as Brothers of St. Birgitta.)

During the month of July, I was occupied in cleaning and rearranging all the old reliquaries and relics of the Monastery. I felt this was a special privilege: Some of the large cases containing some hundred relics had not been opened for two or three hundred years! When the Arch-Bishop visited the Monastery, the Mother Abbess asked his permission to give me some precious relics which I treasure very much.... I was also permitted to see all the old documents of the Monastery in their archives and letters written by the Fathers of our Order in centuries past, among them letters from Father Mathias Ludwig, written from our Holy Mother's House in Rome to the Mothers of our house in Valladolid. These were the last letters written from the House in Rome to Valladolid, until this humble child of Birgitta wrote from there over a century later!

Until very recently, the custom of burying the dead Sisters in the cloister had been kept up, so that whenever one walked along the broad cloister, leading to the Choir, one had to walk over the dead. (Even Mother Inez, the foundress, was buried in the Sacristy, without a name—under the red tiles.) This was undoubtedly a beautiful thought for those who had in this life, humbly looked forward to being thus trodden on and forgotten (desiring nothing but their Union with God).

Saint Teresa, who was a friend of Ven. Marina de Escobar, visited this our Convent when making her foundation in Valladolid. She spent some time with our Sisters in the *Sala di Lavoro* where the Sisters sit and work together for certain hours of the day, according to Brigittine custom, and it is recorded that she expressed admiration for the *recollection* of the Sisters in God, even when occupied in various manual labors.

During my visit to the Monastery, the Choir was renovated, a new floor and stalls being put in. The floor was some hundred years old and so worn by the kneeling of the dear Sisters, that big holes could be seen before each stall, and the stalls themselves were falling from being so worm-eaten.

In the Refectory was a large wooden Cross bearing the emblems of the Passion of Our Lord. This Cross had stood in the cortile of the house where Ven. Marina de Escobar had lived in Valladolid.

Sister Elisabeth says nothing in her *Notes* about the outside aspects of the convent, standing on a dusty Square named the Plaza Santa Brigida; the high facade of the Chapel has little decoration, since it had not been built as a church but was fitted into the heavy wall of the original *palacio*. But around the corner, on the adjoining street, was the massive, handsome entrance of the convent itself.

Not far away, is the smaller Carmelite convent, founded by St. Teresa, and visited by St. John of the Cross, still active and well preserved with its blue-tiled Chapel. Also within walking distance, is the massive, early-Gothic *San Benito,* and the magnificent, later-Gothic Cathedral, with its museum of priceless sculpture and painting. Valladolid, on the great northern plain, or Llanura, which was the home of early Spanish culture, rivals Madrid as a treasury of art, as well as of religious history.

It was so in the next town that Sister Elisabeth was to visit. Paredes de Nava stands in the very center of the vast Llanura. Modern life seems to have passed it by, but it is a veritable Ghost-Town of culture. Six Basilica-type and Gothic churches of various periods, filled with works of art raise their heads above its small, old houses, many with delicate balconies and carved doorways. This was the home of the famous Berruguete family—painters and sculptors.

The Convent of Santa Brigida rounds the corner of a small square, opposite the Town Hall. Less imposing than that of Valladolid, it was to hold a special place in Sister Maria Elisabeth's experience. Over the door was the slogan *Aquí Mora Jesu, Here Dwells Jesus,* and the words were especially appropriate, as she tells us in her *Notes:*

Paredes de Nava
On the 3rd of August, one of the out-Sisters accompanied me to our

96

Convent in Paredes de Nava. Their Bishop had himself obtained all permissions for me to enter the enclosure and to remain in the Monastery as long as I desired.

This Bishop was a kind friend of our Order, and it was he who had sent the Rector of the Spanish College in Rome to bring me his blessing three years previously, when I had received the holy habit of our Order and made my vows as a daughter of St. Birgitta in *Domus Sanctae Birgittae, Roma.* This so touched my heart at a time when I was going through great humiliations and trials which my position in the House inevitably brought upon me, that I could never forget it. Our dear Lord, whose Heart is ever burning with love for us, inspired this, His good and noble servant, to pour balsam on the wounds of my soul. This good Bishop was, a year later, made Archbishop of Seville, and became His Eminence Cardinal Almares.

As our train passed the city of Palencia, one of the Canons of the Cathedral, Very Rev. Isidoro Lopez, came down to wish me welcome to Spain. By noon, we arrived at Paredes de Nava, where we found a carriage waiting to take us to the Monastery which is not far from the station. The big, iron-bound enclosure door was opened at once on our arrival, and the whole Community came to receive St. Birgitta's humble daughter from Rome, and to escort her to the Choir where the *Te Deum* was sung. After this, we again went out into the cloister, the Rev. Mother Abbess, Mother Isabella and the Mother Prioress, Mother Mercedes, walking by my side, and there, all the Community beginning with the Mother Abbess, gave me a hearty, Sisterly embrace.

My health was better during my stay in this house, so I had the great consolation of going to the Choir daily and of taking part in other Community exercises. This was the smallest and poorest of our Spanish Convents, but I was very happy there as in Valladolid, and I felt at home at once with all the dear Sisters whom I daily learned to love as I had our Sisters in the other houses I had visited. They were all delighted to hear about Rome and our Holy Mother's House. Our conversations during recreation time constantly turned to the History of the Order and our future hopes for it and for God's Glory. The sweet and simple spirit of this little hidden-away Brigittine Monastery impressed me very much, and I carried away with me many useful experiences.

The number of the Community was 18: 13 Professed, including the Rev. Mother Abbess and Prioress, 2 Novices and 5 Lay Sisters. One of the Novices was very delicate in health and there was a question of not giving her the votes for profession. The good Mothers showed me the confidence of calling me into counsel regarding the matter and said they would do as I thought. I felt most unworthy of such a mark of confidence, but I prayed Our Dear Lord to guide me rightly. His Majesty gave me the assurance that He wanted this weak Sister to be a daughter of St. Birgitta and this also corresponded to the natural impression I had regarding this dear child, that she was weakened through the anxieties and doubts she was laboring under, and that all would be well with her as soon as she was certain of being able to remain in the Monastery. She was poor and not able to give anything to the house. I told the good Mothers not to be afraid, but to allow her to be professed. And so they did, to the great joy of the little Novice, who at once began to grow strong and well. The ceremony of Profession was very nice, almost the same as in the primitive observance of our Order.

The October feast of our Holy Mother St. Birgitta, I also spent here. The feast was preceded by a well-attended Novena in the Church; on the eve, a statue of our Holy Mother, dressed in a gray silk and gold-brocaded cowl, was placed in a niche over the High Altar, taking the place of the every-day statue which is sculptured in wood. It was very interesting to help to dress the statue, according to old Spanish custom, and to think of how many of our Sisters during three centuries had touched these garments for which antiquarians had come and offered large sums of money. But our dear Sisters would not part with them for such a purpose, neither with the long, silver pen which a Spanish nobleman had given centuries ago, to be put in our Holy Mother's hand on the day of her feast. An eloquent sermon was preached in the afternoon, followed by Benediction of the Most Blessed Sacrament. In the morning there had been several Masses; during the day, recreation and great joy in the Community.

On the Feast of All Souls in November, there was a procession to the little grave-yard in the garden. All the Sisters carried lighted tapers, the *Miserere* was chanted, prayers were said and the Mother Abbess sprinkled holy water over the graves of our dear Sisters.

In December, I had a severe cold that caused inflammation of the stomach, this part of Spain being colder in the winter than Italy and that year, unusually so. I had been permitted to care for other sick Sisters and had thought I would escape. But no! My turn came, and it gave me the opportunity of experiencing the loving tender care which these dear Sisters gave me. May God reward them!

The Christmas festivals I also spent here, and I was permitted to make a new crib for the sweet little infant King, and to renovate St. Joseph and Our Blessed Lady, two most exquisitely carved statues and very old. This Monastery, like Valladolid, had a little private tribune from which one could see the Blessed Sacrament in the Church. I was permitted to go there when my bodily weakness did not allow me to go to the Choir. What sweet hours I spent there with my dear Spouse, renewing to Him, the offer of my useless self, begging Him to prepare my soul for the work to which He had called me; and so clearly did I see that it would have to be His work alone, because the instrument was worse than nothing, having in itself all the defects which would have proved an obstacle in His designs, if not guided by His Hand. Especially, during the Advent Season (when preparing for the coming of the Divine Infant King) I made use of my little corner in the dimly lighted tribune, where the light and strength my soul received was so much the greater.

In the early part of January, 1910, after consulting my Spiritual Director, it was decided that I should go to England again, so as to spend another six months in the oldest Community of the Order, Syon Abbey. ...Never can I forget what it cost us all to part.

The dear little Community of Paredes de Nava had received this child of St. Birgitta with so much love and sisterly charity! I loved them for this, but still more for their virtue which was so great, their life, so sweet and simple. Once, when I was very ill, and the whole Community was kneeling around my bed, I looked from one to the other, and a joy filled my soul at the thought of dying thus, among them.

After Sister Maria Elisabeth had left Paredes, her influence and her presence lingered on.

A young priest who came to write a cultural history of Paredes, after *Sister Isabel* (Spanish for *Elisabeth*) had gone, was so impressed by what he heard of her, that he wrote several pages about her in his book, and later, went to see her in Rome. The *Chronicles* of the Convent refer to her as "one sent by God" and "the founder of the Apostolic Branch of the Order."

Another more intimate reaction was the love inspired by Sister Elisabeth in the little nun of uncertain health, whose vocation she had advocated. This Sister Navidad felt a strong calling to go to Rome with Sister Elisabeth to work for a foundation there. But she was not allowed to do this; in fact, after Sister Elisabeth left, she was told by her Superior that she must not even speak about her to others, although she was permitted to write to Rome. Her correspondence with Mother Elisabeth lasted many years. The letters have been lost, but a strange, beautiful end to this story was told by Mother Inmaculada, now President of a new Federation of the five Spanish convents.

She had lived with Sister Navidad in Paredes, and when her former Superior was deposed, the little Sister felt free at last to speak of her devotion to Mother Elisabeth. Three nights before she died, in 1967, she said to Mother Inmaculada that she saw Mother Elisabeth holding a basket of flowers, very beautiful and fragrant. "She came dressed in her gray habit with her crown and her commanding presence and smiling face, and said to me, '*Child*—it was the affectionate name that she always called me, *Child, very soon we will be together.*'" With this impression, Sister Navidad passed the last days of her life without pronouncing another word, but in great peace.

VISITS TO VITORIA, AZCOITIA, AND AGAIN, TO LASARTE

Notes, continued:

On leaving Paredes de Nava, an elderly lady, a kind friend of the Community, and the good Canon Rev. T. Lopez, accompanied me to Vitoria, where I remained a few days to visit our Sisters there. They have a very beautiful Monastery and Church recently built for them by the Bishop who had asked for the site of their old, former Monastery on which to build his Cathedral. Our good Sisters at Vitoria had asked me to come to them, and they desired very much to help me in making a foundation in Rome, and some of the Sisters had offered themselves for this work. But when the Bishop heard of my arrival he forbade me to enter the enclosure, so I was left outside among secular people and subjected to many humiliations, for which, "May His Majesty be for ever praised!"

I was afterwards told that the Bishop feared some of the Sisters might have left with me; but his fears were without foundation, because I never would have permitted anyone to do anything that was not in obedience to Superiors. In every house I visited, I always, in words and acts, tried to impress upon all the Sisters the importance of doing all under "Holy Obedience," and I would rather have suffered martyrdom than to do anything underhanded. (This grace Our Dear Lord granted me, as of myself, I am nothing.)

Our Sisters in the Monastery of Azcoitia, near Loyola, had asked me to visit them before leaving Spain, so after three days spent in Vitoria, I travelled with one of the out-Sisters, whom the Mother Abbess had kindly sent me, to Azcoitia in the Basque Provinces near Loyola.

In the Monastery of the Holy Cross, Azcoitia, there was a venerable Sister Josefa Laramendi, who died *in the odor of*

100

sanctity and is buried under the floor in the Choir. A Memorial painting of her shows a striking face in profile, praying before a crucifix, passionate and mystical as only Spanish souls can be.

Notes, continued:

The good Sisters did not realize that the Bishop would also use his authority here (Azcoitia being in the same diocese as Vitoria) and when the news of my going to Loyola was brought to him, he immediately gave orders that I should not enter the enclosure, but leave the Monastery at once.

The poor, good Mother Abbess and the Mother Prioress were so distressed that the tears were running down their faces as they showed me the Bishop's letter through the grating, but His Majesty filled my soul with strength and joy so that I was happy to suffer this new humiliation, and I begged them all not to feel badly on my account.

My infirmities did not allow me to travel at once to Lasarte, near San Sebastián. I had instead to remain five weeks in a little room near the Church at Azcoitia. How very happy I was there, alone with my Lord! Oh how wonderful He is in His Ways! The Bishop, in preventing me from going in among the Community, prepared for me a most desired retreat, and in a place so wonderful!

From the window of my little "cell," I saw below the graveyard of the nuns, in the near distance a grand view of Loyola, the house of St. Ignatius' birth and conversion, and all around high mountains which made one feel as if one was in God's own sanctuary of nature.

Earnestly, I prayed for the help of the soldier-Saint in the battles that I knew were in store for me. I prayed also for the Scandinavian countries and for my two spiritual Fathers in Rome, Fr. Hagen and Fr. Brandi, who had both asked me to pray their Holy Father, St. Ignatius, to obtain for them a happy death.

A dear old out-Sister who had celebrated her golden Jubilee, travelled with me to Lasarte; the good Mother Abbess had given her to me for a companion on the journey. She was joyful and bright, and told me she had taken this journey through the beautiful mountains ever so many times.

This was my second visit to our Sisters in Lasarte, and they begged me to remain with them a few days before proceeding on my journey to England.

The Monastery of Lasarte was founded by a Spanish Admiral who miraculously won a battle on the feast of our Holy Mother St. Birgitta, and his two daughters were among the first to enter the Monastery as nuns. In the Church there are large paintings representing this battle.

A little statue of Our Blessed Lady, which had belonged to the Admiral, is preserved in a niche above the altar.

Our dear Spanish Sisters of Lasarte presented me with a beautiful set of vestments, white, with the Crucifixion of Our Lord worked in gold and colors, for our little Roman foundation....

This is the end of Sister Maria Elisabeth's *Notes* on her stay in Spain. She then returned to Syon Abbey for the second time.

After leaving Spain, she received many letters from the Spanish Brigittines, testifying to the impression she had made on the Abbess and Sisters of Valladolid, who urged her to return, if she wished, just as the Abbess and Sisters of Syon Abbey would have gladly kept her with them.

From the length of Mother Elisabeth's *Notes* on her trip to Spain (shortened by almost half in the present copy) it is obvious how much she felt akin to these Spanish Brigittines with their strong, mystical proclivities. It was Providential, too, that she was forced to stay in the tiny room near the Chapel at Azcoitia, looking over the great Jesuit Shrine of St. Ignatius. For indeed, Jesuits played a leading role in her life; Father Hagen, Father Brandi, and later, Father Rosa; then it was the Jesuit Father Beretta, who took her New Branch to India. Certainly she herself had St. Ignatius' crusading zeal.

Chapter XI

Holland and Germany: Altomünster

WHEN Sister Elisabeth traveled from Spain to England, in the spring of 1910, she stayed in Syon Abbey through the summer. It was in September that she left Syon for the second time, after her visit with Eva, and took a ship across the Channel for Holland.

Here, were two Brigittine convents, Maria Refuge, in Uden, and Maria Hart in Weert. The first was so named because it had received the Brigittine nuns from Marienwater, the earliest monastery of St. Birgitta in Holland, founded in 1434 by a noted Abbess, Mila von Kampen. It was located near Hertogenbosch, in North Brabant. The Abbey suffered greatly during the wars of the Reformation period. After years of struggle to keep their old, medieval site, the nuns were forced to abandon it, and settled in Uden, somewhat to the south, where Catholic influence remained stronger. For their refuge, they built an impressive church to stand between the two wings of their monastery, at the very entrance of the town. Its high walls extend back, enclosing a wide area of field and orchard. A handsome courtyard entrance is flanked by Chaplain's quarters and a guesthouse. It is still the mother-house of the Brigittine Order in Holland. It took the place of Marienwater, and for a hundred years, stood alone, with its Sisters. Finally, in the middle of the nineteenth century, they made a daughter foundation at Weert, a small town in Limburg, where the atmosphere was still strongly affected by the Spanish-Catholic spirit.

Since the priests of the Order of St. Birgitta had been dispersed, the Sisters had no one to help them protect their customs and traditions. The Bishops of Uden and Weert wished the two convents to conform to various other congregations of Sisters in Holland at the time, and did not welcome outside influences. Sister Elisabeth had received no encouraging letters from the Dutch convents, and in her *Notes* she does not describe her visit to Uden, which was not a happy one. It was characteristic of her that she seldom wrote of anything that was negative or that might seem to be critical of a person or situation. She did write of her visit to Weert, however, because of her great joy in meeting Sophia Catherine Ehrenpohl—"The only Swedish Brigittine in existence at that time."

Sister Marie Catherine, as she was called, was born in Stockholm of Swedish and Polish ancestry. She was brought up as a Protestant, but was early drawn to the religious life. She had studied painting, but this had not satisfied her. She left her social and artistic life for the strict enclosure of the Dutch Brigittines. In the convent she painted religious subjects. She had a rather stylized way of representing St. Birgitta, with a heavy border design, setting off her shrinelike pictures. (One is now in the Convent of Djursholm, and another in Valladolid.)

The encounter between the two Swedish nuns was a moving one. Sister Elisabeth must have presented her dream of a foundation in the House of St. Birgitta, and there is a report that Sister Catherine was eager to go to Rome, but was not allowed to do so. Perhaps this was the reason that the Sisters at Weert were wary of her—but she makes no mention of this. We can only gather her feelings from a letter written to Eva, from Weert, quoted in part, in a preceding chapter. It continues here:

From Convent of St. Birgitta, Weert, Sept. 13, 1910
My stay here will not be long, for I will soon have accomplished my business here, and hope to break up my trip to Rome, at Altomünster. Sister Catherine Ehrenpohl was so glad to see a fellow Swede that she was moved to tears.

The only other comments that Sister Elisabeth made on her visit to Weert were in another letter to Eva, written from *Altomünster, Oct. 4, 1910:*

104

The Convent in Weert which you asked about is quite unlike Syon, because it lies inside a little town. But it has a large garden where the Sisters can enjoy fresh air. All the Sisters in Weert are Dutch—except Sister Catherine.

So Sister Elisabeth had gone on to Altomünster where her reception was warm and her visit rich in experience, of which we have her full recording.

Altomünster

Rising out of the rolling farm country of Bavaria, and only about an hour's drive northwest of Munich, the medieval town of Altomünster has miraculously preserved its original character. The railroad has passed it by. Near it, are patches of thick forest, no doubt left over from the time when Alto, an Irish monk and follower of St. Patrick, came to convert this then-pagan area.

Alto lived as a hermit in this forest, which was given to him, as tradition has it, by King Pipin, the Younger. He gradually cut down trees to build the first monastery and church here, which was supposedly dedicated in 760.

Alto died as a saint, and his skull is still preserved in the Brigittine convent here, yellowed and incrusted in heavy gold. Gradually, the little town of Altomünster grew up around the monastery. This was first inhabited by Benedictines, then given over by them to Benedictine nuns, who lived there until about 1460, when the Community died out.

At that time, a certain nobleman, Wolfgang von Sandizell, whose wife had become a Brigittine in the medieval monastery of Maihingen, inspired the Duke of Lower Bavaria to establish a Brigittine convent in his country. Sandizell arranged for the renovation of the empty buildings and the Duke gave the monastery to the Brigittines. He then restored the convent on the south of the church, for the incoming Brigittine monks, and on the north side, built the present nuns' convent. In 1497, fifteen Sisters of St. Birgitta took over this monastery.

It is impossible to include in this simple story of Mother Elisabeth's life, the history of the medieval convents of St. Birgitta.

This has been the study of Dr. Tore Nyberg for the past ten years; published in book form, it makes fascinating reading, and his research still continues. Great, double monasteries built around handsome churches, after the fashion of Vadstena, were found in Denmark, Poland, Lettland, Holland, Belgium, France, not to forget Syon Abbey in England. In Germany, among some ten monasteries, Altomünster stands out as one of the most authentic convents and the most beautiful—the only one surviving from medieval times, and still inhabited by Brigittine Sisters, the direct, spiritual descendants of those who took over the convent in the year 1497.

No wonder, then, that Sister Elisabeth had long desired to come here. The Prioress of this convent had been one of the first to answer her letters of inquiry as to whether their Community might send Sisters to Rome, to form a Brigittine Community there.

Father Hagen had also written to the Prioress, Mother Michaela, and her reply to Sister Elisabeth shows her eagerness to meet him, as well as her openness of mind and heart toward the new idea. (Unlike the Dutch Sisters, who feared any intrusion into their lives.)

Before she had left Rome the first time, Sister Elisabeth had received the following letter:

Altomünster, 21 April, 1907

J.M. J.B.

Very Reverend and Dearest Sister,

Your kind letter I repeated to read with great interest and attention. I must tell, that I find your thoughts and reasons in relation of an humble foundation of our Holy Order in Roma quite right; I also can assure you, that it would be for us the greatest joy and of great progress for all our convents if this wish would become a fact, but with bleeding heart I am obliged to tell you that at present I am not able to fulfill your noble wishes.

... I am not able to send one suitable professed sister without injuring our own convent. Believe me, Dearest Sister Elisabeth, that for instance now, I have difficulty in filling the various house-duties. Our Holy Officium is very exacting and long-lasting, besides, we have a good many other prayers; every week, during the night, Adoration of the Holy Sacrament; we have to manage the washing of altar linens

106

and the baking of the hosts for the churches of the neighborhood. We have a large, extended house, two gardens, and all things are made by ourselves, including the shoes for the community. Some of the Sisters are suffering and aged.

I am sorry to be obliged to make these communications to you, for I wish myself that a community of Children of St. Birgitta could be founded in Rome. How profitable it would be for us Germans that right reverend Pater Hagen is in Roma! If I were some years younger (I am 65 years old) and a little stronger, I would depart immediately for Roma to see him.

Dearest Sister Elisabeth, how much I wish, and will pray, that you may soon find the few Sisters necessary for the foundation. Staying three years with the reverend Sisters of Mount Carmel and by your great piety and zeal, you have certainly already finished the time of proof and your noviciate and I think you have acquired a good spirit, that of the Order and especially that of our Holy Mother.

As sincerely as you have spoken to me, in the same manner, I have spoken to you. Let us continue to pray about this matter remaining full of confidence in our Good Lord.

Enclosing you in the Sacred Heart,

I am most respectfully,

> your
> Loving Sister in Christ
> M. Michaela
> Prioress Ord. St. Birgitta

It was three years since Sister Elisabeth had received this letter. She had been to England and to Spain; rich experiences —and if her short visit to Holland had been less successful, it was perhaps only to increase her joy at arriving in Germany, and finding her way to the unique Bavarian town of Altomünster.

The tall, handsome church of the Brigittines was also the parish church and center of the village. The high stark tower with its large clock, dominated the irregular cobblestoned square which lay below it. The old buildings of the nuns' cloister and the monks' cloister rose like shoulders on either side, their heavy, harmonious lines seemed to fit into the hill above, the whole construction crowning the town with a kind of pre-Baroque beauty.

Sister Elisabeth was greatly impressed as she drove up through the village. Her *Notes* fairly sing with enthusiasm as she describes her visit, the interior of the church and cloister, and the Brigittine life as she found it there after she settled down for a stay of several months. Since this section of her *Notes* terminates the account she wrote at the request of Father Hagen, and leads to the next big decision in her life, we leave it in full:

It was with deep emotion and interest that I continued my journey to Altomünster, the old Abbey which is the only house of our dear Order, besides Vadstena, where there are still to be seen Church and houses built according to the original rule of our Holy Mother St. Birgitta. But for over 300 years, Vadstena has not sheltered any of St. Birgitta's children, whereas Altomünster, in Catholic Bavaria, had not been forced to give them up....

As we drove up to the Monastery, the portress Agnes came to meet us and took us to the enclosure door, where Mother Abbess (Mother Michaela) and some of the older Sisters were waiting to greet us. I was very happy to be permitted to enter that Holy House and grateful to the Good God for the *useful experience* I knew I would have there.

It was a great joy to hear our dear Brigittine Office so well sung, to see the old ceremonies and customs and to take part in them as much as I was able.

The Community numbered 40; 26 Choir Sisters, and 14 Lay Sisters who took care of the garden, the cows, pigs and chickens, etc.

I was sorry to see that the original, so significant, dear habit of our Order, had been changed here, too, from gray to black.

In the Choir, there were beautiful old stalls, carved and inlaid by the Brigittine Brothers centuries ago. The Choir of the Sisters is high up, hanging like a cage in the big Church. Our Sisters had permission to have the Blessed Sacrament there in a beautiful Tabernacle, part of a splendid Altar that was the gift of one of the Sisters at the time of her profession.

On the ceiling were frescoes of Our Blessed Lady, Our Holy Father St. Augustine (The Rule of St. Birgitta was based on the Augustinian Rule), Our Holy Mother St. Birgitta, St. Catherine of Sweden, and Blessed Katerina, the young Indian Princess who died a holy death at Vadstena.

In the refectory, which was a real Brigittine one, they still used the old tables which the soldiers of Gustavus Adolphus had turned upside-down and stamped on with their heels—the marks of which can still be seen—during the devastation of the village at the time of the Thirty-Years War in Germany. The Monastery was spared greater destruction at that time because the Officer in command, jumping up into the reading desk, saw a book lying there and on opening it, read: *Regula Ord: SS Salvatoris et Stae Birgittae de Suecia.* Being Swedish, he felt ashamed to destroy a house whose foundress was his own countrywoman, and so he gave orders for the soldiers to stop and retire.

At the head of the refectory stood an altar dedicated to Our Lord on the Cross and Our Lady of Sorrows; this beautiful Brigittine custom I was so happy to see preserved also that of the Mother Abbess having her place at the head of the table along the right wall and the Mother Prioress at the head of the table on the left. Along the walls were old paintings of the twelve Apostles, at the side of the altar, statues of our Holy Mothers, St. Birgitta and St. Catherine, and the reader's desk stood in the center.

The cells, numbering about 60, were all around the courtyard on the first and second story, forming a perfect quadrangle. The windows of the cells, Chapter room, Community Room Noviciate, infirmary and refectory all looked out over the courtyard and the doors of these rooms opened on the beautiful, wide cloisters. How grand the processions were through those ancient cloisters from whence prayers had ascended to Heaven for over 1000 years!

Altomünster is the only house of our Order that has been able to retain a crypt for burying its dead members. Some weeks after my arrival toward the end of November, I became so ill that my life was again thought to be in danger. The good Mother, thinking I would die, had a place prepared for me in the crypt. But God's time had not come, and I was able once more to leave my bed, and my health became even better than it had been for many years, Thanks to God and the loving care of our dear Bavarian Sisters!

God's ways are not man's way: He takes whom He wishes. After the Christmas holidays, Rev. Mother Michaela became seriously ill and died.

Sister Elisabeth then describes how she had been able to nurse Mother Michaela to the end and the burial ceremonies which were carried out according to the old Brigittine customs.

When the solemn High Mass was finished in the Church, the Chaplain, accompanied by two other Priests, entered the enclosure and the procession down to the crypt was formed.

First came a professed Sister, carrying the Cross, then two Sisters with torches, followed by two carrying holy water and incense. Then came six white-veiled Sisters carrying the remains of the dead Mother on their shoulders under a white pall with a big black Cross. Next to the coffin walked the Mother Prioress, and St. Birgitta's humble daughter from Rome was given a place by her side; then followed the long line of Sisters in black veils, and after them, the white-veiled garden and kitchen Sisters.

It was an impressive sight to see this procession crossing the large courtyard—which was covered with a soft carpet of snow—and going down into the crypt, which was under the ancient part of the Abbey— 1500 years old.

In the crypt the pall was removed and we saw Mother Michaela for the last time. The Priest gave the final absolution, the coffin was lifted into the niche waiting for it and all present sprinkled Mother Michaela's last earthly resting place with holy water before leaving the crypt. R.I.P.

When the election for the new Superior was to take place, a number of the elder Sisters in the Community came to me and told me that they all wanted me to remain with them. I became very alarmed and began at once to prepare for my return to Rome.

No, it was Sister Elisabeth's firm conviction that it was in Rome that her work must be done. Incidentally, while in Altomünster, she had been allowed to look through the ancient attics and storerooms of this rambling double-monastery, and had found some old paintings, and a remarkably expressive Crucifix, which she had been permitted to take for her Roman foundation. The Crucifix now stands in the niche of the Church of St. Birgitta in the Piazza Farnese. To conclude her *Notes* on these journeys, Sister Elisabeth, soon Mother Elisabeth, sums up her gains and new prospects as follows:

With great interest, I had followed the ceremonies and customs of the Holy Season of Christmas at Altomünster, which undoubtedly are the oldest and most like what they used to be in Vadstena. I had now, through a special grace of God, been permitted to live the life of a Brigittine among Holy Mother Birgitta's children in many lands; May God also grant me the grace to use all I have learnt for His greater Glory and our Holy Mother's honor.

In the first week of March (1911) I returned again to our Holy Mother's House, on the Piazza Farnese, Rome. Once more I had had to separate myself from our own dear Brigittine Sisters, and it cost not a little, because a true mutual devotion and affection had sprung up between us.

I had undertaken these long journeys with the consent and advice of my Directors. In 1906 and 1907, before I started, I had had the promise, first from Syon Abbey and afterwards from Spain, that they would send Sisters to Rome. But difficulties had arisen.... However, my relations with all the Convents always remained most cordial....

In all humility, I wish to state that it was *not from a desire for adventure* nor from a love of travel that I undertook these fatiguing journeys; my health at that time was in such a condition that without a special Grace of God, it would have been impossible. After my return to Rome, in 1911 and 1912, I made another attempt to obtain Sisters of our Order, but my renewed attempts also failed.

There remained nothing else for me to do but to make use of the knowledge and experience I had gained during the years that I had lived in the different Brigittine Convents.

Chapter XII

The New Branch of the Order of St. Birgitta

Now comes a very crucial period in Maria Elisabeth Hessel-blad's already remarkable life—the turning point at which Sister Elisabeth becomes Mother Elisabeth, foundress of a new branch of the Ancient Order of Our Most Holy Savior. It was never her intention to found a new Order, but to revive the old, so that it could find a new center of strength in Rome, and in the very House where Saint Birgitta had lived and died. Her further purpose was to bring the Birgitta Sisters back to Sweden and to build up the Order in any country where Providence might call it, to spread the modern spirit of Christian unity and service to others as the far-flung Order of St. Birgitta had spread the Christian culture of its day.

The establishment of Mother Elisabeth's "United Houses" without papal enclosure, and her claim that they are an integral part of the Ancient Order of the Most Holy Savior, commonly called Brigittine, has been the subject of criticism and sometimes controversy. But after thirty years of unceasing toil and perseverance through all kinds of difficulties, her work was crowned by canonical, and later by papal approval.

And not only this, but in spirit and practice, her convents have gradually won the acceptance of the world in general. Their policy of taking guests for a moderate fee, offering hospitality and a lodging for the night, as did the monasteries of old, has quite naturally endeared them to the communities which they serve.

When Mother Elisabeth had returned to Rome after her

journeys to the Brigittine convents, two circumstances made it almost inevitable for her to plunge into the immense responsibility of founding a new Community.

The first was the situation she had found when she got back to the Carmelite convent. Her position there had always been a difficult and delicate one, but it had been made tenable by the extraordinary understanding and affection of Mother Hedwig.

Now, by the strange timing of destiny, during the same month of January, while Sister Elisabeth was nursing Mother Michaela in Altomünster, the noble Mother Hedwig died suddenly at her little convent at Porto Maurizio.

Father Brandi had written of this to Sister Elisabeth. He related that he had hastened to the Piazza Farnese when he heard that Mother Hedwig's *Requiem* was to be held in the Church of St. Birgitta. He had called to express his condolences to the Carmelite Sisters, and said that he had found them in a sad state of grief and confusion. He advised Sister Elisabeth not to come back until a new Prioress had been elected.

When Sister Elisabeth returned in March, she found a changed attitude on the part of the Community. The new Prioress would not allow her to enter the *clausura* nor could she recite the Office with the Sisters in the Choir. She was given a room in the section of the convent usually rented out to strangers, but told that this could only be a temporary arrangement.

Again, Sister Elisabeth had the help and counsel of Father Hagen, as well as of Father Brandi. Through a Monsignor Tonelli, acting as agent, Father Brandi was able to rent a narrow six-room apartment that was vacant on this Monserrato side of the building. Here she could live independently and even envision the beginning of a tiny Community. For both Father Hagen and Father Brandi felt that the time had now come for Sister Elisabeth to take a further step on the path toward realization of the mission which she felt God had entrusted to her; to bring the Birgitta Sisters back to Rome. Since no other Sisters from the convents she had visited had been able to come, perhaps it was God's will that she should find or train others.

113

The second circumstance that made Mother Elisabeth decide to launch her new foundation without further delay, was the fact that Father Benedict had found two postulants for her, and was ready to bring them to Rome.

As was evident on her last visit to Syon Abbey, Mother Elisabeth had observed Father Benedict's own endeavors to found a Community of brothers with the deepest interest.

Father Benedict had appreciated her concern for him, and now it was his turn to help make her foundation possible. He had found two unusual young girls in his parish, where they had enjoyed singing the Liturgy at his Masses. They both had excellent voices and ardent, spiritual natures. He had inspired them with an interest in St. Birgitta and the new work which was to be a counterpart of his own. Catherine Flanagan, whose first name was also that of St. Birgitta's daughter, became Sister Catherine, and Amy Davis, took the name of Sister Reginalda, after Blessed Richard Reynolds.

The apartment which Mother Elisabeth had been able to rent from the Carmelites was quite adequate for the needs of a small convent, as far as space and dignity were concerned.

The entrance was on the Via Monserrato, and so quite apart from the Carmelite Community. Handsome gray stone steps led up from a massive doorway. This was the entrance which visitors had used to reach the rooms of St. Birgitta and St. Catherine on Feast Days or special occasions. They opened on this same stairway, and extended back into the main body of the House. A facing door, a few steps farther down, led into the little suite of rooms that lay along the Via Monserrato as far as the corner of the Piazza Farnese. Of the two small reception rooms, one was used for an oratory. Still smaller rooms served as cells and at the end of the long corridor was a big, pleasant Community room with tall windows on the piazza. This room was directly under the first cell given to Sister Elisabeth when she came to the House of St. Birgitta and found herself in the window which she had seen many years before, in a vision or waking dream.

To the rear of the apartment was a cheerless laundry and kitchen. The only heat was furnished by an old stove for cook-

114

ing. But best of all, in spite of many inconveniences, this was an integral part of that big structure that had grown up around the original Palazzo and Church of St. Birgitta. This little, elongated convent was almost wall-to-wall with the room of the last *Revelations* and of St. Birgitta's death.

To these places so precious to Mother Elisabeth, the Sisters had free access. Sister Reginalda kept a diary of the early days of the foundation. (Most of the story told in this chapter is direct quotation or condensation of what she wrote.) She describes the very moment of their arrival:

Early in the month of September, 1911, we find Sister Maria Elisabeth awaiting the arrival of her first spiritual daughters. It was about half-past seven and she was in the room of St. Birgitta, arranging the altar for Mass, when she heard the door-bell ring. On the threshold was Fr. Benedict Williamson with two English girls who became the first two postulants—Sister Catherine and Sister Reginalda.

A few moments to remove the dust of the long journey, and they all entered the room of St. Birgitta, where Fr. Benedict said Mass and gave Holy Communion to the nascent Community. The record kept is brief. It was a small forward step. But she who on that day, became Mother Elisabeth, poured out her soul in thanksgiving, begging her dearest Lord to accept these humble beginnings and to continue the abundant gifts of grace she had learned to expect from Him.

The last entry in Mother Elisabeth's *Notes* was an evocation of those first days:

I began at once to try to instill the sweet and simple Brigittine spirit into the hearts of the dear spiritual daughters which Almighty God had sent me. God Himself had fitted them with the natural gifts required for the first members of a new Foundation. With their good voices, they have been able to sing the praises of Our Lord and His Blessed Mother according to the chant of the beautiful and ancient Brigittine Office which now, at last, was recited once more in the Eternal City.

(Signed) Rome, month of the Precious Blood, 1918

This was the last entry and end of the *Notes* written down at the request of Father Hagen. No doubt, Mother Elisabeth considered it the climax of this story of her spiritual quest, resulting in her vocation, and then leading on to this point of creating the new branch of an ancient Order. All her future accomplishment stemmed from this, and was merely the cultivation of what she had that day grafted on the old tree of the O.SS.S., trusting blindly that the branch would bear fruit.

The first weeks of the new foundation were truly Brigittine in spirit and practice. Father Benedict stayed on and Sister Reginalda wrote in her diary: "From the very first day, we had the consolation of being able to sing part of the Brigittine Office together, and Father Benedict gave us frequent instructive conferences."

Surely, Mother Elisabeth and Father Benedict, during those days, must have shared the dream of Brigittine brothers and sisters cooperating with one another once more, to build up their work on a larger scale. But then Father Benedict had to return to his own parish and community.

Again, Sister Reginalda provides details of the early struggles to get started:

Life was hard but hearts were fervent. We were delighted to share Our Lord's poverty, and our Mother always consoled us saying, *Providence will provide*—and the next day, some new friend would appear. Indeed, we were never without friends. One brought blankets for our straw beds, another provisions for our poor table, another a sanctuary lamp and candles for our little Oratory.... Useful gifts included an old picture of St. Birgitta from the Sisters at Altomünster. And a Swedish artist who was not Catholic, painted a picture of *Mater Salvatoris,* surrounded by Brigittine Saints.

In March of the following year, 1912, another young girl sent by Father Benedict, arrived from England to become a Postulant. She took the name of Sister Birgitta, and soon after her, came Agnes Beauchamp, who became Sister Richard.

A little later, His Holiness, Pius X (afterwards sainted because of his great qualities as a Pope and as a man) granted an audience to Mother Elisabeth and her Postulants, as Sister Reginalda said: "He greeted them with paternal kindness. . . ."

Mother Elisabeth related afterwards that he had not forgotten her former visits, and her original request to wear the Brigittine Habit, when she thought she was going to die. "Don't forget to

116

die this time," he said, no doubt in a joking manner, but Mother Elisabeth could never forget this rather sardonic jest. Did he mean, perhaps, that she should *die,* more, *to self?* that she was perhaps too presumptuous or ambitious in her plans? In any case, she felt humbled, and was always deeply grateful and full of admiration when she spoke of St. Pius X.

From the very beginning, the little Community attracted the attention and one might almost say, the protective affection of various prelates who could not help admiring Mother Elisabeth and what she was trying to do, in her precarious state of health and with very limited means. Sister Reginalda describes the visit of a Cardinal from England:

"The newly-created Cardinal of Westminster, Francis Cardinal Bourne, visited the little Convent.... The Cardinal said to Mother Elisabeth: 'This will be the first Blessing I give outside the College since I was made a Cardinal!' He was much interested and expressed the hope that the humble undertaking would prosper and receive the Blessing of God. From this time onward, Cardinal Bourne remained a faithful friend to Mother Elisabeth and her daughters and never came to Rome without paying them a visit."

But now the peace of the convent was broken by a notice from the Carmelite Superior that she would require the apartment on the Via Monserrato by the end of August. This was in May, 1912. Mother Elisabeth was also told that she could no longer have access to the rooms of St. Birgitta and St. Catherine, and could not have Masses said there, not even on the Feast Days of the Scandinavian saints, which they had always commemorated with great fervor, often having outside visitors for such occasions. But now the Carmelites even suggested that Brigittines were using their privileges of entry to the rooms, for their own material gain. Probably the Carmelites felt that any small contributions by outsiders should go to them. But this was a bitter blow for Mother Elisabeth.

She laid the matter before Cardinal Falconio, who had learned about the situation and the scope of Mother Elisabeth's concepts from Father Brandi. He had received her very cordially and approved her methods and the constitutions of the new branch of the Order of St. Birgitta. However, he counseled her not to oppose the notice to leave the House, but to seek another home for her Sisters, where they might develop their work for God. He gave her a hearty letter of recommendation.

At this time, Mother Elisabeth was too weak and ill to look around for a house herself, but Father Hagen undertook to do so. On August 18, 1912, his house-man, Carlo, brought news of a small villa near the Vatican, on Via Aurelia, 133. Mother Elisabeth liked the location very much, overlooking St. Peter's, and part of the Vatican gardens. The house was badly in need of repair, but it had much to recommend it. After negotiations with the owner, she arranged to rent it for a modest sum.

Sister Reginalda describes their departure from the beloved little convent on the Piazza Farnese: "Our simple preparations were made. With sad hearts, but complete resignation to the Will of God, and hope that we might someday return, we sang for the last time the hymn, *Ave, Maris Stella* in the Holy House where Birgitta had first sung it."

The custom of singing *Ave, Maris Stella* in Brigittine convents dates back to a dramatic event in the life of the Saint. Birgitta was one of the first to promote devotion to the Virgin, long before this honoring of Mary was popular or generally accepted.

One day, there was a large crowd in the Campo di Fiori, which in the fourteenth century included the Piazza Farnese, and the story goes that Birgitta had pronounced the words *Tota Pulcra es Maria—Mary, you are all beautiful*—when someone suddenly denounced her as a heretic. Led by a Dominican friar, the crowd advanced on her menacingly, and demanded that Birgitta be delivered to them, to be burned as a witch. Birgitta, calm and undaunted, gathered her household around her and sang: *Ave, Maris Stella.* After a few diminishing threats, the crowd dispersed. Birgitta ordered that from that time on, the hymn should be sung every day, in thanksgiving to *Our Blessed Lady.*

Sister Reginalda's account can best give the picture of the

118

convent in its new home, its first, independent little villa, or *Villino,* as they called it:

The first thing to do was to make the house habitable. It had not been lived in for some years, and was in a very bad state. But willing hands and hearts made a quick transformation. Permission could not yet be obtained for Mass to be said in the house, so the Sisters went daily to St. Peter's for Mass and Holy Communion.

Cardinal Bourne, who was in Rome toward the end of October, with a large English pilgrimage, paid two visits to Mother Elisabeth, bringing with him Canon St. John and a Benedictine, Abbot Berge. The Cardinal was very pleased with the new Convent and again expressed the wish that the work should prosper. . . .

On the 17th of December, the house was blessed by Mother Elisabeth's faithful friend and Confessor, Fr. Hagen . . . and on the last Sunday of Advent, December 22nd, Fr. Hagen said the first Mass in *Villino Santa Brigida.*

During December, Mother Elisabeth, accompanied by Princess Cassano, was privileged to be received again in private audience by Pius the X, and to present her children to His Holiness, who gave his blessing to them, and to all of St. Birgitta's children, wherever they were.

The young Postulants, for whose Clothing it had not yet been possible to obtain the necessary permission, were encouraged by Mother Elisabeth to attend the Masses of Holy Week at St. Peter's and to visit the "Altars of Repose," as they are called in Rome, in the famous Churches of the Twelve Apostles, Santa Maria d-Ara Coeli, and others . . . and on Good Friday they went to Santa Croce for the Blessing with the Great Relics of the Holy Cross. Finally on Easter Saturday, they assisted at the great ceremonies of St. Peter's.

On June 7th, 1913, the Supreme Pontiff, Pius X, signed in the affirmative, an appeal made to him by Mother Elisabeth and her infant Community for his approval and blessing of their work. This removed the difficulties that had hindered the Postulants from being given the habit; on the Feast of the Visitation, 1913, a year and a half after they had arrived in Rome, Sisters Reginalda and Catherine were clothed in the gray habit and white veil of Novices. Agnes Lincoln, always a faithful friend, was their God-mother.

The Sisters labored to create some small income, and began reaching out to do work for churches and also for the poor. Many new contacts were made. Sister Reginalda's diary notes that:

119

On St. Birgitta's Feast, the 8th of October, 1913, people of nine different nations, including three Scandinavians, were gathered in the little Oratory to pray for the countries of the North. A relic of St. Birgitta was shown and venerated, and the picture of the Saint, three hundred years old, which Mother Elisabeth had found in a cow-shed at Altomünster was wreathed in evergreens and roses.

A fortnight later, Monsignor Respighi visited the Convent to see that all was in order and readiness for the Preservation of the Blessed Sacrament....

Mass was said on this occasion by Monsignor Ugo Rossi, a priest from the Vicariate, and a few days later, Benediction of the Blessed Sacrament was given for the first time at Villino by the hands of a Scandinavian priest from Norway....

Mother Elisabeth's union with God, her natural talents and her care in nurturing those of others under her charge, made for a very happy and deep religious life.

For in those early days, the Community followed the old Brigittine Office and according to the ancient Rule, much time was devoted to exercises necessary to the Contemplative life, and to the practice of religious music and needlework. The Altar in the Oratory was carved by Mother Elisabeth with the help of her Sisters and all the vestments and furnishings came from the same capable hands. Everything must be as beautiful as possible, however poor and simple it might be. There were no lay Sisters as yet; the household duties were shared by all.

Friends were never wanting to aid, and the constant care of Our Lord was manifest in the talents of the postulants He sent, each one fitted, in her own way, to be a stone in the building of this Community which was to restore the Brigittine Order to Rome.

1914—DEATH OF POPE PIUS X, AND OUTBREAK OF THE FIRST WORLD WAR

The year 1914 brought the death of Pope Pius X, and the outbreak of the First World War. There were no *immediate* consequences for the little convent. Father Hagen wrote:

> The Holy Father has asked the Emperor of Austria not to bombard the open cities, and to spare Monuments and Churches—so in Rome we shall be quite secure. It is a blessing *not* to get war news now. In fact, I hardly know there is a war, and enjoy my quiet and peaceful dealings with the stars.... Of course, the soldiers and sufferers deserve our constant prayers....

Sister Reginalda's diary continued:

In the month of November, 1914, the Bishop of our Sisters in Mexico visited the Convent. He had visited Mother Elisabeth six years before, when she was living alone in the Carmelite Convent....

1915

During these years, Mother Elisabeth's health had been far from good. At times, she suffered great pain and weakness, being able to eat very little and to sleep hardly at all. At the beginning of 1915, she became so gravely ill that her life was again despaired of. She had a return of her severe hemorrhages. She felt herself dying and asked for a priest.

The Confessor to the Convent, Fr. Thomas Braitsch, O.S.A., came at once and heard her confession, but he did not give her the Last Sacraments, as she had recovered a little. The improvement only lasted a few days, and her condition became dangerous again. She received *Extreme Unction* and *Holy Viaticum.* Immediately, she began to recover....

Mother Elisabeth had consulted with Fr. Hagen about taking the Last Sacraments even when it was *not sure* that she was to die, and he had answered her with his usual, loving candor:

"Thank you for telling me about your sickness. It is more serious than I thought, although I am sure that the Lord will save you for completing His work. The answer from the Vicariate is quite right, and I give you the same advice, to have the *Viaticum* with *Extreme Unction,* administered. Then you can receive the *Viaticum* every morning, without fasting, as long as the danger lasts; and it will last many weeks yet, because a new attack may follow at any moment....

"Your children should not be frightened, as many of weak faith are, but *desire* to give you this sacramental help...."

Sister Reginalda's diary now continues:

The month of January, 1915, will be remembered on account of the terrible earthquake that occurred in Italy. It was one of the worst earthquakes Italy had ever known, exceeding even that of Messina.

Thirty-thousand lives were lost, several towns and villages swept away and hundreds of wounded were brought into Rome. The Sisters were saying *Sext* when the quake took place. The little villa rocked; the Sanctuary lamp swung to and fro. All felt sick and giddy. Many children were left orphans and homeless, and the Sisters were asked if they could receive a few. In spite of Mother Elisabeth's weakness, she consented gladly, and felt Our Lord would give her strength. Six little girls arrived and all had sad stories to tell. One had lain for four hours under stones and debris, before she was rescued. Her mother died before her eyes. Another had her little brother, five months old, in her arms when the shock came: The baby was crushed, but she escaped with slight injuries.

February brought fresh anxiety to Mother Elisabeth. She had notice that she must leave the little *Villino* that all now loved so dearly, and had taken such pains to make suitable for a Convent. The owner wanted to raise the rent; not having the means to meet his demand, she found a house further out of town, on the Via Corsica.

The house, though reasonable, at first seemed almost too large. It had a garden, which was desirable, but meant extra work. Later, toward the end of the war, this larger house enabled the Sisters to take in many refugee children.

It was now time for the four Novices, Sisters Reginalda, Catherine, Birgitta and Richard, to make their first Profession, and again, permission had to be asked, as the Order was still awaiting its formal Canonical Approbation. But Mother Elisabeth's good friend, the Benedictine Abbott Berge, helped her this time, to go forward. The distinguished French Father Hattais, who had become the Chaplain of the new Convent, gave the Sisters their preparatory retreat and on the 8th of September, 1915, the four were professed by Père Hattais.

It was a great and beautiful day for Mother Elisabeth when, after so much toil and suffering, she was able to walk in procession behind her four daughters, their white veils exchanged for the black veil and the white Brigittine crown with its five crimson spots, tokening the five wounds of Our Lord.

[Suddenly she realized that this was the very scene of which she had had a pre-view nine years before, when she had first come to the house of St. Birgitta, and as a novice, longing for the habit of St. Birgitta, had been walking along the hallway leading to the terrace.]

In the next year, two Italian Sisters came into the Order, Sister Raffaela and Sister Michaela. Early in 1916 the first Swedish postulant, Sister Elena, entered the Convent on the Via Corsica. It was at about this period that Mother Elisabeth made the change from the Brigittine Office to the Roman Office. The old Breviaries were out of print and almost impossible to obtain. Both Fr. Hagen and Fr. Hattais favored the Roman Breviary, which brought the Sisters into closer participation with the universal prayer of the Church.

By Christmas time of 1916, the Sisters were well established in the new Convent on the Via Corsica. Miss Lincoln sent a beautiful statue of the Christ of the Sacred Heart. Nine Masses were said with many people crowded into the little Chapel. Beginning with the Mass at Midnight, the Sisters sang *Adeste Fidelis* and *Panis Angelicus;* during the Mass at Dawn, *Stilla Natt—Silent Night* in Swedish, and during the third, *Flos de Radice Jesse* and *Quam Dilecta Tabernacula Tua.*

122

Mother Elisabeth had made a beautiful Crib, but she was so ill it was feared she must spend Christmas in bed. Fervent prayers were made by the Community and, with confidence that God would support her, she struggled up at Midnight and was able to go about throughout the day, to the joy of her children.

The Community was now ten in number. Cardinal Bourne, visiting them in the early days of January, 1917, congratulated them, assuring them that Our Lord would watch over them, no matter what difficulties they had to encounter, and added that he never forgot to pray for them.

That life was still often very difficult is reflected in the following letter from Father Hagen:

(His suffering Child-in-Christ had come a long way—He now addressed her with the full dignity of her position as Superior of a Convent.)

Specola Vaticana
Roma   Easter Sunday, 1917

"Reverend and dear Mother Elisabeth:

It is quite natural that you feel the poverty of your saintly Community, which is always pressing on your soul, in a double measure during these terrible times of war. I know it is only confidence in God's loving Providence that keeps you up. You have indeed good reasons to trust in God, working as you do, only for Him and His Church.

As God has inspired you to consecrate your whole life and your work for the Brigittine Order and for the welfare of your country Sweden, and as you respond to the Divine call so generously, under bodily suffering and temporal cares, God is bound by His own Sanctity, by His Truth and Love, to sustain you in all spiritual and temporal needs.

I am always consoled when I read in your letters your unbounded hope and ardent zeal. These are the gifts of God—and how can He withhold the daily bread? You and your good Sisters certainly do *"Seek first the Kingdom of God"* and God in turn will inspire some generous souls to supply the natural means. You and your work for Scandinavia have a permanent place in my daily Mass and I thank God that He allows me to witness the abundant fruit brought forth by the child whom I received into the Church, so many years ago, in Washington.

Pray also for your spiritual father,
J. G. Hagen, S.J."

At this time, the distinguished French priest, Father Hattais, was the Superior General of the Fathers of Mercy and Confessor to the

Convent of St. Birgitta; he was a deeply spiritual and human soul, and had immediately appreciated Mother Elisabeth and her work. In August, 1917, he agreed to interview the Mother Superior of the Carmelites on the Piazza Farnese, and also Rev. Father Lucca, Procurator General of the Carmelite Order, to see if there was any chance of obtaining the House of St. Birgitta.

Both received him favorably and expressed themselves as well-disposed toward the Brigittine Sisters. Père Hattais therefore advised Mother Elisabeth to go and see Father Lucca and thank him for these good dispositions. Though weak from recent illness, Mother Elisabeth went at once, taking with her Sister Richard.

She soon discovered that the only way to dislodge the Carmelite Nuns was with a large sum of money, sufficient to enable them to buy a Monastery somewhere else, superior in every way to *Casa Santa Brigida,* with a large, enclosed garden. "If you had a million lire to give them, they would leave at once," ended the Procurator. "God has the million and we will leave the matter in His Hands," answered Mother Elisabeth.

While living on the Via Corsica, Mother Elisabeth had the visit of Cardinal Almarez, Arch-Bishop of Sevilla, formerly the Bishop of Palencia, who had been so kind to her at Paredes de Nava in 1909. He was accompanied by Mgr. Ramon Barbera y Boada and two other distinguished parties. The Cardinal was very interested and delighted to see the Community so well established, and to give them his blessing.

The Community was steadily growing in numbers, and it was also growing in grace and fervor, impressing not only the people of the neighborhood, but attracting many visitors.

In June, 1918, one of the Carmelite Nuns living in Holy Mother St. Birgitta's House fell ill. The Mother Superior, recalling how much Mother Elisabeth had done for the health of the Nuns during her residence in the House, sent the Mother Assistant over with the sick Sister, to ask her advice. Mother Elisabeth gave it willingly and did all she could for the little Sister.

A fervent Novena was begun in which the Carmelites were invited to share, for mutual intentions, in honour of the Sacred Heart, Our Blessed Lady, St. Birgitta and St. Teresa.

The Novena was just over, when Mother Elisabeth had the privilege of an unexpected private audience with Pope Benedict XV. And she had the opportunity to beg the Holy Father to use his power to get back for her and her children, the House in Piazza Farnese. She explained that it was Sweden's inheritance, given away by one of the former Popes: That St. Birgitta was not only a Saint of Sweden, but a universal Saint, and especially a Saint of the Holy See; and would it not be beautiful, especially in this terrible time of war, to honour this great Saint of the Holy See? "Yes, yes," answered His Holiness. "I wish you every success"—

An interior voice seemed to prompt Mother Elisabeth to continue, and she added: "We will pray God that Your Holiness will help. Your Holiness will have the power and means to do so." The Holy Father gave his blessing, not only to Mother Elisabeth and her companions, but to the whole Brigittine Order.

Mother Elisabeth then wrote at once to Syon Abbey, to the Spanish Monasteries and to Holland, renewing her appeal that they do all they could to help her to get back the House of St. Birgitta for the Order, especially now when the signs of Divine Providence were pointing that way, and the Carmelites had become willing to give up the House. She also wrote to Mgr. Tonarelli, the Deputy of the Cardinal Vicar, urging him to assist in the project.

After three years in the Via Corsica, Mother Elisabeth was faced with the necessity of moving again. She had held the property on a rental basis; now others had bought the place, wished to make alterations and move in themselves. This time, however, the new owners were very considerate, as they realized it was difficult for the Sisters to find another Convent. [It was still not possible to envisage any immediate possibility of returning to the *Casa di Santa Brigida.*]

Many exhausting trips were undertaken by Mother Elisabeth and her Sisters, to try to find suitable quarters for a new Convent, either in Rome or in the surrounding country, approaching a price which they could pay. Should she leave Rome—? No, it could not be God's Will, after all her struggles to bring the Order of St. Birgitta here. The people of the Quartiere Caprera, the district around the Via Corsica, did not want her to leave; they came in a body, to urge her to stay. A large deputation also visited Father Rosa (who had succeeded Father Brandi) at the *Civiltà Cattolica,* urging him to use his influence to find a house in the Quarter where the Sisters were so much loved; the chapel was a consolation and all venerated the Mother Abbess, bringing their sick to her for remedies and seeking her advice in all their undertakings.

The Good Lord must have heard all the prayers that were made on this occasion, for a house, very suitable for their purpose, fell vacant, the property actually adjoining that of the Via Corsica. The owner, a Marchese di Bagno, was willing to sell to

125

the Sisters. The price was very high—the Sisters did not have the half of it—but everything seemed to point to the Villa di Bagno. Mother Elisabeth's faith was strong that Providence would send the necessary money. She thought that perhaps the Holy See would lend the sum needed and she appealed directly to the Pope, through Father Rosa.

His Holiness Benedict XV showed great interest and said: "Of all the works I would like to have represented in Rome, it is one for the Scandinavian Countries, I would most value—I would like to see a Scandinavian Colony formed." He added that he would like to see the Mother Abbess himself, and she was received in private audience, once more, this time with Sister Richard (February 19, 1919) in the Pope's study. She told him briefly of the scope of the work, and how it was now growing. His Holiness was most gracious. Finally, he agreed that a certain, generous sum could be made available as a loan from the Holy See. (After five years, this loan was entirely paid back!)

The joy and gratitude of the Sisters was very great. A few days later, the Marchese di Bagno sent his car for Mother Elisabeth who, with Sister Richard and Sister Catherine, went to his office to sign the contract for the house, 34 Via delle Isole. It was to be the mother house of the Brigittines in Rome for the next twelve years.

The move was accomplished by the Sisters themselves, as they carried their beds, furniture, and possessions through the hedge separating the two properties.

On April 6, 1919, the Mass of Inauguration of the new chapel was said by the Reverend Père Hattais, in the presence of a congregation of at least 180 persons.

The Community had the happiness of Exposition all day, and at five o'clock in the afternoon, Reverend Father Rosa, S.J., gave Benediction of the Most Blessed Sacrament, preceded by a short but very appropriate discourse. Several Scandinavians were present, among them the consuls for Norway, Sweden, and Denmark, Mr. Solomon, a Danish Jewish convert, and Count

126

Wrangel, a well-known Swedish writer. All were entertained at a tea in the convent parlor afterwards—where the Scandinavian flags had been arranged at the feet of a statue of the Blessed Virgin.

For a long time, the indefatigable Mother Elisabeth had been pleading with the vicariate to obtain formal Ecclesiastic Approbation for her Community. Monsignor Mingoli, of the Vicariate, was most kind and expressed himself as being willing and ready to do whatever he could. But everything hung fire.

Father Hagen had also written a letter to be presented to the Cardinal Vicar. In August, 1919, Syon Abbey, at the request of Mother Elisabeth, wrote a petition to the Holy Father, and the Spanish monasteries did the same, recommending Canonical Approbation for Mother Elisabeth and her Sisters as a Community of the Ancient Order of St. Birgitta. The Catholic Bishop Müller also wrote to the Holy Father, thanking him in the name of the Catholics of Sweden for all he had done to help the daughters of St. Birgitta in Rome.

Father Rosa, S.J., then director of *Civiltà Cattolica,* who had now become Mother Elisabeth's confessor and staunch friend, undertook himself to present the letters from the Brigittine monasteries to the Pope.

But many visits had to be paid to the vicariate; many difficulties and discouragements still lay in the way....

The Cardinal Vicar himself said to Mother Elisabeth on one occasion: "C'e tempo, c'e tempo, abbiamo tutta l'eternita!" (There's time, there's time—we have all of eternity!)

"Oh no! Your Eminence," she replied, "we have only a limited *time* in which to work for eternity!" She also said, more than once, that the hearts of the Scandinavian people could be touched in a special way through St. Birgitta; that not even priests, bishops, cardinals, nor the Pope himself could inspire in them the great respect and love that they felt for Birgitta.

Another year dawned, and there were still delays. At last, at the end of January, 1920, Monsignor Tonarelli sent for Mother Elisabeth and read through the Constitutions with her. He made a very few and unimportant changes. In February, the news came that all the papers were in the hands of Monsignor Mingoli at the vicariate.

Mother Elisabeth then wrote a letter which was signed by all the Sisters, saying that the Community was anxiously awaiting the document containing the Canonical Approbation, desired for so many years, and promising, on the part of the Community, fidelity and loyalty to God, the Pope, and ecclesiastical superiors.

Sister Reginalda concludes: "On March 4, 1920, it was at last possible to gather together the whole Community and to sing the *Te Deum:* Monsignor Mingoli had called, bringing with him the *Decree of Canonical Approbation!*

"Mgr. Mingoli was extremely kind, and shared the joy of the Sisters, saying that it was the first decree of this kind that he had prepared since he had been in office.

"This was a great day in the history of the renewal of the Brigittine Order. Mother Elisabeth was now Mother Abbess of the Order of the Most Holy Savior, in Rome. She who had for sixteen long years contended valiantly *in the strength of the Lord,* against ill-health, poverty, humiliation and persecutions of all kinds, now saw her children safely and surely established upon the old Foundation—"

Chapter XIII

Via delle Isole

THE new convent at the Via delle Isole proved to be the corner-stone of the expanding structure of the Order of St. Birgitta for the next ten years. Now Mother Elisabeth had come into her full stature as Superior of an established Order, linked with the past, but looking toward a future of active, apostolic work.

Sister Richard, who had always remained especially close to Mother Elisabeth as assistant, now kept a diary of those days which gives an insight into the day-by-day life of the House and shows how its influence was developing. Scattered throughout this chapter, her notes are freely transcribed and necessarily shortened; quoted but not indented, they follow, for the most part, a chronological order beginning in October, 1920.

"After the first year in the new Convent at Via Delle Isole, it became necessary to build a bigger Chapel for our growing Community ... and the neighbors who came to worship with us. All building materials were extremely expensive, and the masons' work as well. ... So we could not afford to employ more than *one* man. ... All the Sisters began to help according to their strength and capacities; the lay Sisters made the cement for the mason and several of the choir Sisters helped to put the plaster on the walls, and afterwards, did the inside painting of the Chapel, pillars, walls, etc. Our dear Mother herself built and carved the altar and the altar steps; she was the engineer for the whole building and had to direct the mason, as well as help with the painting and mixing all the colors.

"On October 7th, the Feast of our Holy Mother Birgitta, Don

Rossi from the Vicariate, came to bless our new Chapel. He carried the Blessed Sacrament from the old Chapel to the new altar, the Sisters walking in procession carrying lighted candles and singing the *Pange Lingua.* . . . There was a large congregation; at 4:30 P.M. our Cardinal Protector, His Eminence Cardinal Billot, S.J., came to give us Benediction. There was a great number of Scandinavians present.

"October 18th. The Parish Priest of *Porta Paradiso,* in Florence, came to say Mass. His church was part of the ancient Brigittine Monastery of that name, founded from Vadstena in 1394. It was the second Convent of our Order, and the original buildings still stand, as does the church of which he is pastor. But he told us that the once-sacred Cloister is now used for the storage of wines.

"In November, the Swedish Baroness Lagerfelt came to see Mother Elisabeth and said she had come in the name of the Swedish Government and certain ladies of the Nobility who would like to buy our Holy Mother's House on the Piazza Farnese. They would be willing to give our Community the rooms sanctified by Our Holy Mother St. Birgitta, and also the Church, and certain other rooms for our use. But the rest of the House they would use as an Institute for studies. Mother Elisabeth told her that she thought it might be possible to divide the House in this way . . . but evidently, nothing came of it."

Such rumors showed, however, that there was a revived interest in Birgitta among her own countrymen, and it had no doubt been stimulated by the fact that there was a new branch of active Brigittines in Rome, led by the remarkable Swedish nun Elisabeth Hesselblad.

Indeed, earlier than 1911, a certain Countess Mary von Rosen had come to Rome, and sought to see the lone Brigittine Sister whom she had heard was living at the Piazza Farnese. She was one of those noble ladies who had a great personal devotion to Saint Birgitta.

In June, 1911, Sister Elisabeth wrote to her as follows (in part):

130

Good Countess von Rosen:

Your friendly letter received and I heartily thank you for it. You ask if I will be in Rome for some time? It depends on whether I can arrange all as I hope, in our Holy Mother Birgitta's honor.

I am very sorry that I did not have the opportunity to meet you when you were in Rome; I was away, studying the life of our Holy Birgitta's Convents in Spain and England.

The remaining Convents of our Order are too poor to help us with the building up of St. Birgitta's memory here. . . . Some months ago, I came back here to see if there was not some corner where her own daughters might find a place to work for our beloved Mother's memory and for the good of our fellow men. . . .

A section of the House, with entrance from the via Monserrato, which you may remember, is now free—it is just at the side of our treasured Birgitta and Catherine's rooms—I have taken it for the purpose mentioned above, and also so that as a Swede, I may try to protect our historical treasures here, before they are taken still further from us. . . .

St. Birgitta is our country's Mother and in a double sense, my Mother, as I am both Swedish and her spiritual daughter—even though unworthy to wear her Order's habit. . . ."

Then, with the greatest tact, Sister Elisabeth begged the countess' help in carrying out her project, saying she would be grateful for large or small contributions from interested Swedes. The countess responded graciously, and from then on began a truly deep friendship which was to bear much fruit.

In 1920, when Mother Elisabeth heard of the renewed interest in Birgitta, she considered making a very small foundation in Sweden, if it were possible. She began to pray about this with her Sisters—but the time was not yet ripe.

"In the next months, several new Postulants entered the Order, and a number of friends of the Convent were taken into the Catholic Church, by way of the new Chapel," continues Sister Richard.

The story of Sister Mary Magdalena emerges from the *Convent Diary* and begins with her dramatic entrance into the Order.

"She was a gifted young student at the Ursuline College

nearby, and felt drawn to the Order of St. Birgitta, but her Mother and Father were violently opposed. They were rich and worldly Neapolitans, and when they came to take her home from the College, Gilda, the daughter, ran away and took refuge at the Via delle Isole.

"She arrived breathless at the gate, and begged to see Mother Elisabeth. Though Mother was sick in bed at the time, she arose to talk with Gilda. Since she was over 21 years old, Mother decided to let her stay, for she said that returning to her parents again would be like going back to a virtual prison. Cardinal Billot was visiting that day, and he also interviewed Gilda and encouraged her to stay. The next day, she was given a Postulant's dress and the name Sister Mary Magdalena. She said she felt she was in paradise!

"But her mother had hired a detective to find out where she was. He came to the Convent and was allowed to see Gilda, who assured him that she was there of her own free will. He left, but the next day, her mother arrived at the gate of the garden with a number of relatives, shouting and demanding: *bring me my child!*—following her words with terrible insults.

"Mother Elisabeth felt it would not be safe to let her in and sent for the *Carabinieri.* When they came, it was dusk, and they asked that Gilda be sent to reassure her mother, through the gate, that she wished to stay. By this time a large crowd had gathered. Gilda came out quite calmly, saying *Mama, Mama,* very affectionately, but her mother refused to speak to her. Then Gilda spoke out in a loud, clear voice, to the people outside the gate, saying that she had entered the Convent of her own free will and that she was more than 21 years of age. She wished to remain there, as a Spouse of Christ. Her mother continued to scream so loud that she had to be taken away in a cab, with two men to hold her down. Gilda's father said: 'You will see that I will find a way of getting her out!'

"It was quite dark when they left. Gilda remained outwardly calm, but it had been a terrible ordeal for her, as well as for Our Mother and for all of us." (Her story is continued later.)

"The high-ranking Prelates of Rome seemed to love to visit

this unusual Convent, especially when they could bring Nordic guests. One day, Monsignor Rocca called and brought with him Count de Paus, a Norwegian gentleman whom he had taken into the Church and who became a very good friend of the Order. A little later, he in turn brought the Swedish Baron Fleetwood, a Protestant, who also became a good friend to Mother Elisabeth when she came to Sweden.

"On the Feast of St. Ansgar, Feb. 6th, Mother Elisabeth invited a Norwegian priest who happened to be staying in Rome, before returning to Norway, to give a talk in Norwegian on this great Scandinavian Saint, for the benefit of all the Scandinavians in Rome. Mother sent out many invitations, with the result that many came. . . .

"Father Kjelstrup gave a very good conference, and all stayed for Benediction and tea, which followed. (It was this Father Kjelstrup who later became the means of bringing Sigrid Undset into the Catholic Church.) A certain Baron—in the name of all present—formally thanked our Dear Mother for what she was doing to honor the memory of St. Birgitta and added how much Scandinavians enjoyed these little reunions. . . ."

This was among the first large gatherings that Mother Elisabeth organized for Scandinavians, but by no means the last. It was part of her warm, sentiment-rich nature that must find expression—an overflowing of the love of God in her, for others, and particularly those of her native Sweden.

However, such joys were not enough to satisfy the mind of Mother Elisabeth, nor to distract her from the firm purpose of acquiring the House of St. Birgitta for her Order. She had again approached various Church authorities concerning this. The first document we have specifically stating that the Carmelite Sisters were willing to move is one signed by D. Jorio for the Chapter of Santa Maria in Trastevere and confirmed by Monsignor Mingoli, of the Sacred Congregation of Religious, with whom Mother Elisabeth was constantly in contact.

It was this Chapter that had originally taken over the House when it was abandoned by the Brigittine monks of Altomünster, in 1828. The Chapter had never given up its ownership, but had given the Carmelites a very long lease. Now the Chapter stated that it also wished compensation, if the Brigittines were to take over the House! But Mother Elisabeth was not one to be easily discouraged. Her work was developing its own momentum. Of the many new postulants and Sisters who began to come to the Via delle Isole, some were outstanding in their background and subsequent fidelity. One of these was Anna K.: "She was of German origin and, during the war of 1914, she had been interned eight years in a small house in the depths of Italy. The house had been lent to her by Italian friends, but she lived entirely alone. She spent her time in prayer and work, picking herbs and greens in the garden, for her food. When the country people got to know her, they saw that she was an innocent girl, and brought her a little flour and oil from time to time, for which she was very grateful. The Police used to come regularly to see if she was there, knocking at the door sometimes by day, sometimes in the middle of the night, and she was obliged to come to the door to show herself.

"She had chosen the smallest room in the house for her bedroom, which was like a cell. She used to pray late at night, by the light of an ancient Roman virgin's lamp. Her parents died during the war, but she did not know this until afterwards, when she returned to Germany, as all correspondence was stopped during the war. She had always had a great longing for the religious life, to give herself to God. She came to us, and when Mother gave her the Postulant's dress and cape, she gave her the name of Sister Mary Agnes. She was very happy.

"A quiet accomplishment of Mother Elisabeth's at this time was the claiming of two French Sisters, martyred at Valenciennes during the French Revolution, as true Brigittines. They had been forced to flee from their own Convent, took refuge with a Community of Ursuline Nuns and were put to death with them. The canonization of these Sisters was about to take place, and they were all to be considered Ursulines. But when Mother Elisabeth heard of this, she worked tirelessly through Fr. Rosa, and others in the Vatican, to bring out the fact that Sister Anne-Marie La Croix and Sister Marie Françoise had belonged to the Order of St. Birgitta, then existing in France. They were subsequently declared both Saints and Martyrs of the *O.SS.S.*

"The following year, Mother Elisabeth heard from the Parish Priest of Pont-sur-Sambre, France, that a great Feast was to be celebrated in honor of the Ursuline Martyrs and the two Brigittine Martyrs. Sambre was the birthplace of the two Brigittine Saints. At that time, an elderly French woman, staying at the Convent on the Via delle Isole, expressed a desire to join the Order, and was accepted. She was to go back to France to settle her worldly affairs, and so Mother Elisabeth asked her to attend the celebration at Pont-sur-Sambre, which she was very glad to do. She took the name of the two martyrs, and became Sister Anne-Marie.

"Besides Saint Birgitta herself, and her daughter St. Catherine, St. Anne-Marie La Croix and St. Marie Françoise are the only woman-Saints of the Order. St. Richard Reynolds, recently canonized, together with the other English proto-martyrs of the Reformation, has become the fifth Saint in the Order of Our Most Holy Savior."

Further notes from the *Convent Journal:*

"*Holy Week, 1921: Maunday Thursday,* Our Dear Mother washed the feet of all the Sisters, so sweetly and humbly, in imitation of Christ.... Fr. Rosa gave us another beautiful conference on the Passion of Our Lord and explained how each soul had its interior passion to go through....

"*April 3, 1921:* At an invitation from Mother Elisabeth, the brother of the King of Sweden, Prince Oscar Bernadotte, with his wife and their two daughters, came to visit us.... They were under the impression that we were all forced to stay in the Convent, whether we liked it or not.... In our conversation, we were able to clear away many prejudices. Another strange idea they shared with most Swedes was that Catholics never read the Bible. Knowing this, Our Mother had placed all the Bibles we had in the house, on a table, so they could see them. There were some in Italian, in English and in Swedish.

"*October 8th:* The Feast of our Glorious Mother St. Birgitta ... Fr. Rosa preached a beautiful sermon on Our Holy Mother; he said, after the death of St. Birgitta, Almighty God had chosen her daughter, St. Elisabeth, as His instrument for the great work of continuing the Brigittine Order. Fr. Rosa meant to say *St. Catherine,* but we took his words as being prophetic and that our Beloved Mother Elisabeth whom God had chosen as His instrument to *revive* the great Brigittine Order would one day be honored on the altars.

"Fr. Rosa also explained how, as in the days of old, our Convent continued to give hospitality to Scandinavians, giving them food and lodging for as long as they desired. ...

"Listening to Fr. Rosa's talk, was a young Swedish sculptor, who was desperately looking for a room in Rome, with his wife and small son. He appealed to Mother Elisabeth who gave him a tiny room which had been used as an emergency parlor. But then Mother had a better idea: that of converting a small stone house on the grounds into a livable bungalow. It had its own entrance on the street. The mason who helped us build the church came to our assistance, and with the aid of the Sisters, and especially Mother Elisabeth herself, who did a great deal of hard work, a fine little abode was arranged, with wooden floor, water, etc. The sculptor was over-joyed and promised to make a Statue of St. Birgitta in return. ... Some months later, he was baptized a Catholic in our Chapel, with his little son.

"Now comes the end of the story of Sister Mary Magdalen whose name had been Gilda, and whose parents had so fiercely opposed her entrance into the Convent. She was suffering from tuberculosis, but she did not wish to leave for a sanatorium where she would have no spiritual consolation. Mother Elisabeth undertook to nurse her, bringing her special meals and washing all her dishes herself.

"In February, she received the Last Sacraments. Mother Elisabeth asked a certain arch-bishop Morretti, who had accidentally come to call, if he could *profess* her at once, since she was in a dying condition and wished to make her final vows. The whole Community of Sisters gathered on the terrace outside her door.

136

The simple ceremony of her first and last *Profession,* made together, was most impressive and beautiful.

"The next day her mother came to see her for the first time since she had screamed outside the Convent gate. She asked Mother Elisabeth to pardon her, for she realized that her poor Gilda had lived a short but holy life. She seemed completely reconciled to her death, for Mother Elisabeth helped her to believe that her daughter was still alive in the spiritual world.

"The distinguished Father Hattais had now left the Community as Chaplain, as he was sent by his Order to America. In a retrospective letter, he said: "No Community has ever given me as much consolation as that of the Via Delle Isole. And I am convinced that the Good Lord thinks as I do. There is there an *elite* of souls which is really remarkable. . . ."

Once more, in the *Diary,* comes the recurrent theme of Mother Elisabeth's desire—her deep prayer and endless efforts—that the House of St. Birgitta should come into the hands of her own Order. Second only to her wish to serve God, it was the drive and dream that never left her—because she also believed that it must be the will of God.

How many times already she had been near death, and the drive remained; if only she could live until this was accomplished.

"*June 12th, 1922:* Our beloved Mother wrote to our Cardinal Protector, to ask him if he would not use his influence to help us obtain our Holy Mother's House which was still inhabited by the Carmelites of Papal Enclosure.

Our dear Mother felt that we could honor our Holy Mother's memory so much more if we were in that House. . . .

"*June 17th:* Our Mother went to see Fr. Rosa, to ask him if he would not speak to the Holy Father Pius XI about the House in Piazza Farnese. She suggested that we could be caretakers of the house for the Holy See, and at the same time have charge of the rooms of Our Holy Mother St. Birgitta and St. Catherine, in order to spread devotion to our Holy Mother and make her better known. . . .

137

"*June 27th:* Monsignor Zonchi came to pay a visit to our Convent. He was then Rector of the College of the *Nobili Ecclesiastici.* As His Eminence, Cardinal Iacci had an apartment in the same college and the Church of St. Birgitta was one of his titular churches, our Mother asked Mons. Zonchi if he would speak to His Eminence about *Casa di Santa Brigida.* . . . Mons. Zonchi promised to speak to His Eminence, Cardinal Iacci.

"All that summer of 1922, Mother Elisabeth was sick with very high fever. Doctors prescribed quinine and various powders, but nothing seemed to help. We stormed heaven with prayers. . . . Finally, on the fifth of August, her temperature went down to normal. This was a turning point."

During this time when she was so ill, Mother Elisabeth composed a *Supplica,* a very long and beautiful letter to His Holiness, Pope Pius XI, asking him to help her reclaim the House of St. Birgitta and giving him all her reasons and hopes for the Order.

Father Hagen also wrote a letter, recommending Mother Elisabeth and her Community, and personally presented both letters to the Holy Father. Father Hagen was still director of the *Specola Vaticana,* and his fame as an astronomer had grown. He was, as ever, a faithful father to his child-in-Christ, but he was growing too frail to go around freely. Father Rosa had become Mother Elisabeth's confessor and advisor, but Father Hagen never failed to write or give advice whenever she requested it.

There was no immediate result to her writing of this letter, but it was Mother Elisabeth's first step toward attracting the attention of Pius XI. Ten years later, the contact brought fruit! (The wheels of the Vatican turn slowly!)

In October of that year, Mother Elisabeth was desperately ill once more. In spite of prayers and medicines, it seemed as if she must recurrently go through these terrible periods of suffering, with frequent hemorrhages from her old ulcers, and not able to take anything but liquid foods. Anyone in her condition would normally have died long before. Certainly it was only

138

her willpower, and the will of Destiny, that allowed her to survive.

JANUARY, 1923

The New Year started off as usual—this year that was to mark another great turning point, or advance, in the story of Mother Elisabeth.

After describing the usual Christmas and New Year's festivities, the *Diary* notes that Pastor Nordmark from Stockholm came to visit for the first time. He had been in Munich, Germany, attending the consecration of the Bavarian Monsignor Müller as Bishop of Sweden. Mother Elisabeth had been in correspondence with this Swedish priest for some years, as he was very much interested in her foundation. The following Sunday, he preached in Swedish, and many Scandinavians, whom Mother had invited, were present. Among them was the Protestant pastor of Maribo, the former Church and Convent of St. Birgitta, in Denmark, of almost the same age and proportions as Vadstena.

A month later, the new Bishop Müller of Sweden came to visit Mother Elisabeth. He was most cordial and spoke to the Community saying, among other things, that it would be a great joy to him when the Brigittine Sisters could return to Sweden and he prayed that the time was not far off. . . . He told them that for his Bishop's Pectoral Cross he had chosen the Brigittine Cross; it was of plain gold with five rubies set in it, in honor of the Five Wounds of Our Savior.

The following day, Bishop Müller had a private audience with the Holy Father, and asked Mother Elisabeth to meet him at the Vatican with three or four of her Sisters, to share his audience. The Bishop first had a private talk with His Holiness and then Mother Elisabeth was called in, with her children.

The Holy Father spoke to Mother about the House of St. Birgitta and said that he had read her *Supplica* (which she had sent six months before) and made inquiries. He had learned

139

that the Carmelites were willing to leave, but not until they had another large house with a garden. He added that houses were difficult to find at the present time in Rome; however, he would pray over the matter and see what could be done. . . .

A week later, as Bishop Müller was leaving Rome, he asked Mother Elisabeth to come to see him. He said he was *most anxious* for her Community to have the Casa di Santa Brigida and he would like it to be a center for Swedish visitors in Rome. (Of course, this had always been her desire, but the Bishop did not fully realize that she had been working and praying for this, for over sixteen years!) He told her he had spoken to Cardinal Billot about it, and also to Cardinal von Rossum of the *Collegio Propaganda Fide,* and urged her to follow up these contacts, which, of course, she did with joy. At least now she was not so very much alone in her zeal and efforts to reclaim the beloved House.

Then, toward the end of May, came a letter which precipitated a chain of events leading to Mother Elisabeth's return to Sweden with the Order of St. Birgitta.

It was a letter from Mary von Rosen, devotee of St. Birgitta, who had been corresponding with Mother Elisabeth ever since 1911 when, after her return from Spain, she found that Countess von Rosen had tried to find her in Rome at the Casa di Santa Brigida.

In the meantime, a group of distinguished Swedish friends of Birgitta, most of them High Church Lutherans, led by Count and Countess von Rosen and encouraged by Bishop Nathan Söderblom and other churchmen, had founded a *Societas Sancta Birgittae,* using the Latin name which connoted their historical interest and the fact that they admired classic liturgy. They had determined to gather each year at Vadstena on the anniversary of Birgitta's death, and to honor her by wearing gray Brigittine robes for this occasion, marching in procession to the old convent church, where medieval singing and ceremonies emulating those of Birgitta's day were held.

That year, in July, the 550th anniversary of Birgitta's death would be celebrated, and the von Rosens invited Mother Elisa-

140

beth, with another Sister, to attend, saying that all expenses would be paid and she must first come to visit the count and countess in their own home, at Rockelstad. At first it seemed like nothing more than an exquisite courtesy and a wish to see two Catholic Birgitta Sisters in the crowds that would be present at this historic commemoration. However, it proved to be an event with far-reaching consequences for Mother Elisabeth and her revival of the Order.

Secretly, at first, but deep in her heart, she resolved that if she went to Sweden, her own beloved country and that of St. Birgitta, she would not leave until she had made a new foundation there—planted the flag, so to speak; in this case, the Cross of the Brigittine Order in the land of its origin.

But she was far too humble and too astute to do this without the approval and help of her superiors. She first wrote to Bishop Müller, who heartily approved of this idea, particularly as the Protestant *Societas St. Birgittae* had invited her, so that it could not be said that the Bishop had asked her to come for purposes of propaganda.

Mother Elisabeth went to the vicariate in Rome where Monsignor Mingoli encouraged her and arranged another private audience for her with Pius XI, who gave her his blessing for her undertaking and also granted a singular request. She asked if she might be allowed to have Mass said in the old Church of Vadstena, on the very day of St. Birgitta's death, if this were possible. For this purpose, she prepared a small, portable altar, with a consecrated stone set into its top, to take in her baggage!

With great hope, Mother Elisabeth started off for her northern homeland.

Chapter XIV

Sweden—Djursholm

ON July 8, 1923, Maria Elisabeth Hesselblad set foot once more on the soil of her beloved Sweden. It was just past midsummer, and she must have been thrilled to see the long, Nordic twilight; to hear the birds twittering at ten o'clock in the evening; to see the birch leaves trembling, alive in those white nights that hold a magic all their own. Even the fragrance of the air at this season is something indescribable to those who have not experienced it.

Bishop Müller was on hand to greet this visitor from Rome. Even though she had broken the long trip at Munich and at Berlin, he could see that she was tired and insisted that she first come to rest at his country residence on Lake Mälaren. Then they returned to Stockholm, luminous at this time of year, alive with boats and waterways between its handsome buildings. Here Eva came to meet her sister Maria, with much rejoicing.

Mother Elisabeth visited the French Sisters who ran an excellent private school for girls in Stockholm, but did not wear habits, as after the Reformation the law of the State forbade religious Orders to exist or wear nuns' dress in Sweden. She also called on the German Elisabeth Sisters who wore the plain, semi-uniform of deaconesses or Swedish nurses.

Count Erik and Mary von Rosen came to escort Mother Elisabeth to their country estate of Rockelstad, a typical Swedish manor house with two wide, round towers, set-in terraces and lawns, with the forest nearby.

Mary von Rosen was a slender, gracious figure, with the

142

assured simplicity of Swedish aristocrats. Count Erik was a handsome sportsman type, genuinely cordial and deeply religious, as was his wife. They showed Mother Elisabeth their prayer room in one of the towers; around the ceiling were painted scenes of St. Birgitta receiving some of her *Revelations.* A small altar, erected between two columns, held a picture of Our Blessed Lady, four candles, and a Bible. Here all said prayers, together reading from a book entitled *Oremus,* by the venerable Jesuit Father Benelius.

A few days later, they went on to Vadstena, for the formal commemoration in honor of St. Birgitta.

Vadstena

The very name evoked all that Birgitta meant, not only to Mother Elisabeth, but to Sweden, and now especially to the *Societas St. Birgittae* who was gathering to celebrate its third annual reunion, this time exactly 550 years after the death of Birgitta in Rome, July 23, 1373.

Vadstena was then, as it is now, a stretched out, quaint village of low stone or stucco houses along a central, winding cobble-stoned street. Care has been taken to preserve its character, so that its great medieval monuments stand shoulders above its humble roofs; there is the round-towered castle of Gustav Wasa with its moat swinging around it, filled with water from Lake Vettern, and older still, the high Blue Church, Birgitta's church, also near the lake, with its convents on either side; the restored nuns' convent and refectory to the north, and to the south, the remains of the monks' monastery.

Birgitta was cousin to the Swedish King Magnus. Born of noble parents in the province of Uppland, she was only twelve years old when her mother died, and she was brought to live with an aunt on an estate near Vadstena, in the province of Östergötland. (This was just across the lake from Västergötland, where Mother Elisabeth was born!) Birgitta was married at the age of thirteen, and lived with her husband on another estate

143

near Vadstena—indeed, she lived in Östergötland from 1314 until 1349, almost half of her life. During this time, she often took part in the life of the court. Vadstena was one of the favorite residences of the king, and Birgitta, as the queen's lady-in-waiting, lived at the castle, even though she was hurt and scandalized by the dissipated manner of living there. She had a deep, mystical nature, and even as a child she conversed with Our Lord, who talked to her as she knelt before her crucifix.

She was inspired to tell the King that he should repent and build a great monastery at Vadstena to take the place of the wicked court. Although the king and his young Flemish wife would listen to Birgitta and promise reform, they went on in their dissolute way. But the king finally gave her the land for her project and Birgitta envisioned and planned for her new monastery and church before she left on her long pilgrimage to Rome.

The Blue Church, so called because of the bluish tint of its limestone blocks, was built in an early pure Gothic style, with a high pointed roof—no towers, but a tall spire which could be seen far out over the stormy Lake Vettern.

Inside, its nave has great width and majesty. Its massive, octagonal pillars hold lofty vaults; the capitals are plain, unsculptured, but of beautiful proportions. High on the east side had once been the nuns' choir and gallery. The broad apse around the altar toward the west formed the monks' choir. A few, low, platform steps led up to it. Here was a perfect setting for religious drama.

In this year of 1923, the church was well preserved, and work was in progress to restore the remaining portions of the nuns' convent. Thanks to the revived interest in Birgitta, the *Societas St. Birgittae* had been founded, and also the *Birgitta Stiftelse,* led by Prince Eugene and the art historian, Professor Andreas Lindblom, aiming at a restoration of the convent at Vadstena.

So on this third anniversary celebrated by the S.S.B., a bigger

144

gathering than those drawn only by religious interest had come to Vadstena; historians, musicians, art lovers, and intellectuals of many sorts, as well as journalists and photographers.

It is easy to imagine the feelings of Mother Elisabeth and Sister Reginalda as they came into the Blue Church, and later found themselves among this crowd of Birgitta followers, with men and women, also clothed in gray habits, bringing to life some of the long, dramatic past of this monastery.

The *Diary* kept by Sister Reginalda is understatement indeed, but its genuine quality also feeds the imagination: "Arriving in Vadstena, we were taken to see the memorable old Church. We were left alone in it for about half an hour. We walked down the broad aisle and knelt and kissed the paving stones, thanking Our Lord for permitting us to come here."

They must have seen two early statues of Birgitta, treasures of the church, one a sturdy, seated figure carved in wood, and another representing St. Birgitta in an ecstasy, her head thrown back, as if she were leaning against one of the octagonal columns, in a particularly beautiful pose. There were other wooden altarpieces of medieval times, one showing scenes from the life of Birgitta, one where she is giving out the rule of her Order to brothers on one side, Sisters on the other. In the apse was a handsome chest, or reliquary, containing the bones of the saint. It was pointed on top, like the roof of the church, covered with red velvet and studded with silver medals, the coats of arms of Birgitta's families, and other designs of the day.

On the vigil of the Anniversary of St. Birgitta, there was sacred music in the church, the opening ceremony of the occasion. Sister Reginalda tells us of the concert: "It was made up of Brigittine music that was sung in the olden times by our dear Brothers and Sisters—some of which we sing now." Then she gives her account of the main event: "The next day, the celebration was still greater. We were present at the function in the afternoon, which was made up of an historical lecture about our Foundress, the Order, Vadstena Church and its construction. After this, there was the laying of wreaths around the

145

very wooden coffin which had carried the remains of St. Birgitta from Rome to Sweden."

(This blackened wooden chest, usually kept in the nun's convent and larger than the reliquary, had been placed on the altar steps with four large candles around it.) "The first to bring his wreath was Prince Eugene of Sweden. There were two beautiful gray ribbons hanging from it, on which he had made designs himself in gold. On one was the Monks' Cross; on the other, the Sisters' Crown, in colors. As he laid down his wreath, he said: *'To Sweden's greatest woman—*

"The Prince also presented a handsome silver cup which he had designed.

"The next to lay a wreath was the Lutheran pastor of the Church, Rev. Turner; then came our dear Countess von Rosen. On her wreath were two wide ribbons with the words in gold: *Societas St. Birgittae;* here was also the Brothers' Cross; on the other ribbon, the Sisters' Crown.

"Others then followed with flowers. It was a beautiful sight to see the many colors spreading around the stark, wooden chest between its candles, the large silver cup standing in front of it. We were deeply impressed by what these Swedish people were doing out of love and devotion to our Holy Mother Birgitta. There must have been some two thousand souls—and some hundred more who could not get into the Church, big as it is, but stood in the doorway."

We can also imagine how it must have looked to the crowd to see these Brigittine Sisters from Rome in their classic gray habits, with black veils and white, crimson-dotted crowns, standing quietly near the altar with their Swedish brothers and sisters of the *Societas St. Birgittae,* also in their gray costumes for this occasion, making a guard of honor, among the throng of laymen, intellectuals, art lovers, and townsfolk of Vadstena.

Historically interesting as it must have been for many to see them, they also represented a living spiritual force.

At this time, Mother Elisabeth was fifty-three years old. Her lovely face with its even features had become more strongly defined, the mouth thinner and a little drawn, because of her many hours of suffering and amazing self-control. There was great peace and dignity about her figure, a presence that all could sense. She stood slender and straight as a young novice; in her heavy, handsome, gray habit you could not see that she was sometimes emaciatedly thin. She had a modest way, when photographed, of holding her head down as if she were reading a book, but her eyes met others with a warm, level look; eyes that were brown, not dark in a Latin way, but full of light. They were disarming, strong when she was challenged, but thoughtful, kind, full of tenderness and compassion when she smiled.

Sister Reginalda was tall and handsome, then in her early thirties. She had a low speaking voice, a rich alto when she sang, with a fine sense of music, a perfect voice for liturgy, which she loved.

Then, the morning after the great ceremony, came the secret Mass for which Mother Elisabeth had been preparing ever since she had asked in Rome for permission to have it said. She did not dare to seek local consent, for she was almost sure it would be refused, yet who could understand—except for a few of the High Church members of the *Societas*—how much it would mean to these daughters of Birgitta to attend a Mass in her own Blue Church? Countess von Rosen had fully concurred in the idea, together with her husband and a little band of devout friends. A priest, Father Assarson, had come down from Stockholm the night before. Here again, Sister Reginalda gives us the unforgettable picture of what took place.

"On Tuesday, the twenty-fourth, we left the house where we were staying at about half-past four in the morning. It was already light. We had our parcels with altar ornaments and vestments. As we walked across the fields, we could see the steeple of our beloved Vadstena Church. Soon we came in sight of Countess von Rosen. Just before five o'clock, Count Rosen appeared with the key to open the door. We immediately began to prepare for the Holy Sacrifice of the Mass. Who can tell what joy there was among the Angels at the sight of Brigittines preparing for the Holy One to descend upon the altar here once more. . . .

"Everything was very touching in the secret and silence of the early morning. The sacred words uttered by the Priest echoed through the Church; the very atmosphere was changed and the Sanctuary, which had seemed cold and barren, was filled with a fullness that human tongue cannot explain!

"The persons present were Rev. Fr. Assarson, Erik Ihrfors, Sister M. Louise, Mrs. Elbert, Mr. Blom and his wife, Countess Lagergren, Mrs. Eklund, Count and Countess von Rosen and Baron Fleetwood. As in early Reformation days, when the Holy Mass had to be celebrated in secret, so it was on that memorable morning. Count von Rosen and Baron Fleetwood kept watch and held the key in the Church door, for fear that someone might force an entrance. All were deeply moved and said afterwards that it had seemed right for us to be there."

Sister Reginalda was too modest to say that she had sung the Swedish *O Gud, min Gud* (O God, my Lord) and the Latin *Ecce Panis* at the dawn Mass.

Before Mother Elisabeth left Vadstena two days later, she wrote in tiny letters, crowded on the back of a post card of the Blue Church, this message to the Sisters in Rome:

Vadstena, 26 July, 1923

Tomorrow we are leaving Vadstena on our way back to Stockholm. One more greeting from both of us.

Here we have been able to pray on the very spot where our dear fellow Sisters, long ago, praised the Lord with ardent hearts. After more than 350 years we have had the blessing of participating in the Holy Mass in the very Abbey, and of receiving Holy Communion. It was almost overwhelming. But we must pray very, very much, Dearest Daughters. There is still no place for us here. The Daughters of St. Birgitta must wait and pray with the utmost patience. The Lord bless you all. Yours in Jesus Christ,

Mother M. Elisabeth of St. Birgitta

For God, a thousand years are like a day.

A prayer answered after 40 years. I prayed as a child to be permitted to see Vadstena one day.

As all were leaving Vadstena the next day, a friend offered to drive Mother Elisabeth to Alvastra, the remains of the famous monastery where St. Birgitta had lived with Ulf, her husband, during the last years of his life, and where she had stayed on after his death to receive some of her first and most remarkable *Revelations.*

Mother Elisabeth also stopped at Sturefors, the estate of Count and Countess Bielke; indirectly descended from the count buried in the Church of St. Birgitta in Rome.

Then at last, she was able once more to visit with her own family, the dear mother whom she had left at Fridhem almost twenty-two years before. The old lady was now almost eighty-two years old, living at Lindesborg, with her daughters Eva and Agnes. A few days later, she met her eldest brother Gustav in Stockholm. All were delighted that she might now be able to stay for a while in Sweden, and promised to help her in any way they could. Her beloved family—her heart had never left them and they had never ceased to love and admire their *wonderful Maria.*

Then followed consultations with Bishop Müller. He fully backed Mother Elisabeth's calm determination to found a small convent or guest house nearby, now that she had been able to bring the Sisters of St. Birgitta back to their native land. She first found a suitable house in Stockholm, but the bishop was afraid that this might seem to be too close to the *unofficial* Sisters already working there and facing their own problems of adjustment to the old Swedish regulations. On the other hand, Mother Elisabeth was afraid of moving too far away from the city, because of the difficulty in getting priests to come out to them. At last, a compromise was found—a fine, solid house in the residential suburb of Djursholm, twenty minutes by electric train from Stockholm.

It was Gustav who helped his sister find the place, and she was always grateful to him for this.

No one could see from the outside what planning, what daring, what prayer, and what sacrifice went into the establishing of the new *St. Birgitta's Vilohem* (St. Birgitta's Rest Home) in the quiet, beautiful *villa-stad,* or residential Djursholm.

It was a handsome, stucco house, standing on a wide gravel driveway sweeping in from a lower gate on one side and a

149

gatehouse archway on the other, a secluded and typically Swedish piece of property, with flower beds and fruit trees on one side and a shoulder of forest on the other, tall pines standing over gray rocks, shrubs, blueberries, lingonberries.

There were three stories under a heavy, Nordic roof. From the farther side of the house, there was a broad view toward the water, the inner reaches of the rocky, harbor approach to Stockholm. Comfortable parlors on the ground floor opened out on the garden, trees, and distant villas; this was an ideal place for rest and retreat.

In calling her new foundation a rest home rather than a convent, Mother Elisabeth was bowing to the Swedish prejudices of the time. And indeed, she was inaugurating a new apostolate. The convents that she had had so far were primarily for her own growing branch of the Order, and although some guests had been accommodated at Via delle Isole, it was not as a separate work of hospitality. But now her scope had suddenly broadened. She could practice that free reaching out to all who wished to come, of any creed or nationality, and give them a place of spiritual rest and refreshment, parallel to, but independent of, the life of her own Sisters who would serve and pray beside them. And so, with this double purpose, according to the unpredictable timing of destiny, *the Brigittine Order had come back to Sweden.*

To Via delle Isole, which was now the Mother House, she sent for two more Sisters for the new foundation. They were Sister Richard and Sister Margherita. When they arrived at the Central Station in Stockholm, Mother Elisabeth and Sister Reginalda were on hand to meet them.

Sister Reginalda wrote: "We were all in our Brigittine habits with the gray cloaks. Our beloved Mother is the first religious to wear her habit in Sweden, and walking in the streets —the first since the *Reformation*. What a surprise for the people of Stockholm when they saw four Brigittine Nuns in full Brigittine dress, walking from the station. We wore a black veil over our crowns so as not to attract too much attention."

Pastor Nordmark came out to give the Sisters Mass as often

as he could. He also gave them furniture and linens which he had inherited from an aunt; Mother Elisabeth's own family sent her furniture and pictures, as well as a small organ or harmonium which they had had in their Fridhem. Eva and Agnes were fascinated by the new home, and spent some time there, helping the Sisters get settled. Soon they had several rooms ready to take guests, as well as a small chapel for themselves.

Visitors began coming to the rest home. Although it was not yet officially dedicated, Bishop Müller and the Jesuit Fathers from St. Eugenia's Church enjoyed coming out to give them Masses and Benediction. They gave the Sisters every encouragement and sent guests and friends, so that by the end of the summer the Vilohem was a well-known place.

The days did not pass, however, without certain threats and difficulties. The world has changed so much since 1923, and moved away from religious preoccupations in general, that it is hard to believe that many Swedes in those days thought of Catholics as possessing some kind of black magic, and presenting a danger to the community! A few weeks after the Sisters settled in Djursholm, an anonymous letter threatened to kill them if they did not move out within a week! A few days later, Mother Elisabeth was raking the drive, when a tall, menacing-looking man suddenly approached her. She asked him what he wanted in a friendly tone—noting that he stood between her and the house, and might overpower her at any moment!

He grumbled that he wanted something to eat, and she led him up the wide entrance stoop where there was a bench. Asking him to wait there, she went in. She then calmly prepared a heaping plate of hot food, and took it out to him. He merely glared at her, and could find nothing to say as she continued to to look at him with kind seriousness. She was praying for the right word to say to him, but she admitted that she herself felt tongue-tied. She went back into the house, and a few moments later he had disappeared, leaving his plate untouched.

Another incident which occurred during those early days, and might have been serious, but because it was not, seemed comic and had the effect of endearing the Sisters to their neighbors, was a collision between a taxi, in which two of the Sisters were riding, and another car. At the jolt, both doors of the taxi flew open and both Sisters fell out. They picked themselves up, luckily without injury, and a bystander reported that "those funny-looking Sisters never made a sound, never got mad—all they worried about was whether the taxi man was hurt!" The driver of the second car was also impressed with their courage. He drove them home, and congratulated them heartily. As a matter of fact, one of the Sisters suffered a badly wrenched shoulder, but made no complaint about it. The story of the little accident went the rounds of Djursholm, and was remembered a long time.

An entry from Sister Reginalda's *Diary* introduced the theme of oblates, first called brothers and Sisters *ab extra* when associated with the old Order of Our Most Holy Savior. Gradually, a large group of oblates grew up around the Vilohem, and this was their beginning:

"Rev. Pastor Nordmark came to pay us his first visit in our new home, bringing with him four young men and two young ladies whom he received as Oblates in the little Chapel we had prepared. Our Beloved Mother pinned the scapular of the Cross and five wounds on each newly received Oblate. After the little ceremony, all had refreshments in the guests' dining room and returned to Stockholm, very pleased and so happy for their reception as Oblates of our Holy ancient Order."

On the Feast of St. Birgitta, October eighth of that happy year, 1923, the Sisters of St. Birgitta came into Stockholm to hear a special pontifical high Mass sung by Bishop Müller, assisted by four other priests in the beautiful Church of St. Eugenia. They spoke of the history of the Brigittines and officially thanked Mother Elisabeth for having brought the Order back to Sweden after a lapse of 400 years!

Five days later, on the thirteenth of October, the Vilohem was officially inaugurated, Bishop Muller presiding.

It was an exciting year for him, his first year as bishop. As he wrote in his diary (later found at Indersdorf, where he died): "After the quiet year of 1922, a year of great happenings was

152

to follow. The most important were: arrival of the new Bishop in April, celebration of the 550-years Jubilee of the Death of St. Birgitta, the founding of a new branch of the Order of St. Birgitta by a Swedish Convert, visit of Cardinal Rossum. Prefect of the Congregation of the *Propaganda Fide,* his trip through the Nordic lands, and, after long years, the calling together and conference of all the priests in Sweden, through the Bishop. . . ."

In his diary, he also quoted an article from the magazine *Credo*: "Who would have dreamt of such events a year ago! There is no longer need to be afraid nor to doubt. Holy Birgitta has not forgotten her praying children. With hope and trust we look to the future. Surely all Catholics in Sweden unite in a warm greeting to the Sisters who out of love for the land of St. Birgitta have been willing to leave the warm, Catholic South. . . ."

It was indeed a turning point for the Catholic Church in Sweden.

In November, Mother Elisabeth was taken desperately ill. Again it would seem as though she must pay for each new step in her progress with more suffering and a temporary setback. A well-known specialist was called in and he said there was only one remedy, an operation; either that, or she would always be an invalid, suffer much pain, and be obliged to live on liquid foods. She tried to explain to him that her illness was of twenty years' standing; a great specialist in America had told her years before that an operation was useless and there was no hope for a recovery. Now she felt that an operation might terminate her life entirely, whereas she had confidence that if God wanted her to live on, she could do so, even though she would suffer and be limited in her diet and activity. To her Sisters, she said: "You see, the doctor does not understand that I have a reason to suffer and offer up my pain; I am willing, if my Lord will accept it, to offer all my present suffering and pain for the sake of this work and for Sweden. . . ."

But even when Mother Elisabeth had to spend long hours and days in bed, her time was not lost. Her mind was working, planning; her will-power was bearing her on, the mysterious

153

forces of prayer, of her pain turned into wordless supplication, the psychic forces of desire, which we understand only partially, were operating, and had been operating all through these years toward the accomplishment of her aims. Since these aims were not personal but a part of what she felt that God wanted her to do, she had a right to believe that this work would come to fruition, even though she must strive often only in this seemingly ineffectual way. But she was sustained by the conviction that Destiny, or Divine Providence, was fulfilling a design by means of her frail life.

If publicity is any sign of success, it began to come unsolicited that fall to the new foundation. The Sunday supplement of a leading Stockholm newspaper (*Dagens Nyheter, November 25, 1923*) came out with a two-page feature entitled "The First Nuns' Convent in 400 Years." It gave an account of the newly opened rest home in Djursholm, and the story of the "remarkable Swedish woman, Mother Elisabeth, who after twenty-one years, with an undiminished love for all things Swedish, came back to the North."

There were photographs of the house, the Sisters, and a strong but somehow touching view of Mother Elisabeth on the terrace, in which one can read the self-control in her small, dignified figure, her firm features, and far-seeing eyes. (She had struggled to get up from her bed to meet these unexpected journalists.)

An interior photo of the chapel showed the heavy crucifix symbolic of the Order and a large painting of St. Birgitta made by the Swedish Brigittine Catherine Ehrenpohl of the Dutch Convent of Weert, whom Mother Elisabeth had visited in 1909. She was still alive at that time, and the Swedish newspaper was very interested in her. Several weeks later, the paper gave a full story of her life, reproducing the picture of her painting and an old photograph of her which they had been able to secure. They also mentioned the book written about her by Fanny Cederblad in 1900. Strangely enough, the magazine *Idun* picked up the story of Sister Maria Catherine Ehrenpohl once again, in 1951, claiming that they had first published her biography. The newspaper feature was entitled "A Swedish Woman's Destiny," and as such, gave the account a certain import which also reflected on Mother Elisabeth's work.

In December, Mother Elisabeth was somewhat better, and received a number of visitors at the Vilohem. Among them was her faithful friend Countess von Rosen, who stayed for some days and took part in all their services. Count von Rosen brought his flute on another occasion, and gave a delightful musical evening for Sisters and guests.

Other visitors included Marquis and Marchioness Lagergren, Baron and Baroness Armfelt, a group of the Children of Mary, and four Finnish ladies who wished to become oblates and had the intention of forming a group when they returned to Finland. Pastor Nordmark continued to bring his six oblates with others who were drawn to the new chapel.

In the meantime, Mother Elisabeth had called another Sister from Rome, to aid the growing household. A number of guests asked to stay for longer periods; all the Sisters were studying Swedish and, as Christmas approached, they prepared to celebrate it in true Swedish, as well as Catholic, style. Mother Elisabeth made the decorations. It was her first Christmas in her homeland for many years.

The venerable old Jesuit Father Benelius came out to celebrate midnight Mass. He was then about eighty years old. At that time, there were three Catholic families in Djursholm who came to Masses. But the little chapel was often crowded to overflowing.

It was interesting to note that the Von Rosens and others of the *Societas St. Birgittae*—the Society liked always to be called by its Latin name—enjoyed the Catholic forms of worship and felt no prejudice against Catholics, since they believed in ritualism as a way of renewing and enhancing the religious spirit. The news of their movement had even reached the Vatican, and had been noted by Father Hagen, who had kept in constant touch with his spiritual daughter and also kept contact with the House in Rome. He wrote to Mother Catherine, who had been left in charge; the following shows his continuing concern and faith in Mother Elisabeth.

Extract of letter from Father Hagen to Mother Catherine, in Rome:

Specola Vaticana, Jan. 25, 1924
Several times a day, I kneel at the Shrine of the Divine Infant and remember your house.... From a printed report, it appears that there is a strong movement in Sweden, first in the shape of ritualism which necessarily diminishes the old prejudices, as it did in England and Germany.

I always maintain that Rev. Mother Elisabeth is not guided by human counselors, but by the Holy Spirit directly. That explains why everything she undertakes, succeeds. I hear most Swedish ritualists strongly defend the Brigittine Foundation near Stockholm.

In the new year, the little community at Djursholm was glad to celebrate its first baptism. The event was recorded by the Sisters with enthusiasm: "The young man made such a profound genuflection before the Altar that one could just sense his belief in the Divine Presence.... How good of Our Lord to let all this take place in our humble little Chapel. We pray that this young man may be true to his faith til death. He is a student at the University of Stockholm. His parents do not yet know of the step he has taken."

Actually, both this young man and Jack-Adams Ray, another convert who served at the altar that day, proved to be staunch friends of the Order. (Indeed, this was Oskar Eklund, who wrote the first part of this book, and was a lifelong friend and helper to Mother Elisabeth.)

On February eighth of that year, Karin Hesselblad, the old mother whom Elisabeth had visited in Lindesborg, passed away after a sudden stroke. Eva and Agnes were at her bedside, and it was a great disappointment for her daughter in Djursholm that she could not come to assist her. But she was not well herself and would not have been able to reach her in time. She ordered a large cross of pine boughs, with twenty-one white flowers tucked into it to represent the Sisters in Djursholm and in Rome.

From the beginning of what she felt was her call to renew the Order of St. Birgitta, Mother Elisabeth had always hoped that the old foundations could be persuaded or inspired to lead such a revival themselves; as a first step, to send Sisters to Rome. But in spite of her visits to Syon Abbey, the convents in Spain, Holland, and in Altomünster, she had not been able to bring this about. Now that she had brought the daughters of St. Birgitta back to their own country, she felt that she might try once more to interest the older Houses in coming to help her in Sweden.

For some time she had been in correspondence with the Lady Abbess of Syon Abbey (at that time, Mother Teresa) and had also met the Bishop of Plymouth when in Rome, who was a close friend and protector of the abbey. He had written to one of the Sisters: "Mother Elisabeth's story, her vocation, her wonderful opportunity to enter Sweden, and all those many in-between providences, must fill her heart with adoration. Do give her my most warm blessing and ask her to pray for a distant friend. . . . Keily, Bishop of Plymouth."

Finally, with the bishop's approval, the Lady Abbess graciously consented to sending two Sisters, one (Sister Mary Francis) who had been at Syon for fourteen years, and another (Sister Cecilia) who had been there for ten.

But after they had been there only two weeks, Mother Elisabeth was sad to see that they did not seem happy out of their own cloistered Community.

Actually, the Sisters from Syon Abbey stayed at Djursholm about one year before they returned to England. It is to their credit that they helped the new foundation in its first critical period, and afterwards others could replace them. They had no doubt made a sacrifice in giving up the relative peace and quiet of their strictly contemplative life.

Mother Elisabeth had begun to prepare for her return to Rome when a new blow struck her; as she was walking in the garden, she coughed, and blood filled her mouth. Calmly she motioned for Sister Reginalda, who was with her, to get a small sleigh which happened to be in the garden, as there was still snow on the ground. Pulled slowly back to the House, Mother Elisabeth went straight to bed and waited for the doctor, who told her she had broken a vein in her bronchial tubes. . . . It was not until Easter Saturday, three weeks later, that she could come to the chapel again, and her trip to Rome was postponed indefinitely.

Many friends came to see her, and it was perhaps providential that she stayed on to further consolidate her work. Increasingly, the Vilohem filled a need. Baron Armfelt brought his mother to become a permanent guest, and said that the convent was "a real Providence for Sweden." Edith Unnerstad, a popular writer living nearby, rented a room where she could work in peace. The *Convent Journal* records the visit of Sigrid Undset, among many others:

On Saturday, April 26th, 1924, Mrs. Sigrid Undset came on a visit of ten days. She is the well-known Norwegian authoress; she had been recommended to come to us by good Pastor Kjelstrup, who visited the Sisters in Rome and who is rector of a small church in Norway, St. Olav's. He is instructing Fru Undset in the Catholic Faith. Her coming into the Church is a wonderful Grace, and will no doubt cause a great sensation, but also do much good (especially to those souls who hesitate to come into the Church through fear of what people will think of them). . . .

Countess von Rosen went to meet Fru Undset at the station and carried her bag for her; Fru Undset seemed very pleased to come to St. Birgitta's *Vilohem;* she is very humble and simple and endears herself to all who know her. During her visit she spoke at length on several occasions with our beloved Mother and she found it very helpful to her soul.

Mother Elisabeth wrote to her sister Agnes: "It was a great joy for me to have you and Eva here, but I am sorry that you did not meet Sigrid Undset (who came just afterwards). She is a delightful person. She has the warmest conviction that the real truth lies in the Old Faith of our fathers."

158

Another summer went by before Mother Elisabeth was able to undertake her trip to Rome, but it had certainly been fortunate for the new foundation that she had stayed so long. It was a good summer. The guest rooms were filled, with other visitors waiting to get in. By frugal management Mother Elisabeth had been able to make a payment on the heavy debt she had incurred to purchase the house.

At midsummer, Bishop Müller had come out to "consecrate the whole of Sweden to the Sacred Heart"—the devotion very close to the heart of Mother Elisabeth. On July second, the anniversary of the day she had left Rome to come to Sweden, a statue of Our Lady was carried in procession through the tall pines of the beautiful property. It was a wood carving almost black with age, which had been given to Mother Elisabeth, as she was leaving, by a devout, old Italian woman, and she had taken it with her as a sign of blessing on her trip.

Then on the fifteenth of August, Feast of the Assumption, Mother Elisabeth organized a procession which has been repeated at Djursholm ever since. Bishop Müller himself came out to inaugurate it, carrying the Blessed Sacrament from the chapel, and out of the driveway, to pass a few hundred feet on the road and then back into the grounds, under the graceful archway of the gatehouse, which was now a chaplain's cottage. The Sisters, with their gray habits and Brigittine crowns, followed the priests, one with the swinging censer of incense; children carried flowers and many people who had come out from Stockholm for the occasion made up a joyful crowd, singing hymns to the Virgin.

How long was it since there had been such a procession in Sweden? Certainly nothing like it had happened before in Djursholm, and now it is hailed as a happy, annual event.

Yes, *the ice had been broken*—nothing terrible had happened to hinder the simple life and service of the Sisters of St. Birgitta in their rest home. It was even urgent to plan a larger house and chapel for the future. Mother Elisabeth left with a full heart. She took Sister Richard with her and Sister Reginalda became Mother of the Djursholm Vilohem.

Chapter XV

The Flowering of the Order:
Lugano—Rome—Iver Heath

AFTER she had established the House at Djursholm, and left Sweden in September, 1924, Mother Elisabeth entered into a further period of expansion—a true flowering of the Order.

Instead of returning immediately to Rome, Mother Elisabeth stopped in Italian Switzerland where a foundation had been proposed to her by a Bishop Bacciarini of Lugano, whom she had known in Rome; he was eager to have the Brigittine Sisters in his diocese. Finally, she found a lovely villa, above the Lake of Lugano, in a section called Paradiso. Here was a romantic guest house in a garden of palms and colorful plants, with a smaller gardener's annex which could be converted into a Sisters' convent and chapel. The property had belonged to Madame Tetrazzini, a famous opera singer, and there were traces of artistic taste everywhere. There was even a certain amount of furniture left in the house, mirrors and chandeliers of elaborate design. Some of these were sold, to help get the convent started!

Much hard work had to be done before Mother Elisabeth could move in. Mother herself arranged the chapel with canopy and carved missal stand—all put together with old nails which she had first straightened out! Then two more Sisters were summoned from Rome, and a third Foundation was made. On the first of December, 1924, it was dedicated by His Lordship.

Bishop Bacciarini remained a close friend of the Sisters. He was a saintly old man, who, when he developed tuberculosis of the bones, worked as long as he could without complaining. He loved to say Masses in the little chapel of the Brigittines. When the regular chaplain showed reluctance to listen to the confessions of children who came to the convent, the bishop volunteered to hear them. His kindness and humility were so great that, after his death, many wanted to promote his cause as one worthy of sainthood. Mother Elisabeth came all the way from Rome to attend his funeral.

The guest house at Lugano continued to develop until it became one of the most popular and remunerative of all Mother Elisabeth's convents.

When Mother Katherine came to take charge, in 1929, there were as many guests as could be managed; she undertook additions to the main house, and also to the chapel. As one of her Sisters said, "She was not afraid of anything." She was popular with the guests and, at this time, many young students and priests from the American College in Rome began to come for their vacations, and ever after, Lugano was a favorite spot for the seminarians.

Among Scandinavian guests who stayed for long periods at Lugano was a former Swedish minister of the government, Ekstrand, and Monsignor Schaulis, a refugee bishop from Lithuania.

Another guest was Mother Elisabeth's old friend, Marie Cisneros-Potter. She had married an Englishman, middle-aged as herself; they had no children and, during the war of 1914, they had adopted eighteen Belgian boys left orphans by the invasion of their unfortunate country. (Mother Elisabeth used to chide the Potters because she said they were bringing the boys up like "little gentlemen" instead of preparing them to earn their living.) For a while Marie seemed to be threatened with tuberculosis, and came to get the mountain air of Lugano. She must have recovered completely, however, for she later returned to England where she had a home at Iver Heath, near London.

ROME—1925–1928

With great joy, the Sisters on the Via delle Isole welcomed their Mother who had been away for almost two years. During

161

that time she had made two new foundations, but the longest and most difficult challenge was still ahead of her.

Her departure from Lugano had been hastened by a letter announcing the good news that there was now a possibility that the Carmelite Sisters might move out of the House of St. Birgitta, as the Holy Father himself had stated that he wished to have the House ready to receive Scandinavian pilgrims who would be coming to Rome that summer of 1925—a Jubilee year.

Mother Elisabeth went at once to see Monsignor Maganesi who said that there was hope that her Community might be in their Holy Mother's House by the following May; he had been looking for suitable houses for the Carmelites and had found two that he hoped they would consider, and there should be no further difficulty in getting them to move.

A letter from the Vatican, dated April 21, 1925, to Reverend Father Lucca, Procurator of the Carmelite Order, stated the wish of the Holy Father, and so it was only a question of satisfying the Carmelite Sisters with a new convent.

Unfortunately, however, the houses that had been suggested to them were not according to their aspirations, and the whole matter was again blocked. It would seem as though they wished to procure land and build an entirely new convent for themselves.

This meant raising still more money; Mother Elisabeth said that she was even willing to sell the convent on the Via delle Isole to obtain enough to satisfy the Carmelites' needs. In an optimistic mood, she had already made announcements in the Swedish papers that the Pope desired to acquire the House of St. Birgitta for her Daughters, and requested contributions to help with this cause. One of the newspapers had asked her for an article on the subject—what should she reply? She put this information into a letter to the Holy Father, dated August 9, 1925. The answer was an *Aide-memoire* (Memorandum) handed to Martin Melvin, secretary to the Pope, at an audience on October 10, 1925, which read as follows:

"The Holy Father, Pius XI, has several times expressed the wish to create a Pontifical Hospice for the Converts of the Scandinavian countries in Rome (in the *Casa di Santa Brigida* on the Piazza Farnese). For this intention, the Count de Paus has placed in the hands of His Holiness an important sum, which is, however, insufficient to reach the goal.

The afore-mentioned Count de Paus has interested Mr. Melvin in the desire of the Holy Father, and he has volunteered his services to procure the capital that is lacking. He declares that for this, it is necessary for him to have a letter which authorizes him to raise such an important sum. His Holiness, in an audience granted to Mr. Melvin on October 10, 1925, thanked him for his good will and encouraged him to procure the means necessary to bring to effect his announced project, which is much on his heart.

It is requested that the contents of this Pontifical audience be put into a letter for Mr. Melvin.

It should also be noted that in the Scandinavian countries, many newspapers have spoken of this desire of the Holy Father and that some have spoken about this as an established fact. Therefore, it would be advisable to proceed with the raising of the necessary capital.

But even after this, the matter of buying the Casa dragged on.

In the spring Mother Elisabeth made another attempt to speed the decision of the Carmelites to move. A piece of property had been found for them, and now it was necessary to raise a larger sum of money, so that they could build, as they wished to do.

She appealed to Mr. Martin Melvin, who had promised six months before to help raise money for the purchase of the House from the Carmelites. On April 20, 1926, he had written to Monsignor Maganesi of the Vatican to ask him for more information and pictures of the Casa, so that he might launch an appeal for funds—why had this not been done earlier?

That spring, the convent was involved in a dramatic event that, but for Mother Elisabeth's impressive personality, might have proved disastrous. Mussolini had come into power in 1925, and already the threatening atmosphere of a police state prevailed. Sister Richard relates in her Journal for 1926:

On April 7th, at 11 A.M., there was a violent peal of the gate-bell; the Portress announced to Mother Elisabeth that there were five detectives in the garden. They asked if there was an Irish lady in the house. The only Irish person Mother could think of was Sister Katherine. They looked her up and down and said: "No, she is not the one; there must be another." Then we thought of a guest, Miss Violet Gibson, whom we had quite forgotten in the shock of the moment. Yes, that was the name; the detectives looked grave.... Mother asked them if anything had happened to Miss Gibson, but they would not give any information, only demanded to see her room. Her trunks were locked, but the detectives burst them open with their sticks, and pulled everything out. Her garments were examined piece by piece, and her books, which were all spiritual reading. These things, together with money and jewelry, were confiscated by the police.

It was not until they found her passport that they would answer our repeated inquiries: Was she ill? Had she been run over? Was she dead? *No, she had attempted to kill Mussolini with a pistol!*

We could not believe it was possible. Miss Gibson was one of the quietest and sweetest of persons, refined, gentle, considerate of others in every way! She lived the life of a poor Franciscan, though she had means enough to live very comfortably. (It was said that she went around with a shopping bag, filled with paper-bills, *lire,* which she gave out right and left, going through the worst sections of the city, poorly dressed—and it was in this bag that she had concealed her revolver!)

Finally the detectives left, leaving one man in Miss Gibson's room. Later, the Commissioner of Police arrived with 20 policemen, saying they had come to "protect" us. He told us that several houses had been wrecked, and riots had taken place, led by fanatical followers of *Il Duce.* Actually, Miss Gibson had shot Mussolini through the nose. He bled profusely, but his life was not endangered.

The Commissioner began to make an examination of all the Sisters and guests, beginning at 8:30 P.M. and going on till past midnight. We feared that the Fascists would make a raid on our house during the night. We were questioned closely by the detectives, on various other occasions, and Our Mother had to go to the Palace of Justice to be questioned by the Judge.

After some months, it was decided that Miss Violet Gibson was mad, and not responsible for her acts. She was released from jail and sent back to England, where she was confined in a Sanatorium.

What the Sisters did not relate was that the secret police attempted to hang a huge, international plot on the shoulders of this odd woman. The convent was watched for a long time, and

164

it was a wonder that Mother Elisabeth or some of the Sisters were not imprisoned.

Later in the summer, Mother Elisabeth undertook a trip to visit her convents in the North. She spent only ten days in Lugano, and started to paint the shutters with her Sisters; it was not to show them an example of her energy, which was not lacking even though she was never physically strong—but because she had a strong sense of order and really loved to do practical work. The beautiful little house was full of guests, and soon she went on to Sweden.

Arriving at the Vilohem in Djursholm, Mother Elisabeth lost no time in talking over plans for additions to the house and chapel. The work here was flourishing under the capable guidance of Mother Reginalda and there was urgent need for more guest rooms and a larger chapel. With builder, engineer, and the practical advice of the Sisters, a project was soon underway. Only limited funds kept the Vilohem from becoming even larger than its present size. The house had become a center for various activities, and very popular with Catholics and non-Catholics alike.

A large group of oblates had grown around the Community at Djursholm. Bishop Müller was himself a member, and had drawn up some additional rules which Mother Elisabeth promised to seek to have approved by the Sacred Congregation of Rites, when she returned to Rome. It was gratifying to find this earnest band of oblates supporting the work of St. Birgitta in Sweden. They met once a month at the Vilohem, for their day of spiritual study and refreshment, and many came more often, to attend services or to assist the Sisters with various tasks.

Mother Elisabeth would gladly have spent the winter of 1926–1927 in her beloved Sweden, but she felt that matters in Rome required her attention.

Stopping off in Lugano on the way back to Italy, she was taken ill, however, and at this time discovered that she had a heart condition which demanded rest. On the doctor's orders she remained in Lugano for some months, resting, as far as her physical activity was concerned, but writing letters, planning, and praying with her great force of spirit, to forward the work which she felt that God had given her.

It was spring before she could return to Rome.

IVER HEATH

Before Mother Elisabeth's last efforts to regain the Casa di Santa Brigida in Rome bore fruit, a different opportunity opened for her in England. Her lifelong friend, Marie Cisneros Potter, offered her the house where she had lived with her husband, just outside of London.

It was a small, timbered house of gracious, Tudor style, standing on the quiet Fulmer Common Road, running out of Iver Heath, not far from Uxbridge—the end of the London subway line southwest of the city. A high hedge shielded the house and garden from the road. Behind it were woodlands and a country lane leading to the historic little town of Fulmer.

Now that she was alone in the world once more, Mrs. Potter lived there only for short periods. She went every winter to San Sebastian in Spain. She also made trips to America. When she decided to give the house over to the Sisters of St. Birgitta, she built an annex for herself, which was eventually to go to the Order. She also owned another house across the road which proved of great use later on, during the Second World War.

But when the Sisters came in 1931, they found the house very cramped for space. The first chapel was the tiny parlor in the center of the structure. The most urgent task was to build a chapel and choir on the west side of the house, and to add a few small rooms for cells.

It was Mother Katherine Flanagan, one of the first two Sisters that Father Benedict had brought from England, to whom Mother Elisabeth entrusted this new foundation. She had always been a fervent and utterly dedicated soul, imbued with the spirit of her Mother Foundress, who sometimes, half in jest, half in affection, called her St. Peter.

She had been put in charge of the Via delle Isole when

Mother Elisabeth and Sister Reginalda left for Sweden. When, in 1927, Mother Reginalda was suddenly taken sick in Djursholm, Mother Katherine was sent, on a few moments notice, to help her. It was Christmas Eve. As she was preparing to leave, a sharp, earthquake shock wrenched off the door of a wardrobe, and set the windows rattling. Mother Elisabeth at once asked her if she was not afraid to travel that night, since another shock might cause a railroad wreck or other disasters. She simply answered: "I am in the Hands of God," and departed for the station.

It was after Mother Reginalda recovered that Mother Katherine was put in charge of the convent at Lugano. Here she had presided until she came to England in 1931.

At Iver Heath, Mother Katherine soon endeared herself to everyone. As soon as she had arranged the small chapel and procured a priest, unknown worshippers seemed to spring up, as there was no Catholic parish nearby. The chapel had to be enlarged three times during the following years. There were also a number of English vocations.

There were unexpected difficulties in the early days because Mrs. Potter, who had promised to help them get started, was often away, and when at home, seemed preoccupied by many other problems. She had a business advisor who called on her frequently, and her chauffeur, a distinguished domestic on whom she relied completely, was always in attendance.

However, Marie Cisneros Potter was always the devout and pious character who had first taken Elisabeth to Europe, to the Cathedral of St. Gudule in Brussels, and whose sister was a Nun of the Visitation. She was a complex, but attractive personality; she dressed simply but well; of medium figure, her dark, beautiful eyes gave her the Spanish look of her forebears. She who had opposed her friend's entrance into a cloistered life, partly for reasons of health, but also because of her personal attachment to her, was now reconciled and proud to be her associate in this founding of the new branch of the Order in England. She spent long hours in the chapel, and would let no one interrupt her when the mood for prayer overtook her.

It was only in 1937 that Mother Elisabeth came for the first time to visit the convent at Iver Heath. Marie Potter was there to welcome her and plan for further extension of the house and grounds.

In the meantime, Mother Katherine had managed the first hard struggle to put the convent on its feet. They had gone through days of real poverty and privation. But neighbors were kind. Certain mysterious gifts of food and flowers were left in the chapel at times, and finally it was discovered that these came from a devout Irish maid employed by a wealthy family in the neighborhood. They had permitted this charity because of their own large gardens and oversufficient supplies. Many others became loyal friends of Mother Katherine, until she left in 1935.

Chapter XVI

Casa di Santa Brigida

WHEN Mother Elisabeth returned to Rome after her forced period of rest in Lugano, it was to take up once more the matter of acquiring the Casa di Santa Brigida which had been pending so long.

This had been her hope, her impossible dream, ever since she was in the Carmelite noviciate; how many prayers and aspirations had she poured into this deep desire! Finally, it had become a project, a practical objective on which she had worked for years and months, and the wheels of the Vatican had slowly begun to turn to bring it nearer realization.

She had been greatly encouraged by the assistance of Martin Melvin, secretary to the Pope, but this had been in 1925, and a year later the appeal that he had promised to make for funds had not materialized. But Mother Elisabeth had kept on trying to collect money to add to the sum contributed by Count de Paus and others, so that it would be possible to satisfy the Carmelite Sisters in their desire to build an entirely new, suitable convent, and so be willing to leave the Casa di Santa Brigida for St. Birgitta's own daughters.

Father Rosa, who had taken Father Brandi's place as Mother Elisabeth's firm friend and adviser, was now editor of the Vatican journal, *Civiltà Cattolica,* a post he had taken over from Father Brandi when the latter was taken ill and soon after died. Father Rosa was a thoughtful, kind man with enormous, dark eyes and thick white hair. Mother Elisabeth was far too full of respect and tact to try to rush him in any way; she had accepted his promise that he was trying his best to bring the matter of the *Casa* to the attention of the Holy Father himself. She prayed for patience; yet it seems incredible that another year went by without any tangible results.

Then Mother Elisabeth heard indirectly from Sweden that there was talk of a project to take over the House so sacred to the Order and to her, for an entirely different purpose! It was to reward the Swedes for what they had done in an attempt to rescue the Italian explorer Nobile, and the Zeppelin *Italia* in which he tried to reach the North Pole some years before!

Father Rosa advised Mother Elisabeth to put the situation in a letter which he himself would bring to the attention of important persons in the Vatican. She wrote immediately; her remarkable self-control, but also a certain amount of desperation, can be read between the lines:

Most Reverend Monsignore:

As His Reverence has asked me for news regarding the House of our Mother St. Birgitta, I must tell you that a Senator, and other Italian friends of his, wish to propose to the Italian Government the offer of this House to the Swedish Archeological and Geographical Institute in Rome, as a tribute of gratitude for that which Sweden did at the time of the wreck of the *Italia* at the North Pole.

As we know, the Swedish people consider this House as a National Monument. We have knowledge of another Senator of Italy, a good Catholic; does your Reverence not think that we could approach him, to prevent the other negotiations?

Thanking you in advance for a few lines to answer to this matter, with the most respectful greetings,

Humble servant in Christ,

M. Elisabetta di St. Brigida, O.SS.S.

July 16, 1928   *Monasterio di Santa Brigida*
34 Via delle Isole
Quartiere Caprera
Roma, 27

After this, there must have been some action, for we next hear of Mother Elisabeth talking with engineers and experts about the building of a new monastery for the Carmelites.

170

It seems strange to think that with all the able-bodied priests and *Monsignore,* who had expressed interest and support for Mother Elisabeth in her worthy desire to reclaim the House of St. Birgitta for her Order, *it was she, a very sick, weak woman* who had to do the practical work of bringing this question to a final showdown. We have another letter which she wrote to the *Monsignore* in the Vatican saying:

I have talked with Dr. Romeo regarding the property of the S. Pancrazio district; the Doctor, with an engineer of the Government, offers to construct a monastery and a Chapel in this district, a location that is high, healthy and good, according to modern hygienic conditions, for the price of 700,000 Lire, and to have it ready in six months. The Doctor is even disposed to advance credit for the sum, in order to facilitate the matter of the *Casa di St. Brigida.*

To buy a villa would only be a loss of time and of money. The Doctor found the land near the Church of San Pancrazio....

M. Elisabetta di S. Brigida, O.SS.S.

Dec. 6, 1928

After this, it would seem that Father Rosa had stepped in and his Audience with the Holy Father (or possibly he had had several occasions to talk with him informally) had finally resulted in a decision that Mother Elisabeth was to have the treasured House.

Father Rosa told Mother Elisabeth that the time had come to hand over to the Holy See all the funds that she had been able to collect; to have confidence that her wishes would now be fulfilled. He said that no formal agreement was necessary, since he personally had made all clear to His Holiness, who intended to bring the whole matter to a conclusion.

Thus the great burden of financial worry rolled off Mother Elisabeth's back, as far as paying further for the building of the Carmelite monastery. The Carmelite Sisters began preparing to leave the Casa di Santa Brigida. They finally did so, in October, 1930.

Father Rosa, with Mother Elisabeth, made all the final arrangements. She always felt, thereafter, that she and the Order of St. Birgitta owed him a great debt of gratitude for ending this matter that had been on her heart for twenty-five years—ever since she had first been able to speak about it to Pope Pius X. . . .

Father Rosa, himself a very important figure because of his direction of the *Civiltà Cattolica,* the semiofficial organ of the Vatican, had the deepest respect and admiration for Mother Elisabeth, recognizing her exceptional vocation as had Father Brandi before him. A noted writer, he was an astute observer of human nature, and a fearless fighter for his ideals. A memorial booklet says about him: "His energetic attitude is not forgotten, at the time of the Fascist persecution of 1931. His courage won the *Civiltà Cattolica* the honor of confiscation and suspension. He was stricken with paralysis of the face. . . . but the very last week before his death, the *Osservatore Romano* reproduced one of this articles on 'The Persecution of the Concordat in Germany.' (He died in 1938.) As heated as he was in combat, he no less always preserved the greatest charity toward individuals." It was this charity which he showed to Mother Elisabeth. The last letter he wrote concerning the House was typical of his regard:

October, 1930
La Civiltà Cattolica

Reverend Mother Abbess:

I thank you sincerely for your good letter and for the present. But I don't want you to go to any more trouble. . . .

I have already asked the Holy Father, personally, what costs would remain—he wishes that you should keep the same house as you have now, for the Brigittine Noviciate; and in the Piazza Farnese at the Rooms of St. Birgitta, you should open another house for their custody and the head offices of your work, to serve, at the same time, for the reception of visitors, especially for those coming from Scandinavia.

It seems to me that the Holy Father takes all this into consideration with much goodness. . . . He also added that he was very devoted and grateful to Santa Brigida, because this Saint had predicted that which now has come to pass, concerning His Holiness, by means of the *Concordato.* He alluded to one of the famous prophesies of the Saint, of which even the newspapers have spoken, recently.

This Concordato was the "reconciliation between Church and State, brought into effect by agreement between Pope Pius XI and Mussolini, when he first came into power and was anxious to ingratiate himself to the Italians. The Vatican Palace, St. Peter's, and a certain amount of land was ceded to form a papal state, independent of the government.

Six hundred years earlier, St. Birgitta had seen, as in a vision, this center of the Church, taking the place of those random papal estates, administered by bishops or cardinals, sometimes dissolute, or defying the rule of the Pope. In her *Heavenly Revelations,* Book VI, Chapter 74, Birgitta says:

I saw Rome, from the Pope's Palace near St. Peter's Church to the Angel's stronghold; from the Castel Sant' Angelo to the Church of the Holy Spirit, yes, even right up to St. Peter's Church, as if it were one big plain, and the strongest wall was built around this plain protecting it, and various dwelling places lay inside the walls.

Then I heard a voice that said: "That Pope that loves his Bride (the Church) with the same love with which my friends love her, shall own this place with his fellow-workers, so that he can call together his counselors more easily and in peace."

These are almost the exact boundaries of the present Vatican City.

The distinguished old Father Hagen died in 1930. He had not lived to see his spiritual daughter move into the House of St. Birgitta, but he knew that her great dream was about to become a reality. In one of his last letters concerning her, he wrote:

Specola Vaticana, July 20, 1925

Rev. Mother is probably staying in Lugano for her health and not because of difficulties in the new foundation, I hope.

Her sufferings are to me a living example of how to get holy. If her body were as strong as her mind, she would not be so full of humility and charity as she is. I know a similar saint in America doing apostolic work, stretched on a couch for the last 40–50 years. (This was Mary Merrick, of Washington, a life-long invalid, founder of the *Christ-Child Society.*) I look up to these saints with awe; they give a severe lesson to healthy people.

After Mother Elisabeth had written her *Notes* at his request, he wrote the lines quoted at the beginning of this book: "You have promoted the glory of God by writing this *extraordinary*

173

vocation. I have thanked God that he allowed me to witness the graces that He has poured upon your soul and body, and I thank you for writing them down. This ms. must remain a document in your Order and will increase in value with time. Pray for your father, J.G.H."

It was this remarkable man who from the very beginning had discerned in Maria Elisabeth that special quality of a soul permeated and led by God. He had consistently sustained her with his own great mind and lofty spirit. It is said that *it takes genius to recognize genius*—so Father Hagen had recognized the genius of his spiritual child.

In October, 1930, the Carmelite Sisters moved out of the Piazza Farnese to their new monastery in the Parioli section. But there was much to be settled before Mother Elisabeth and her Sisters could move in. It was only the following spring, of 1931, that the House was officially theirs. A note in Mother Richard's *Diary* says: "On the 8th of April, Easter Wednesday, our Beloved Mother Elisabeth Hesselblad received the keys of the House of our Holy Mother Birgitta, from the hands of Monsignor Mariani."

And then a vigorous program of restoration was begun. Mother Elisabeth had planned every detail during the long months of waiting. Everything had to be repainted; central heating was put in for the first time, and adequate plumbing, bathrooms, which had not previously existed, and new electric installations. For this, Mother had to take out a large mortgage, so that new financial burdens were taken up. But oh the joy of having the beloved House, secured at last, and of preparing for its new life, as a Scandinavian Hospice and the Mother House of the new daughters of St. Birgitta!

In the fall of 1931 it was ready.... And then came the acclaim of the press—in Italy, but most of all where Mother Elisabeth wanted it, in Sweden!

BIRGITTA'S HOUSE IN ROME—Again in Swedish hands.

There had been articles before about Birgitta Nuns on the Via delle Isole. But this was different. As Mother Elisabeth had always hoped, the Swedish people responded to this revival

174

of their old national shrine; the House, the whole work of the Order, took on a new life, color, and importance.

By 1932, Mother Elisabeth had organized the House on the Piazza Farnese so that it could become the official Mother House of the new branch of the Brigittine Order. It now united five convents; those at Via delle Isole, Djursholm, Lugano, Iver Heath, and Casa di Santa Brigida, Rome. She decided to place the Noviciate there, since there was ample room, and the choir was spacious enough for a large Community. It was wonderful to have this choir now filled and resounding with the Divine Office. Mother had always given special care to the recital of the Office; she now followed the Roman breviary, with certain Brigittine prayers included. Her deep, impressive speaking voice was not one for singing, but she loved the musical voices of her Sisters, and trained them to strive for perfection in tone, pronunciation, and rhythm; the psalmody was not rushed; the Divine Office was sung whenever possible.

Many new vocations had become attracted to the expanding Order. One of the first postulants to come to the new Roman convent was a Swedish girl, tall, blond, and gifted, intellectually and musically. Her report, which follows, gives an interesting side light on the new mission of Birgitta's House on the Piazza Farnese.

This Swedish Sister had first heard of Mother Elisabeth when attending school at Linköping, not far from Vadstena, where Agnes Hesselblad was her teacher. Agnes had been to Rome to visit her sister, who was a nun in a convent—her pupil wrote:

To hear such a thing was almost shocking! I felt cold all over and shivered—then, some years later, I read about this nun in the Swedish paper, when she had come to celebrate the 550th Anniversary of our great Saint.... Then I heard that she had established a guest-house at Djursholm. Now I knew that a Swedish Mother had a Convent in Sweden. Years later, when I decided to enter the Religious Life, there was no doubt where I should go. In May, 1932, I went to Rome, to Casa di Santa Brigida, as the first postulant in that historical house which Mother Elisabeth had re-acquired for her newly-founded branch of the Brigittine Order. Mother Elisabeth possessed all the great characteristics of the Foundress of a Religious Order. She was very broad-minded, tolerant, and warm-hearted. She had great charm and a sense of humor; in business matters she was a genius....

Mother had beautiful, dark eyes full of goodness and compassion. She was reserved, but always just. Her voice was low and melodious, and her laugh was very catching. How many trials and sorrows our dear Mother had to suffer.

Mother Elisabeth loved the solemn Liturgy of the Church. It was said in Rome that the two best Choirs were those of the Sisters of Mary Reparatrix and the Brigittine Sisters.

Every year on St. Stephen's Day, the Scandinavian Colony in Rome was invited for a Christmas Party. First they all took part in Solemn Benediction. Mother Elisabeth usually invited a Scandinavian Priest to preach a short sermon in one of the Sandinavian languages. After Benediction we sang Swedish Christmas Carols; then all the guests were invited up to the large reception Hall, where coffee, and Swedish cakes in many forms, awaited them.

On one such occasion, there was a young Dane present. He took a great interest in the Liturgy and at the tea-party questioned the Monsignor about many things. As there were many people there, the Monsignor said: "If you will call on me tomorrow, it will be easier to answer your questions."

The next morning, the young Dane presented himself—and that was the first of many meetings. First, he was received into the Church; then he became a Benedictine.

Years later, he was back in Rome for higher studies, as a Priest. Often, he would come to say his Mass in Our Holy Mother's Room, and I would make the responses. One day, he came with his Abbot, and I happened to open the door for them. The Abbot said: "Do you know who this is?" "O yes, certainly I know, it is the Danish Father." "Yes," the Abbot replied, "He was until yesterday. Today, he is the Bishop of Denmark!"

"We always counted Bishop Theodor Suhr, O.S.B. as one of 'ours.' He was always a faithful friend to Mother Elisabeth."

The work of Mother Elisabeth had found a new center of expansion; it is no longer possible to follow the progress of each convent, the treasured notes and diaries which recorded each visit and each vocation. The Casa di Santa Brigida led them all in activity and in its prestige as a Swedish national shrine.

Chapter XVII

Vadstena, 1935

WITH the impetus she had gained by her success in acquiring the House of St. Birgitta, Mother Elisabeth felt that the time had come to make a foundation in Vadstena. What did not seem possible in 1923, was now a logical step in the development of the new branch of the Order of St. Birgitta; to go back not only to the country of her origin, but to the very site of the first foundation.

For some time, Mother Elisabeth had been looking, through friends, for a suitable place, and finally, in 1935, one became available on the drive that skirts the lake within sight of the Blue Church.

The house had been built only twenty years earlier in the pure, spacious style of a country manor. But at first, old prejudices threatened to mar the peace of this ideal spot. They were reflected in a letter from Sigrid Hult, a kind, devout member of the S.S.B. She lived just outside of the village and had undertaken to supervise repair work going on at the convent-to-be. She was, like Countess von Rosen, a High Church Lutheran, who loved the liturgy and had no prejudice against Catholics. But she wrote with trepidation from her home, Gamla Gården:

People are uneasy about Rome's daughters who intend to·make their entrance into Vadstena. The Pastor gets anxious letters every day and hears unpleasant remarks. He is discouraged and tired out, and the Bishop also lacks understanding.... I think you should know the situation into which you are coming. Your holy and quiet life must talk its silent language and give the inhabitants confidence.... You must not expect to be welcomed with open arms. Still—*God is with us. Who, then, can be against us?*

May 2, 1935   Sigrid Hult, Ord. S.S.B.

Mother Elisabeth was not one to be disheartened by such negative reactions. She had encountered them in Stockholm and Djursholm, but she knew that although there were still persons in Sweden who did not wish the work well, others had shown positive reactions far exceeding her expectations, and circumstances had gradually broken down many prejudices and misunderstandings. As always, she had the courage to proceed.

In the beautiful days and endless evenings of midsummer, Mother Elisabeth arrived in Vadstena to take over the handsome house on the lake. She brought several Sisters with her and she had sent for Mother Katherine from Iver Heath, to replace her when she herself would return to Rome.

First of all, a chapel and choir was arranged, so that the Mass and the full cycle of the liturgy could be taken up once more in this place where, six hundred years before, Birgitta had envisioned her convent; here it had flourished, and here also its remaining Sisters had been forced to disband in 1595. After all these years of exile, a Swedish woman, Maria Elisabeth Hesselblad, had brought them back again. Through the strange circumstances that had made her a Catholic and a nun of St. Birgitta, she had nourished the old vine of her Order. And she was rooting her new branch, a shoot carefully prepared for planting, in its native soil of Vadstena.

The Swedish intellectual world was not slow in responding to this; even before the Sisters arrived, there had been a full picture article in the leading illustrated weekly *Vecko-Journalen,* which read in part:

Almost three hundred and fifty years ago, in 1595, Vadstena Convent was closed—and now we have learned that the Sisters of St. Birgitta, already living in Djursholm, have bought a beautiful shore-villa in Vadstena, right near Birgitta's Church. They are opening there a *Vilohem,* for tired souls. So once more, Vadstena's narrow cobble-stoned streets will be adorned with gentle, silent Birgitta Nuns who, with their habits, will set a new—or rather a medieval—*stamp* on the old Monastery town. As absurd as is all religious persecution, it would be equally narrow to deny this addition to the atmosphere and the beauty which this new invasion will bring to this historically saturated milieu.

Indeed, at that time, the sleepy little town was awakening to its own history. Since Mother Elisabeth had come there for the first time, the *Birgitta-Stiftelse* or foundation, had been active in trying to recover the former nuns' convent, to the north of the Blue Church. It was later discovered that the building to the north had actually been the former castle of King Magnus and Queen Blanche. When Birgitta stayed there, tradition has it that she inhabited a room in the northeast corner of this large structure.

In those days there was a large yard, or *grass court,* between this castle and other medieval buildings to the south of it. Toward the east was the entrance and, through the grass courtyard, people entering could see glimpses of the dissipated life of the castle. Birgitta wanted it to be the other way around; that people should enter here and receive God's blessing and inspiration to lead a better life. This was Birgitta's concept, as she expressed it in those revelations, called *Revelationes Extravagantes.* In them she describes her vision of her church, built in the center of the grass court, with the outlying houses given to the convent, the nuns to be housed in the former castle and the priests in the buildings to the south, both properties running down to the lake and both having access to the church in the middle.

There followed a time of desolation in Vadstena, when Birgitta went as a pilgrim to Rome, and remained there almost twenty years. King Magnus seems to have regretted his donation of the castle and grounds to Birgitta. Probably the castle was damaged during internal wars about 1356–1357. Finally, when a knight in the service of Birgitta came there to start the building of a convent in 1369, the big stone castle was almost a ruin.

Birgitta had ordered that the former high walls be lowered, since they represented too much pride (*superbia,* as the old

179

Latin has it). So the Chapter room and workroom of the nuns were reconstructed in the parterre of the old castle, and above was only the long, low dormitory of the nuns.

Around 1370–1375, a wooden chapel was built on the grass court in the place which the Blue Church later occupied. In 1388, this first chapel was destroyed by fire; many old things were consumed or damaged, and a lay Brother lost his life. The partition of the convents had been carried out by this time, the nuns to the north, the priests and brothers to the south, and then the building of the Blue Church began. It took a long time; they started to build from the west, with the choir of the priests which was vaulted by 1398. It was not used until 1405. The main walls were standing by 1414, the vaulting finished six years later, and the final consecration of the church took place in 1430.

All these facts had begun to come into people's minds again, because of the new discoveries. The Birgitta *Stiftelse* had excavated some ruins to the west of the monk's choir. The monk's convent was restored, first with the intention of making it a hostel for young people and the many tourists who come each year, at all seasons, to visit this famous spot. The nuns' convent was later freed from secular use and the larger structure to the north took on a special importance as the work of restoration proceeded; in 1932, the Chapter room of the nuns was reopened; a library, *Biblioteca Birgittina* was established. Later, when the north wing of the nun's convent was recognized as identical with the old castle of King Magnus, it came under Public Monument Protection. The conventual buildings were handed over to the Birgitta *Stiftelse,* or foundation. In this way their permanent safekeeping was assured. The old palace is now a museum.

In many respects, the time had become very favorable for Mother Elisabeth's new venture. The formal inauguration of her convent turned into an unexpected event; historians, newspapermen, and almost all the friends, both old and new, that Mother Elisabeth had made in Sweden, came to this gracious house which became that day a revived convent of St. Birgitta in Vadstena.

It was a perfect day. Sunshine danced over the blue lake, and the plants and roses in the large, walled garden were bright with color. Mass was held out-of-doors, with an assistant and four altar boys. Six professed Sisters and two novices made a striking picture. The same feature writer of the *Vecko-Journalen,* who signed himself Tigram, made a three-page story of this happy day, calling it a "Pilgrimage to the Birgitta Sisters," and printed almost the full text of the priest's talk, as well as his own interview with Mother Elisabeth. Father d'Argenlieu is seen in the photos he took, tall and impressive in his white Dominican habit.

An interesting aftermath of the opening of the convent at Vadstena was the offer of Count von Rosen to deed a plot, belonging to his own family, to the Sisters of St. Birgitta. The following letters show his loving thought, which Mother Elisabeth deeply appreciated. (Mother Catherine, who died suddenly in 1941, is buried there, beneath the very walls of the Blue Church.)

Rockelstad, Sparreholm,
2/12/1935

Good Mother Elisabeth,

First let me send my warm, heart-felt thanks—as well as those of my wife—for the friendly hospitality we experienced when we visited Vadstena last fall. That was an unforgettable day.

And then I would like to inform you that my wife and I, for a long time, have had the intention of offering to Mother Elisabeth's branch of the O.SS.S. the burial place in the Vadstena Cemetery which belongs to us. We will soon have a valid letter drawn up concerning this gift, and send it to you. It gives my wife and me great joy to be able to give to Saint Birgitta's children, as a Christmas gift...the first little piece of ground inside of their ancient Convent grounds in Vadstena.

My wife and I, Erik and Anna, wish Mother Elisabeth and all the Sisters a good and joyous Christmas. We send our warmest greetings to you all.

Your admiring and devoted,
Erik von Rosen

181

Slowly, the new convent at Vadstena began to be known and loved, accepted as a natural part of this quaint and beautiful little town. On the side toward the village, a small gardener's cottage made a fine chaplain's residence. It was connected to the property by a high, white stucco wall with a graceful arch. Against it grew roses and the ample garden was filled with flowers and a sizable vegetable patch. On the other side, a few feet across the driveway, was the gray-blue, windy, changeable *Vettern*—that lake called a *Troll-Sjö,* or Lake of Trolls, because of its uncertain and sometimes wildly stormy weather, and also because of its great depth, so deep in places that it can not be sounded. People say that it is connected to a Swiss lake by an underground river, for pieces of Viking ships had been found there. Perhaps this lake is typical of the spirit-ridden atmosphere of this ancient town, which before Christian times may have been a place of pagan worship.

At any rate, the shimmering lake and the fascinating town have a great drawing power for visitors and tourists, and its center is the Blue Church, with its austere beauty and its traditions. It was only a few steps to go over there from the rest-home convent.

Later, a certain elderly Polish nun, who was half-guest, half-refugee, used to go every day and sit quietly in the sun when the weather was good, selling Brigittine rosaries, not in front of the church, but on the side toward the lake, where there were steps and grass-grown ruins of the brothers' convent.

All through the little town, the fields and groves of white birches, and especially along the lake and by the Blue Church, there was an atmosphere of other-worldliness, stemming from long ago and not yet lost.

Under the wise and loving leadership of Mother Katherine, the guest house at Vadstena flourished and became a religious point of gathering for many Catholics; even more than Djursholm, it seemed to attract intellectuals and students of culture. It obtained a distinguished chaplain, and the writer Johannes Jörgensen came here to work on his long biography of St. Birgitta. He expresses the feelings of many who came here, with less important projects than his own, but who relished the atmosphere of this unique place: He writes in the introduction to his monumental work, published at last in 1954:

There is a big *thank you* to be said to St. Birgitta's daughters in Vadstena, in the *Home of Rest* by the shores of Lake Vettern and in the shadow of the *Blue Church*. With them I found a place to work which I could not have imagined to be better. From the Chapel next to my studio, the clear voices came into me, singing Birgitta's hymns, *Ave, Maris Stella* and *Rosa rorans bonitatem*. And if I looked up from my paper, my glance went out between the white birches, across the blue lake or, when the sleepless water of the *Troll-Sjö* were bound by frost, out across the white desert of ice toward the coast of *Västergötland*, blue-toned in the distance.... I thank you, Mother Elisabeth down in Rome, because for so long you gave me shelter.... I must also thank the town of Vadstena, the citizens of Vadstena! Year in, year out, they saw me walking in the streets and lanes of the town and wandering along the roads of *Östergötland*.... It was said that the Danish professor was writing a book about St. Birgitta, and the years passed ... but they still believed in me, showed me kindness, amiability, all *on credit;* the keeper of the archives, Dr. Sten Engström, treated me like a colleague, and Harold Thorngren, the writer with the greatest local knowledge, took me up to Granby Hill, where in the old days the pilgrims took off their shoes, to walk barefoot down to the holy city. Last but not least, I thank my wife who, for my sake, became a resident of Vadstena...."

So Professor Jörgensen and many others made a haven of this re-living Convent of St. Birgitta.

Chapter XVIII

India

THE most surprising move in Mother Elisabeth's unpredictable career was the launching of her Swedish Order—in India!

It happened through an Italian Jesuit, Fr. Edward Beretta, who had been sent as a young seminarian missionary to Calicut, in Kerala Province, in southern India, a region first Christianized by Thomas the Apostle. Fired by the deep, spiritual quality of Indian Catholics, and at the same time, up against the grave difficulties of dealing with pagan traditions and primitive conditions of health and food, Father Beretta had a great obsessing dream; he wanted to establish a convent of Perpetual Adoration in Calicut, to act as a spiritual powerhouse from which the Catholic work in India could draw life-giving strength.

Father Beretta was visiting the north of Italy where Mother Francesca, then Superior at Lugano, heard of him and invited him to give a retreat for the convent at Paradiso. He was very much impressed with the spirit of prayer he found among the Brigittines; he expressed his *dream* to Mother Francesca and, afterwards, went to Rome to see Mother Elisabeth. Would she consider sending a group of her daughters of St. Birgitta to make a foundation in Calicut? He promised to build her a church and a convent, and to be personally responsible for getting the Order established in India.

Mother Elisabeth, with her pioneer spirit and daring intuition, accepted Father Beretta's offer. He volunteered to search for Indian postulants to train in Rome and found four devout young girls whom he brought to the Casa di Santa Brigida.

184

If Mother Elisabeth had been stronger, and not already near her seventieth year, she would no doubt have led this new venture. The Sisters all realized that the dangers of tropical diseases, extreme heat, and other difficulties awaited them. Yet many had volunteered to be in the founding Community; the appeal was not only to their imaginations, but to the sense of sacrifice which Mother Elisabeth had always emphasized in their religious training. The Superior was to be Mother Francesca-of-the-Cross, herself frail in health, but strong in spirit. Ever since she had met Father Beretta at Lugano, she had felt a compelling desire to work for India.

Of the four Indian Sisters who had entered the noviciate in Rome, one had returned to India for reasons of health. The other three were eager to start their service to their own people. Mother Elisabeth found a very deep love in her heart for her Indian children. She never tired of telling them and others that they were not the first Sisters of St. Birgitta of Indian blood. And she wrote out this little story for them in her own hand:

Sister M. Katerina of the East (called in the Order, the black Sister Katherina) was born of noble Indian parents who were taken prisoner during some eastern war (about 1370) and she was brought with them to Naples. At the death of her parents, Queen Johanna gave the little girl to St. Birgitta of Sweden who at that time was visiting the Queen at Naples (she was her distant cousin). The girl came with Birgitta to Rome and lived in this holy House, *Casa di Santa Brigida,* with her and her daughter Katherine. At her Baptism, the little Indian was given the name of Katherina. After the death of St. Birgitta, she went to Sweden with St. Katherine and became a Religious there in the first House of our Order at Vadstena. She lived a life of heroic virtue and a saintly priest, at the moment of her death, saw her soul rise to heaven, like a bright star.

The old monastery of Altomünster has a painting of this holy death.

After some delays, a pioneer band of twelve Sisters and nine Italians, embarked at Brindisi for Malabar, on April 10, 1937. This appealed to the imagination of a Swedish journalist, who wrote: "The first Brigittine Convent to be founded in Asia—the new Convent is not, however, the first to be founded outside of

185

Europe, as there have been foundations in Mexico—but now there will be one across the Indian Ocean, near Malabar's chief city of Calicut. . . . Now Mother Elisabeth has seven Convents. Many languages are spoken in them—but all must learn a few words of Swedish, and the Rev. Mother herself speaks with the accent of Dalarna."

There was not much Swedish atmosphere on the high rise above Calicut, where the Jesuits had placed the new Convent of St. Birgitta. It was not far from their own noviciate House, but stood on the opposite side of the main road, approachable by means of a long, dirt lane which rose gradually and then swung left along the top of a hill long noted as the site of a pagan temple. Strange cries were said to have been heard here, and the place had been called the Devils' Hill. Now it was christened *Marikunnu* (Hill of Mary).

When the Sisters arrived, the convent was completed except for doors and windows, and the church was just rising behind a high, white facade, dramatically flanking the entrance to the long compound of the convent. Arrangements were still quite primitive. Water flowed slowly out of a single faucet, and it was several years before electricity was brought into the buildings.

But space was adequate and well laid out. Rooms opened off a long, wide veranda, and, above, a second row of cells stood along an equally broad and shaded balcony. Behind the airy rooms was another, inner courtyard which looked onto the main compound; the ground fell away behind tall palms and cashew trees, so that no wall could be seen, but only the wild tangle of treetops below. Father Beretta lived in a small stone house nearby, and there were workmen and women to help the Sisters in the daytime. A chapel was improvised in one of the large workrooms, so that Adoration of the Blessed Sacrament was started as soon as the Sisters arrived. The Sisters were filled with courage and a determination to adapt themselves to all circumstances. . . . However, one of the most trying was the presence of snakes in the new compound and even in the rooms of the convent.

186

Every night, when the Sisters went to bed, they would take their petrol lamps and search their cells for snakes before extinguishing the light. When they found a snake in their room, they put the light down on the floor, where it seemed to immobilize the snake. Then they would summon help, and one of the Indian Sisters, who was hardened to such unwanted *visitors,* would arrive with a strong stick and kill the snake. It was only after the building was completed, and the compound cleared, that snakes were not a daily sight to the Sisters. But these, and the insects and excessive heat were all accepted in a spirit of penance, and only one case of malaria, and occasional sickness, marred the singular life of prayer and sacrifice which developed on the Hill of Mary.

At first, Adoration was maintained only in the daytime, but later, for many years, it was also kept up at night—making *Marikunnu* a special source of spiritual power, as Father Beretta had wished. Indeed, the convent became a place of pilgrimage for Catholics in Calicut.

It was not long before Indian postulants from the region joined them, and the Sisters found a side vocation in accepting the care of orphans. This was Father Beretta's idea, for he was always seeking to meet human needs, and the Indian children appealed to his heart. He arranged for some forty or fifty girls to live in a large bungalow near the convent, where the Sisters could provide them with clothing and loving care. He had an equally large group of boys under his own supervision, and provided food for all the children, with some help from the bishop and a native assistant.

Father Beretta also started a small dispensary for the poorest families of the district. A woman with some medical training helped him at first, and then, with several lady doctors, he gradually started a primitive clinic. Finally, an excellent Italian, Dr. Fasana, felt inspired to take over the work. He developed an airy, rambling hospital with outbuildings, and persuaded the Sisters of Charity of Milan to provide nurses and to staff the whole complex.

Father Beretta remained for several years the devoted chaplain of Marikunnu. This convent chapel also took the place of a Catholic parish for Calicut, and in this way the Sisters were also involved in parish work, as they were later, in Kalamassery and Madras. Indeed, from the very first, the Sisters in India tended to take up whatever activity seemed most necessary to meet local needs. Some Sisters of intellectual bent later studied theology at the *Mater Dei* Institute in Goa. Others took courses in cooking, poultry raising, or nursing.

In spite of various activities, however, none of these Indian convents gave up the practice of Adoration, at least during the daytime hours. This was the great concept of Father Beretta, and he had surely left his stamp on the Order of Our Most Holy Savior in India. None of those who knew him could ever forget his serious, intense, and loving gaze. His tall figure and distinguished face with its small, pointed beard, was that of a monk and a visionary. It was a hard blow for all when he was taken ill and obliged to return to Italy where he died in 1951.

When there were more than forty Sisters at Marikunnu, another convent was opened at Bangalore, in 1960; next, a foundation, which had long been sought by the Archbishop of Verapoly, was made at Kalamassery, in the very heart of the devout, Catholic colony of Kerala, from which many vocations had come. Here the chapel was a shrine to the memory of the Pope, now St. Pius X, who had first recognized the founding of Mother Elisabeth's new branch.

The story of the development of the Order in India is marked by its *Silver Jubilee* book—a remarkable testimony to the vitality of the prayer life of the Convent of Perpetual Adoration and its subsequent Sister convents, which still continue to multiply.

Many exceptional Sisters have been formed or lived out their lives in these Indian convents. Mother Francesca held out for fifteen years, in spite of great weakness and suffering. She, like Father Beretta, was not permitted by destiny to die in the land of her adoption, but was forced to return to Italy, to endure a long illness, offered up for her beloved India.

Two important convents have been founded since 1962; one in the teeming city of Madras—a beautiful House built for

European Carmelites, who were obliged to leave for reasons of health.

Another rest-home convent has recently been founded in the suburbs of Mysore, the city famous for the temples and palaces of this former principality. Here, to fill urgent needs, a dispensary was opened.

The Indian convents of St. Birgitta are now entirely independent and self-supporting; Indian Sisters have responded generously to the call of the spiritual life. A number of Catholic convents are now flourishing in India; notably a large teaching Order of active Carmelites, all of Indian ancestry. The naturally spiritual natures of the *old souls* of Hindu and Buddhist tradition are easily drawn to a life of prayer, and lately a Community of Sisters of Hindu Religion has been formed for the first time in *Madya Pradesh,* the central part of India. Communities of non-Christian priests and monks have always existed; the solitary hermit and the sage or guru has also been a constant symbol of Indian spiritual mindedness. However, it may have been the Catholic Orders for women that have inspired a Hindu Sisterhood.

In any case, the deep, mystical atmosphere of India, particularly in the southern states, where Catholic faith has existed since the days of St. Thomas the Apostle, made a happy soil for the old Order of St. Birgitta, and its contemplative character has been brought out because of this practice of Perpetual Adoration, so dear to the Eastern soul. There are now almost one hundred Indian Sisters in the Order of our Most Holy Savior, and many have come back to Italy, Switzerland, America, to bring their special quality to this truly international Order.

So it was by another God-given intuition that Mother Elisabeth accepted this far-flung call to India for the Order of St. Birgitta. It has yielded fruit, one hundredfold, not only for India, but for the unifying world of today. This concept would not have been alien to the spirit of Birgitta, who was a genuine Swede, but traveled in many lands, and spent her last twenty years in Rome, the home of universal faith.

By the circuitous ways of destiny, she had included the

little Indian Sister Katerina, in her household of the Casa di Santa Brigida, and so prepared the way for her to be taken into the first foundation of her own Order, made by her daughter, St. Catherine, at Vadstena. This link made in the thirteen-hundreds, between India and St. Birgitta, was a little omen of the rich interrelationship developing today.

Chapter XIX

The War Years

BEFORE the Second World War actually broke out, Mother Elisabeth had already suffered under the oppression of Mussolini's Fascism. From the time that Violet Gibson had called attention to the little Community on the Via delle Isole, because of her abortive attempt on the life of *Il Duce,* military police had come from time to time to inspect the convent. Mother Elisabeth had always had a keen mind that followed world affairs, and while she did not spend much time reading newspapers, a glance at them now and then was sufficient to keep her abreast of current events. She was fearless in expressing her opinions.

She wrote to Count von Rosen from Lugano in December 1935:

I have read with great interest, your excellent article on the horrible conflict going on in Abyssinia. In Rome, I have had many conversations with highly placed persons who have been just as blinded by false patriotism as the ignorant crowds. I have even asked the Holy Father to take a stand against modern Caesar, and I know that he has done so—several times, the Vatican's newspaper has been confiscated, and once, after a speech of the Pope, there was a real thunderstorm around Caesar—he wanted to lock up the Pope so that he could not move around freely any more. But through wise and good people, he was calmed down again. Mussolini has done much, but I think that almost everything he does bears the stamp of pride and arrogance, and I doubt whether he has had a pure purpose in what he has done for the Church, but has only done it to draw the mass of Italian people with him.

Again, she wrote to Count von Rosen in January, 1936: "We still seem far away from peace on earth.... Many people seem completely hypnotized by the modern Nero and take this horrible *modern warfare* as something quite natural, and necessary for humanity!"

Before the war years, Mother Elisabeth had obtained a small house with land and a vineyard at Genzano, a little over an hour from Rome by electric train; here the Sisters could get away from the heat of Rome in summer, and also raise vegetables, fruits, and keep chickens. It was a simple place, not intended for winter use, but during the war it proved a godsend. The ground was fertile, and the air excellent, as it lay on a hillside with a distant view of the sea.

In 1938, Mother Elisabeth had been offered the chance to buy a villa on the island of Capri, through Dr. Axel Munthe, Swedish author of the noted work *The Story of San Michele*. He was a devotee of Birgitta, had visited the convent in Rome several times, and greatly admired Mother Elisabeth. Although nothing came of this project in view of gathering war clouds, it further strengthened the friendship between these two remarkable Swedes.

The following summer, Mother Richard records a new crisis and the concern of Mother Elisabeth: "This year, full of sadness and tremendous pain, I prefer that we do not have a play for the Feast of St. Elisabeth; let us have, instead, only some small refreshments. We must think, dearest daughters, of the suffering of thousands of priests and religious of all Orders, in all parts of the world."

In 1940, few travelers could come to Rome, and the Sisters were left with very little income. They were glad when an English family arrived to settle in an apartment on the Via Monserrato. Another family, recommended by the Vatican, came to take over the flat originally used by Mother Elisabeth for her first foundation. Later, two more guests arrived from Kenya, Africa.

Mother Elisabeth was very happy when she had news in March

of that year that the Sacred Congregation of Religious, which was meeting in formal session, had approved her request for *Approbatio cum Laude,* with a full, unanimous vote. This was an honor added to the formal Canonical Approbation she had received in 1920, and it seemed to justify the many years of prayer, work, and suffering offered up for the Order of St. Birgitta and Scandinavia.

That spring, two young Scandinavians were ordained priests, and said their first Mass in the Church of St. Birgitta. A scholar, Adalbert Frederickson, arrived from Sweden to do research concerning the Casa di Santa Brigida. Mother Elisabeth had long sought to have the archives of the House given over to her Order, but the canons of Santa Maria in Trastevere, who had owned the House, would not give them up. They could be seen only at Trastevere, and copied by hand, if necessary. (At present, they have been transferred to the Vatican Archive.)

At this time, a Signora Armfelt, Swedish by nationality, but an Italian citizen through her marriage to an Italian, came to see Mother Elisabeth about a proposal for peace that was being arranged by some prominent Italians, and they wished Sweden to take part in it. . . .

This was the beginnng of a deep interest and work for peace which Mother Elisabeth pursued for many years.

In May of that fateful year, 1940, France was invaded; Italy was drawn into the War by the Nazi compulsion, and what is history, now, became a horrifying, daily reality to the Sisters in Rome, as well as to all the convents of this international Order —although the Houses in Sweden, Switzerland, and India were relatively safe.

In Rome, there was first wild confusion; the British ambassador told all English citizens to leave Rome. Eighty-two young seminarians of the English College left in a group. They asked the Sisters of the Piazza Farnese to keep their boos and vestments for them.

Outside the Piazza was full of police who feared demontrations against the French Embassy in the Palazzo Farnese. The American College also closed, and sent forty young men home. Fr. Francis Kennedy came to say goodbye to Mother Elisabeth. The Sisters were advised to put what little money they had in the Vatican Administration, for custody.

In all the anxiety, there is note of a conference given by a Capuchin Padre Dionigi, who quoted the words of St. Teresa: *"Let nothing affright thee; Let nothing disturb thee. . . .* He said we should live abandoned to the Will of God in all things and not allow the things of the external world, the general up-heaval caused by War, to disturb our inward peace."

Mother Elisabeth obtained a private audience with Pope Pius XII, and took with her Mother Richard, Mother Reginalda, Mother Agnes, Sister Benedict, and Karin von Horn. The Pope showed great interest in Mother Elisabeth's work and as he had heard what a great sufferer she was, he gave her a special blessing.

Air-raid alarms grew frequent, and Mother Elisabeth was obliged to go down in the cellars with the Sisters, although this aggravated her condition. For a while, these let up but were resumed from time to time until the end of the War.

In the month of August, 1940, Mother Elisabeth was so ex-hausted from the great heat in Rome that her Sisters insisted she go to rest in Genzano. Father Ströjny, the Polish priest who had taken an apartment in the Casa di Santa Brigida, came to visit Mother Elisabeth in Genzano, and was impressed with the little convent there.

Under the direction of Mother Elisabeth, Sister Veronica, who had studied gardening in Sweden before entering the Order, did a great deal of work to establish the garden at Genzano. She pruned, scraped, and medicated trees and bushes, digging around their roots, and transplanting, arranging flower beds, etc. She was remarkably capable and reliable, one of the first Swedish Sisters to enter in Rome; afterwards, she served in Djursholm, until she returned to Rome in 1940. After the War, she was sent to Lugano, where she continued her exemplary service, until she died there at the age of seventy-eight.

After she returned to Rome from Genzano Mother Elisabeth heard that Dr. Munthe was seriously ill with heart trouble, and

194

though not able to receive visitors, asked her to come to see him. She went to his apartment over the garage of the Villa Svezia, where Queen Victoria had lived when in Rome. She found him suffering greatly; he felt as though he were suffocating. Mother spoke words of comfort to him, and he allowed her to place a small crucifix in the pocket of his vest, near his heart.

At the Via delle Isole, Mother Elisabeth visited three blind women for whom the Sisters were caring. A young Jewish woman was received into the Church at the chapel there.

The terrible news of the bombardments in London reached Rome, and Mother Elisabeth and all her daughters prayed earnestly for the Sisters at Iver Heath. All news of them was cut off, and only later, through the Red Cross, came news that they were unharmed, but it was at this time that they experienced the terror of nightly air raids and rockets which, for the most part, passed over their heads.

In November, air raids were again announced in Rome almost nightly, and experts came to arrange a shelter for the Sisters in the crypt, under the Chapel of St. Richard Reynolds. It was very hard for Mother Elisabeth in her state of health and at seventy years old to leave a warm bed and pass down the draughty stairways, into the cellar. Again, Sister Richard relates:

November 24, 1940, The Holy Father said Mass in St. Peter's to implore the Mercy of God on the World. Every Priest offered his Mass for the same intention, all over the Catholic World. St. Peter's was crowded, but he gave orders that there was to be no acclamation when he entered. He walked behind the Bishops and Cardinals; all were vested in purple as a sign of penance and mourning. The Mass was low and the Holy Father preached a wonderful homily on the Gospel of the day, applying its meaning to the events in Europe just now.

November 28th, The cold is beginning to make itself felt. On account of the shortage of coal and the terrible price it costs, we shall not be able to have coal this winter. All the Sisters are glad to have this mortification to offer up to Our Lord, to help to obtain Peace. (And so it was—no heat for the next four years!)

December 8th, Dr. Munthe came to see Mother Elisabeth and thank her for a Bible she had sent him. He had his valet, Vittorio, with him, seemed better, but said he was very lonely. He looked at a small apartment in our house, but did not decide to take it. He was eighty-three years old. Later, Mother sent him two pairs of wool socks and two caps, made on our knitting machine, because he suffers so much from the cold. A little later, he suddenly left for Capri.

During these grim days, Mother Elisabeth had had news that Mother Katherine in Sweden was very ill, after an operation which was supposed to have saved her life. Permission was obtained for Mother Reginalda to pass through Germany, to go to her assistance.

At Djursholm, Mother Katherine had been told that her illness was cancer and any further operation would be useless. She wrote from her heart to Mother Elisabeth:

Djursholm, Dec. 17, 1940

Beloved Mother:

I heard last evening that I am beyond cure, other than by miracle. You can imagine I got a big shock—I had not the slightest idea that things were so bad.... Well, may God's Holy Will be done—if he wants me to die now, before going to America, He will send someone else. It's very good of Him to give me time to prepare, even though it's hard. But beloved Mother, don't you think I had better go to the Elisabeth Sisters' Hospital after Christmas?

I humbly ask pardon, Darling Mother, of you for all my faults of the past ... and ask you all most fervently to pray much, much for me that I may with patience and merit bear the sufferings prepared for me and die a holy death in the arms of Jesus Mary and Joseph. I hope one of these days soon, Father Burczyk comes for Confession and I hope with God's Grace to make a sincere, general confession with perfect sorrow for all my sins. God's ways are not our ways, that's quite certain.

The Sisters had not had the courage to tell me themselves, but got the Chaplain to do it, and then last evening we spoke freely of it to one another. I suppose really from the beginning it has all been a failure, the operation, etc. In some cases it's good; in others, too late. Only pray, and get prayers for me, to face it all with peace and joy. One shouldn't really mind it; after all, life should have been one continued preparation for death, and yet we put it off. I offer the Sacrifice of not again seeing you, my precious Mother, nor dearly beloved St. John. What that costs, Our Dear Lord knows well. I offer it for the success of your work.

And so beloved Mother, a very peaceful Christmas, full of graces and blessings and a big embrace, thanking you most heartily for all you have done for me in my life....

Your poor St. Peter

As Mother Katherine had mentioned, she had been designated to undertake a foundation in America, near Minneapolis, Minnesota, with the help of the St. Ansgar's League for Scandinavian Catholics, active in New York and other cities. But the whole project was abandoned, not only because of Mother Katherine's illness, but because of the War.

When she signed herself *St. Peter,* Mother Katherine was recalling the early days of Mother Elisabeth's foundation when she would tease or encourage her Sisters by giving them the names of the Disciples; Katherine was St. Peter and Sister Richard, St. John; Mother used these names affectionately, in some of her own letters.

A last note from Mother Katherine reached Mother Elisabeth after the New Year: "I try to suffer all for our beloved Order and your work. Pains are very bad sometimes—*Fiat*—pray only that I may take one day at a time until the decisive moment when I go to God. The Order needs *you*—more than anyone else. Lots and lots of love from your own St. Peter."

She died on the nineteenth of March in Stockholm, at the Nursing Home of the Elisabeth Sisters, who cared for her with much love. Her body was brought to the Church of St. Eugenia, where a Solemn Requiem was celebrated in the presence of Bishop Müller. The Church was crowded by Catholics and Protestants who knew of her dedicated life.

It was then that Mother Elisabeth took advantage of the generous and unique gift made to her by Count von Rosen, of his burial plot at Vadstena, under the very walls of the *Blue Church.* Here is Mother Katherine's grave, with the Brigittine Cross above her name.

Shortly afterwards, the Swedish government declared that this burial ground was now part of the historical monument of Vadstena and no more internments could be made in it. So the splendid Sister Katherine is perhaps the last and only modern Brigittine to rest there.

No diary was kept after 1940, until 1943, but much went on at the Casa di Santa Brigida. Many persons had taken refuge there, and after the entry of the Nazis into Rome during the disastrous African campaign of Rommel and the arrival of the Americans in the Mediterranean, tensions were still greater. A number of Jewish friends, and also strangers, were taken in and hidden in the House, even inside the Sisters' living quarters.

Once a Nazi officer arrived to inspect the House. Mother Elisabeth met him, and spoke to him in her low, self-possessed voice. She allowed him to visit all the guests' quarters, but when he still wanted to go into the Sisters' cloister, she said to him in German and in her most serious tone: "We are nothing but a group of defenseless women, living in a Convent. I do not believe that a German Officer will violate our privacy." He looked at her, meeting that level, penetrating look of her brown eyes, deepened by suffering. Then he went away.

In July, 1943, the *Diary* of Mother Richard takes up the story of the dire bombardments which finally ended the rule of Mussolini.

July 19, 1943, This morning at 11 A.M. the alarm sounded. The heavy bombardment of Rome began in the direction of St. Lorenzo (Station) and surrounding districts. Five hundred aeroplanes (American) came over. The ancient Basilica of St Lorenzo was damaged. Also the graves in the Verano Cemetery. Many houses and big buildings were brought down. 10,000 people were killed, many being crushed under the debris of the fallen houses.

His Holiness, Pope Pius the XII, went out in person to console the sufferers—he went in a small automobile, accompanied by Monsignor Montini [the present Pope!] quite privately. His Holiness wept when he saw the great destruction and terrible suffering of his beloved children. Many graves had been broken up, among them the family grave of the Holy Father, Pius XII. His Holiness had a lot of pasta, rice and bread distributed among the poor, homeless people. The whole quarter of the Tiburtino had been almost destroyed; a wing of the Polyclinic brought down and one side of the University.

The bombardment had lasted two hours. We spent the time in our air-raid shelter, saying the rosary and other prayers.

Seventeen days later, 43 persons were taken out of the debris, alive. During the time that rescuers had been trying to release them, they were fed with milk and kept alive with syphons of oxygen. Some days later, we heard that our tomb at the cemetery, which we had bought three months before, had been completely destroyed, but we were thankful to know that the coffins containing the remains of our dear Sisters had been found and placed in a morgue, until things could be arranged and a new tomb prepared.

August 1st, Rome was bombed again by the Americans and English. The Station of St. Lorenzo was again the target, also the Central Station and the aeroport of Littoria.

September 8th, The Commander-in-chief of the Italian army in Calabria asked General Eisenhower, Commander-in-chief of the Allied Forces, for an armistice.

September 20th, Rome completely occupied by the Germans.

October, 1943, These months of German Occupation have been full of events, and it has been a time of horror and intense suffering....

The poverty and hunger in Italy took on calamity proportions toward the end of the War, and the years following. The Casa di Santa Brigida became a center for distributing food and clothing, which was sent from Sweden. A charity organization called *Rädda Barnen* (Save the Children) collected vast amounts for Italian families.

Toward the end of the War in Italy, Mother Elisabeth wrote a long letter to Eva:

Down here it is still very difficult for many, but our Lord has let us help, and just lately we have received over 1,000 pieces of clothing for boys and girls. Some of them are only stapled together, and there will be much sewing to do—some of the mothers will have to help us. We work all year long for the poor, but during the war years it has been hard to get material—how frightful is *modern war*—it is horrifying to see the small towns and villages in ruins.

Genzano, where our little convent lies, was bombarded from the air and from Anzio, where the Allies for four months sent off cannonshots from the beach and from gun-boats. All the streets of the town, which had 12,000 inhabitants, had disappeared. Many thousands of people were buried alive in caves and on the hillsides where they had gone to seek shelter. Cannon shots came and blocked their entrances.... Our Sisters had to walk for three days, under fire from cannons and bombs, until they reached Rome. By the time I was able to go out by car to see what had happened, all our furniture, doors and windows had disappeared. Partisans had dragged in some beds and were sleeping in our rooms at ten o'clock in the morning. But our good Minister Lagerberg got them out. When they left the house, they wrote on the walls: *Till we meet again! Long live Lenin!*

When I came out, some had come back again, but they were all very nice and said: "Welcome, Dearest Mother!" and kissed my hand. Many came to get help and advice. Italy is in a bad position.... Deserters of every nationality are roaming around over the whole country—it is hard to put an end to it. I enclose a little prayer for peace, and beg you to join us in our *Peace* band.

The letter of Minister Lagerberg, authorizing Mother Elisabeth to use his car and visit the house at Genzano, reflects these unsettled days:

Swedish Legation

The undersigned, Royal Minister of Sweden, certifies that Rev. Mother Elisabeth, Abbess of the Order of Saint Birgitta, a Swedish subject, who is using, together with two of the Sisters of the same Order, my diplomatic car, is going to inspect the house belonging to the Order situated at Genzano.

The Allied Military Government, Office of the Public Safety Division (Major Battersby) has taken the necessary steps in order to put the said house, unduly taken into possession by intruders, at the disposal of the Abbess.

The undersigned begs to recommend Rev. Mother Elisabeth and trusts that the Allied Military Authorities will give her all possible assistance for the fulfillment of Her mission,

Rome, July 18, 1944

Royal Legation

Sven Lagerberg,
Minister

At the end of the War, Mother Elisabeth, as many figures of world stature, had the great desire to work for peace, for some great organization that would educate people's minds and hearts, so that never again would there be such a disaster on the earth.

Writing to her dear friend Mary von Rosen, she said:

Roma 2/8/1946

Dearest Daughter in Our Lord:

The enclosed writing will explain the reason for my letter.

For so many years, our prayers have gone up from St. Birgitta's House in Rome. I see it as an (indirect) answer that the Lord has now inspired right-thinking, broad-viewed, big-hearted people all over the world to work for *Peace* as *Knights of Peace*. Surely, our Peace-loving Land will be among them? Earnestly I beg you, my daughter, collect as many well-known names as you can, on the petition which I enclose. Do you think it would be possible to get the signature of our

Peace-Loving King? Princes Carl and Eugene, and some of the Princesses? Count Folke Bernadotte, who has worked so much in Germany (with the Red Cross)? Former State-Minister Undén, Sandler, etc. The Professors in Uppsala—Prince zu Wied, and others from Germany? Catholic Bishops and Protestant Bishops, The Rabbi of the Synagogue in Stockholm, and others? All, provided they believe in God, can be members in the *Knights of Peace*.

In a letter one month later, she writes in part: "There is so much suffering in the world that one can hardly be happy about anything, if one has sympathy for one's fellow men. . . . Quite a few well-known people have signed for Knights of Peace. . . . There is a growing interest here in founding a University of Peace in the Eternal City. . . .

Although nothing came of Mother Elisabeth's project of Knights of Peace, it shows her nobility of spirit. The following thoughts about war, were recorded at the end of her diary:

If war is considered one of the calamities of life—the punishment of sin, like disease—why should it not be combatted by the training of the will to something better and nobler? The desire for War is a perverseness of the will. As disease is combatted by medical science and as criminal tendencies are combatted by religion and educational systems, so war should be combatted by educating people to something better—to works of mercy and love which enoble human nature.

Chapter XX

Mother Elisabeth's Harvest

AFTER the difficult war years, Mother Elisabeth entered a period of relative calm; her work had come into its full maturity and she began to reap honors, publicity, and recognition of all kinds. And, what alone was important to her, a certain spiritual harvest, parallel to all this, was manifest through her many contacts, her correspondence with people of every sort, the subtle influence of her love and desire to help, which drew many toward her.

Soon after the War, on the birthday of the ninety-year-old King Gustav, she was awarded the Service Cross, First Class, of the Order of Malta, for the help offered to refugees in Rome. The Swedish newspaper *Svenska Dagbladet* reported: "The honor was given as a sign of deep gratitude toward the Swedish people for the volunteer assistance in food and clothing which was given out in 1948, to the poor and needy in Rome.... The Swedish Minister's wife escorted Mother Elisabeth to the Palazzo Chigi, where the Order's Grand Master, Prince Chigi, received her in private audience and handed her the handsome Decoration of the Maltese Order."

During the last year of the War, and years following, Mother Elisabeth and her Sisters had given out food supplies and countless thousands of bundles of clothing, which were sent to them from Sweden for distribution. Long lines of women and children seeking help would often be seen standing outside the convent door. The Sisters took huge piles of clothes out on the roof terrace of the Casa di Santa Brigida and sorted them, washing and mending when necessary, and then saw that they got into the right hands.

This was shown when Ingrid Bergman and the director Rosselini made a short film in 1951, for *Rädda Barnen* (Save the Children) as an account of this Association's help to the Italian children. "The film is taken in the Convent of St. Birgitta in Rome and the Sisters under the leadership of the Swedish Abbess, Mother Elisabeth, take part in the film."

This report, in the *Svenska Dagbladet* for November 28, 1951, showed a still of Ingrid Bergman and Mother Elisabeth, with Mother Richard in the background.

It was in 1955, that Mother Elisabeth received the highest honor of the Swedish nation, and one seldom given to a woman —that of the Order of the North Star, with rank of Commander.

This was given for her accomplishment as a Swedish woman, in general, and in particular, for her success in obtaining the ancient House of St. Birgitta and restoring it to Swedish hands. At this time, all the Swedish newspapers gave her great praise; in an interview with the Rome correspondent of the *Svenska Dagbladet*, Mother Elisabeth answered quite simply:

Now almost fifty years ago, I came to Rome to die. . . . But in His goodness, Our Lord gave me strength and health again and I have tried as best I could, to carry out a work in His spirit. . . .

Now we are glad to say that many Swedes find their way to Birgitta's House and Chapel. In our social work we have always had support from our Homeland. . . . In a moving letter of thanks from the mountains of Albano, they spoke of the *Noble Swedish nation*—this was written by people who before the war didn't know the difference between Sweden and Switzerland. . . . This honor which I have received from my Homeland makes me very happy and I share it with my beloved daughters. The Mother Convent has now twenty-five nuns, three of whom are Swedish.

It remained for the Swedish Minister in Rome to express his full admiration and that of his nation (Informal speech by the Swedish Minister in Rome, Johan Beck-Fries; quoted in part):

We have come together today for the reason that His Majesty the King has been pleased to name you *Commander of the Royal Order of the North Star.*

But let me point out that you have, all your life, devoted yourself to a humanitarian work of the most impressive quality. Even as a young girl of twenty, alone in New York, without protection, you visited the sick in the worst sections of the city. Danger did not exist for you.

It was almost a half century ago that you began your exhausting efforts to win back for the Order of St. Birgitta this wonderful, old house in which we find ourselves today.

This House, where Holy Birgitta lived and worked and ended her life in 1373, is the most remarkable Swedish memorial outside of our country, not only in Rome or Italy, but in the whole world. It will come to be, for all time, a place of pilgrimage for countless Swedes, irrespective of their religious attitudes—

You have saved this House, and we thank you for it!

UNITAS

One of the many intellectual friendships that Mother Elisabeth inspired grew out of her acquaintance with Dr. Piero Chiminelli. He was a convert, having formerly been an Italian Baptist clergyman. He had written a beautiful article on St. Birgitta for the *Osservatore Romano,* entitled "The Roman Characteristics" (*Romaneità*) of St. Birgitta. He later wrote a study of her life in Italian. Dr. Chiminelli was instrumental in bringing into Mother Elisabeth's mature life a work which she had long desired to make part of her own mission; indeed, one in which she had always been involved and carried in her heart, ever since, in the forest of Dalarne, she had longed to understand the mystery of the *One True Fold.*

First this yearning had led her through her long search for a spiritual family, which she found in the Catholic Church— but now, as she had matured and developed through the years of experience and inner struggle, she sought an even broader manifestation of Christian unity—the *ecumenical movement,* just beginning to develop in those days, and of which she had always, consciously or unconsciously, been a part. But to go

204

back to a simpler story of what she was now able to do in Rome, the convent record relates:

Jan. 5, 1947: Dr. Piero Chiminelli brought Father Charles Boyer, S.J., to see us. Father Boyer is a prominent theologian and Director of Studies at the Gregorian University. He is also the president of *Unitas,*—the great movement that is going on for the union of the churches, by means of special prayer, first of all, and literature. He is editor of *Unitas,* which comes out four times a year and contains learned articles on the different churches.

Fr. Boyer said he was in great need of helpers for *Unitas.* As it is a work for which our beloved Mother has prayed since she was a child, the visit of Fr. Boyer seemed an answer to her prayers after so many years. After this, we began at once to cooperate with Fr. Boyer in the great work of reunion.

A room on the ground floor was given over to be the office for this work, and soon Father Germanus, an Atonement Father from the Franciscan Friars of the Atonement, at Graymoor, in Garrison, New York, was put in charge.

This had first been an Anglican Order, and had gone over to the Catholic Church, almost as a body. It was psychologically a very broad-minded group, and is still today in the foremost ranks of the ecumenical activities taking place on every level and in relation with Protestants and Orthodox leaders all over the world.

At this early date, Mother Elisabeth was plunged into the full stream of this onrushing work. From that time forward, many Masses were offered up at the Church of St. Birgitta, for Unity. Preceding Pentecost of the same year, a novena was held with a different, distinguished speaker each day, including Monsignor Etteldorf (now a bishop), Orthodox Fathers, and His Eminence, Cardinal Tisserant.

On the eightieth birthday of Mother Elisabeth, Father Boyer spoke at the Casa di Santa Brigida (Rome, 4th of June, 1950) in these words:

I wish to express my gratitude to the Mother General, for what she has done for our work.

When we were starting, we were looking for a place to work, and she said, "Why not here?" We asked if she had a typewriter and she

205

said—"Not only a typewriter, but a Sister to write on it!" And we got not only a Sister, but many Sisters who worked for us; they pounded the typewriter, they mailed out our publication, they translated it, because our review is published in English, French and Italian.

And we did not get material aid only, but that of prayer, and of the life of suffering of the Mother General, offered up for our intentions.

I am sorry that she is not with us today, but at the same time, I am glad because I can speak freely without offending her humility; the Mother General is our benefactor, but in saying this, I do not say enough; she is our sustaining force in our work. And I am sure she sustains us, because it is miraculous that we have been able to develop so quickly. Today, she has completed her eightieth year, and we wish her all the best, that the Lord may grant her many more years to continue to do such great good.

The work of *Unitas* continued in the Casa di Santa Brigida until it outgrew its office and moved to larger quarters, near the Piazza Navona.

With the many Protestant friends who corresponded with Mother Elisabeth, she was always forthright in telling them of her own Catholic experience, but also granting them their rights of dissent. One lively exchange was hers with Dr. Harald Schiller, from Västergötland, like herself, and he never forgot this bond between them. He wrote regularly for the *Sydsvenska Dagbladet* (the South Sweden newspaper) and frequently sent her his articles. She wrote him from Rome, July 15, 1953:

Hearty thanks for the two numbers of the *Sydsvenska Dagbladet*. The one, with its fine description of your visit to Ostia, with its memories of Holy St. Monica; the other, about your visit to Assisi. Forgive me if I make a few remarks about your critical comments on our Holy Churches' relics.... When I read what you said about the relics in Assisi, my mind went back to a day 63 years ago, when I stood by the sick-bed of a prominent professor and scientist. He had had his foot crushed, and we had just made him comfortable in his bed and put his watch on the night-table. We took his clothes to the garde-robe. When I came back, he was looking around, restlessly. When I asked: "Is there anything you want, Professor?" He answered, "Yes, Sister, in my vest-pocket, there is a little stub of a pencil." I went back to see if I could find it. To my surprise, I found a very small stub, with the color almost worn off. When I placed it beside his watch, his face beamed with pleasure.

206

When he was better, he told me that this little pencil stub was the last thing his father held in his hand, as he was dying, about 30 years earlier. His good father, who had stroked his head when he came home from school with good marks, and who was the first to embrace him when he had passed his student exams. This little pencil-stub was a relic. It reminded him of the biggest thing we human beings have on this earth, the clean, true love which radiates out from God. Protestants, who talk so much about the fact that they depend only on the Bible, forget that it says in the Holy Writ that people who touched the prophets' bones were cured of their diseases. It says also that people were cured when the apostle's clothing was laid on them. My thought is, that it is neither bones nor clothing, but the almighty God's great love that radiates out and permits these wonders. Those people whose souls possessed a body which is now only bones were, during their life-time, one with God (united to God) in love. God's love is the strongest thing in the whole universe. God has permitted the little people in our small world of science, to learn of certain rays which heal the sick. How much stronger and more powerful are the rays of love that radiate out from Our Lord Himself, who is the Creator of the whole Universe, and its Sustainer. It is these rays of love that the "simple-minded" (*enfaldiga*) Catholics kneel and wait for when they pray.

You say, Dr. Schiller, that you don't want to be a Catholic because then you can't talk to God, *directly*—that really surprises me. Ever since my earliest childhood, I have always talked to God. And even if I talk to people, my contact and conversation with God is not cut off....

In a long tribute to Mother Elisabeth, at the time of her death, Dr. Schiller calls her "that second Birgitta, Mother Elisabeth Hesselblad from Västergötland, whom the famous Cardinal Merry del Val called *the most remarkable woman in Rome....* And Birgitta's work bloomed up again after six hundred years, thanks to the girl from Västergötland...."

He recalls how they talked together on several occasions in the spring of 1953: "There radiated from this woman a remarkable strength. She was so completely of another world, and so completely of this one as well....

"She gave me her picture, with a dedication on the back, and I, as much of a *västgöte* as she, had it framed with glass on both sides, so that I can read the dedication and remember: Here, once a hand rested, the hand of a woman that I learned to love

and to admire—she did honor to Västergötland and to her
country—may she rest in peace...."

Sydsvenska Dagbladet—April 9, 1968

As we have seen, Mother Elisabeth had an enduring friendship with Dr. Axel Munthe. He retired to Capri after the War,
where he remained in seclusion, and gradually lost his eyesight.
He was one of the many intellectuals who recognized the
special, spiritual strength of Mother Elisabeth, and the originality of her mind.

Another was Johannes Jörgensen, who stayed for such a long
time writing his book about Birgitta, at the convent of Mother
Elisabeth at Vadstena. He had also visited her in Rome, and
seeped himself in the atmosphere and traditions of the Casa di
Santa Brigida.

The Swedish author, Sven Stolpe, had also written about
Birgitta and was a visitor at the Casa in Rome. He corresponded
with Mother Elisabeth and sought her counsel.

Among Swedish women writers who knew and admired
Mother Elisabeth, were Emilia Fogelklou, Anna Lenah Elgström,
and Karin von Horn. The last two were faithful oblates of St.
Birgitta in the group that met at Djursholm.

Anna Lenah Elgström was deeply attached to Mother Elisabeth and wrote numerous articles about her and the Order. One
long account, printed in the Jesuit magazine *Credo,* brought
out the fact that the revival of interest in Birgitta had developed
parallel to, if not inspired by, Mother Elisabeth's own efforts.
She writes: "In the meantime, Sweden had begun to realize the
national and historical importance of this memorial of the great
Swedish Saint. Studies of St. Birgitta's *Revelations* were taken up
once more. The Royal Librarian, Isak Collijn, who published the
acts of her canonization, and Professor Andreas Lindblom, were
the first outstanding Brigittine researchers; Sven Nordmark,
Trygve Linden followed."

Mother Elisabeth had many friends among Protestant clergy-
men in Sweden. She made a new one when she received a letter
from the pastor of Foglavik in Västergötland, where she was

born. She was moved deeply by the fact that he had remembered her eightieth birthday, because of his parish records. She wrote to him in her direct way, giving testimony of what her life had been:

Rome, 25/9/50

Good Pastor Nunstedt:

Hearty thanks for your friendly letter—very interesting to have information about what stands in the Hudene Parish records about our family....

My own life may seem strange to many of our separated brethren. But I assure you that it was God who led every step....In any case, outside forces never influenced me. On the contrary, all my life I have had the most unbelievable confidence in what my inner convictions told me; to follow God's voice, to do His will!

An unfulfilled dream of Mother Elisabeth's life was her desire to see the priests of the Order of St. Birgitta established once more. It must be remembered that Fr. Benedict Williamson had felt inspired to do this at the very same time that she was a novice under the Carmelites in Rome, and he had come to see her as a fellow devotee of Birgitta. From Spain she had prayed for him and Charles Murphy on the day of their ordination, as they also took vows as Brigittine brothers. When they were subsequently able to form a young group of postulant brothers in Father Benedict's parish at Earlsfield, London, she followed their work with passionate interest.

Father Benedict, who always wore his gray Brigittine habit, aroused an interest for St. Birgitta in his parish. His assistant, Fr. Charles Murphy, and eleven brothers made an impressive group, singing the liturgy or saying their Office in the Earlsfield Church, beloved by its parishioners.

It was from his parish at Earlsfield that Father Benedict recruited two young girl postulants and brought them to Rome, to form Mother Elisabeth's first Community. A few months later, he sent two more to join her. So it was that the Convent of St. Birgitta in Rome and the seemingly further developed parish-monastery of Father Benedict in England became parallel Foundations, already giving each other practical and spiritual support. It must have seemed to Mother Elisabeth that the priests and brothers of St. Birgitta had returned to face the future of a renewed Order, with her.

Alas, this was not to be the case. It was her destiny to follow a difficult and unmapped road, alone. But the breadth of her vision was not limited by a lack of success. She had gone on, still hoping and working for the revival of the priests and brothers.

The Fathers of St. Birgitta might well have flourished had it not been for the First World War in 1914. But as the plight of England grew desperate, all the young men of Earlsfield were called into the Army; Father Benedict became a military chaplain. He was *gassed* three times and returned to London, a broken man. Two of his followers were killed, and the others went back to their homes or entered other religious Orders.

After some time, Father Benedict recovered sufficiently to come to Rome, a city which he dearly loved, and he was able to teach at Beda College. He still wore his Brigittine cloak with its large cross on special occasions, especially when he attended ceremonies at the convent of Mother Elisabeth. He remained her devoted friend and always considered himself a brother of St. Birgitta. But his dream of reviving the Order had faded.

This was, of course, a great disappointment to Mother Elisabeth, but she did not give up hope that some other priest or brother would rise up to try again. During the following years, a few prospects seemed to dawn, but none of the young men in question were able to persevere.

One of these was Peter Schindler, a Danish convert, who had often come to the convent on the Via Corsica when he was completing his studies at the Beda College. In 1916, he became an oblate brother of St. Birgitta and began to teach Christian doctrine to the children of the neighborhood. Mother Elisabeth arranged a little house in the garden for his class, adorned with pictures of saints and scenes from the life of Christ.

Father Schindler felt a strong desire to become a full brother of St. Birgitta. He received permission from the Sacred Congregation of Religious to wear the habit of a Brigittine Friar

210

whenever he was taking part in any ceremony in their chapel. Mother Elisabeth and her Sisters were delighted by his interest. It was arranged that he should be *clothed* in this habit on the Feast of the Presentation of Our Lady, in 1917.

Fr. Schindler was a close friend of Johannes Jörgensen, the celebrated Danish writer who had become a Catholic, and who later wrote a long biographical book about St. Birgitta, which he was already planning at that time. Jörgensen had also visited Mother Elisabeth, and admired her courage in renewing the apostolic work of the Order in Rome. Consequently, Mother Elisabeth, who always saw things in a big way, suddenly had the idea that Peter Schindler and Johannes Jörgensen might not only revive the Brothers of St. Birgitta, but also work with the Sisters to establish a Scandinavian College for Priests. (Actually, there has always been a need for this, since Scandinavians have had to study in German, English, or other Seminaries, in a language not their own.) Mother Elisabeth's letter, written in March 1917, shows her broad vision and boundless hope: She addresses Peter Schindler:

Reverend and dear son in Our Lord:

We have prayed much and continue to do so, for the important matter we spoke about last Monday.... Today, I wish to ask you and our dear friend Mr. Jörgensen to consider, with prudent, experienced men, if it may not be God's Holy Will that St. Birgitta's children in Rome, near the Vicar of Christ, should prepare the way for a Scandinavian College for priests?

Here is a great mission for you, my dear son and brother, to labor for a worthy monument to our glorious Mother St. Birgitta and our three dear Kings and Martyrs, St. Knut, St. Erik and St. Olaf—the revival of our Holy Mother's Order with Fathers and Sisters working together in Rome, could, at the same time, be the beginning of a Scandinavian College.

Alas, nothing came of this noble project. Father Schindler is a prominent priest, writer and spiritual leader in Denmark today.

In 1941, a certain Father Hovers held out a hope to the creative mind of Mother Elisabeth, who, in a letter to him from Rome, throws light on her own acceptance and offering up of suffering, as a means of attaining difficult goals. Father Hovers had been ill, suffering from a heart condition in a hospital in Holland; he had truly hoped to be the instrument for reviving the monks of St. Birgitta, but probably illness and the Second World War prevented him from doing more, just as the first war had blocked Father Benedict. Mother Elisabeth's letter said, in part:

My impression is that your sufferings and your weakness are precious in the eyes of Our Master, Who can use them in the foundation of the Restoration of the Fathers of our Order. He wants you to offer yourself as a victim for this; I believe when you have done this, He may—as He has done in my own case—give you enough strength to undertake exterior work also. There is another Priest who is doing so, a very holy young man who wants to be a Brother: Now with the offering of constant, united prayer and the immolation of ourselves on the altar of His Love, our wishes for the Restoration of the Fathers and Brothers cannot be refused....

There followed another disappointment for Mother Elisabeth. In a letter to a Sister at Djursholm, she said (12/8/48): "You must remember, dear Child, that I have helped over ten students and Priests who, after showing great interest in the Restoration of our Fathers, abandoned everything at the first little trial. Let us continue to pray about this matter."

And in December, 1949, one of the Sisters noted: "One evening when speaking of the revival of the Brigittine Fathers, Our Rev. and beloved Mother said that it would require a Priest who knew how to suffer and support deep humiliations and trials. Only under these conditions would he be fit to carry out such a great work."

As late as 1950, Mother Elisabeth wrote to a Fr. George Anton:

This is to let you know that we are praying very much for you. If the drawing you feel toward Rome comes from God, He will arrange everything. We are working to get some of the rooms free on the Monserrato side. A great scope for the future Fathers would be for the reunion of Christians. We have the office of *Unitas* here now, in this House.... I humbly believe that in our days, the Fathers should be independent from the Community of Sisters and with a rule suitable for our times....

Actually, it was only Father Benedict who had made a brave start toward re-establishing the brothers of St. Birgitta. Although he lived in Rome for many years, his health was never very stable, and he concentrated on literary work, outside of his teaching. He never fluctuated in his devotion to Mother Elisabeth and was a frequent visitor at the convent in Rome. During his last years, he was chaplain for the Blue Nuns Hospital in Rome, and died there, in 1948. He was buried in his gray cloak with the Brigittine Cross. There is a chapel dedicated to his memory at the new Beda College near St. Paul's—outside-the-Walls.

One of the Sisters of St. Birgitta made the following notation about Father Benedict: "Dear Fr. Benedict, about three years before his death, confided to our beloved Mother that he had made a mistake in following the advice of certain people, otherwise he would have been able to keep the Foundation and the subjects he received. No doubt from the Heavenly Country he will obtain light and courage for others to carry out the work he himself had so much at heart...."

The challenge of restoring the Order of Brothers of St. Birgitta is still very much alive. It has been discussed in Sweden and in the United States. May it someday find an answer, perhaps in the urgent, broad resurgence of the Church of tomorrow.

Mother Elisabeth's own words to her Sisters were treasured through the years, her spiritual talks to them written down, sometimes on scraps of paper, sometimes included in the records of the convents.

Her special spirit or spirituality is hard to capture. We have read the story of her actions; she was doing a double task, as Birgitta did before her: living an intense, inner life, and at the same time inspiring her Sisters to take up many tasks, those of hospitality, hard physical work, and the carrying on of an apostolate, often silent, but bearing witness at all times to the

213

power and love of Christ passing through them to all with whom they came in contact.

This is indeed the apostolate that Birgitta and her household of the Piazza Farnese had carried out before them.

Dr. Tore Nyberg, one of the most serious Birgitta scholars working today, has made an interesting comparison of St. Birgitta's first Rule, written down in Vadstena after her early *Revelations,* and that which she asked Pope Urban V to approve after she had lived in Rome and had had twenty years of practical experience dealing with the sick, the poor, pilgrims, priests, and prelates of the day. Since she did not live to establish her first Foundation at Vadstena, it was carried out by her daughter St. Catherine, who went back to the first version of the Rule written before Birgitta went to Rome.

According to Dr. Nyberg, the ideal Rule as worked out by Birgitta in her maturity, and presented to Urban the V in 1370, has never been fully put into practice. Mother Elisabeth tried to do it. But if active work has characterized the new branch of the Order of Our Most Holy Savior, it has not been at the expense of the spirit of prayer and the love of contemplative life, which Mother Elisabeth always strove to instill into her daughters. This can be seen from the counsels she gave them. It was always her intention to balance practical work, human contact, with silence and Divine communion.

Mother Elisabeth held up to all her Sisters the three essential virtues of patience, humility, and love. These are the natural fruits of following the ancient Rule of St. Augustine on which St. Birgitta and most of the medieval Orders based their monastic life—the vows of poverty, chastity, and obedience.

In accord with the cloistered Orders, Mother Elisabeth also emphasized *silence.* In her talks to her Sisters, she calls silence *holy*—*Il Santo Silenzio.* In a beautiful paragraph she said:

Especially, I recommend silence, for whoever does not sin in words, is near perfection.... At the times of silence, God speaks to the soul thus recollected, and fills it with His peace and tender consolation....

Patience, humility, love, silence—virtues precious and dear to God;

God caresses the humble soul, fills it with love and graces...but the proud and arrogant, He spurns.

Jesus did not say: Learn of me for I am powerful and can do great works and miracles, but "Learn from me for I am meek and humble of heart."

Another phase of Mother Elisabeth's spirituality was her acceptance, and even welcoming, of *mortification,* the principle explained to her by Father Hagen at the time of her baptism. Throughout her life, he had witnessed with amazement how she had transmuted her pain and suffering into prayer and spiritual power. The pupil had gone far beyond her teacher in the difficult path of sublimation and self-sacrifice.

In unexpected ways, too, her generosity came out. She was not afraid of any trial or anything that might offend the senses of the normal human being, as she had shown when she nursed the sick in the city hospital.

When she was desperately thinking of ways to reclaim the House of Birgitta, without means or money to do so, she suggested to Father Hagen that the Pope might be interested in a Home for Incurables, such as she had seen founded in New York at the time she was at the Roosevelt Hospital. This was the first institution of its kind in America and attracted much approbation. She wrote from Via delle Isole (2/11/23):

If the Holy Father gives the Carmelites another House, we would use our Holy Mother's House for a home for incurables, in honor of the Holy Father. For such an institution, money could be collected in America. There is great need in Rome for such a home. We have an old lady whose nose has been eaten away by Lupus, and part of her face. She could find no home on account of her terrible appearance, and was on the verge of committing suicide. She has now lived here *gratis* for five years and has become a good Catholic, grateful to God and her benefactors. Such suffering souls are good for contemplatives to contemplate—and I believe they would return into solitude with greater fervor and love.

There is no direct analogy between Mother Elisabeth and her great countrywoman St. Birgitta. The facts of their lives were entirely different, but by temperament and willpower

215

they were women of a kind, measuring up to each other in the originality of their accomplishments.

Birgitta was a practical, sturdy character, and yet she was also the great mystic of the *Revelations,* who felt and projected the *presence* of God and His Son in a remarkable manner.

Elisabeth was less gifted with position and power, claiming no miraculous apparitions nor visions, and yet she had, just as clearly, been aware of some Divine Force directing her and sustaining her in extreme physical need.

Birgitta experienced the Passion of Her Lord, through her intense love and Divinely touched imagination; Elisabeth in a different manner, without attempting description, *shared* the Passion of Christ in a very real way, through the suffering of her own body, offered up to become, as she believed, a tiny part of the continuing, creative work of His *redemption.*

Mother Elisabeth's spirit and that of her Order is singularly appropriate to the needs of the modern age, as was the life and work of Birgitta in her day. It is a work of hospitality, reaching out to all, whatever their race or creed; it seeks to create understanding between human beings, to cultivate unity and love.

At the same time, it clings to those values of the spiritual life of all times; that which so many people, young and old, are seeking today. Some look for the technique of meditation in oriental religions; some seek mystical experience in drugs, or by inventing their own rituals. The way to Truth is always difficult as it was to Mother Elisabeth. But her Order offers its shelter and rest, maintains its daily rhythms of the Divine Office, the holy *Mass,* and without compulsion, leaves its chapels open to guests or strangers for meditation and silent prayer.

As Mother Elisabeth said: *"God speaks to the soul thus recollected—"* This is perhaps the key to her practical spirituality, the active life guided by contact with the *Divine.*

Chapter XXI

The Last Years of Mother Elisabeth

DURING the last two years of Mother Elisabeth's life, her health was failing rapidly and she experienced new difficulties; as in the case of many great souls, she had to traverse a period of deep shadow before she reached the gates of death and transfiguration.

It is also testimony to her strong leadership that when her firm hand began to lose its grip, certain unruly elements within her growing Order caused problems and conflicts.

Mother Richard, her assistant, who had been her right hand and one of her most faithful daughters since the first years in Rome, was by this time in her seventies; she had grown quite worn out from trying to manage a crucial situation and to keep trouble away from her beloved Mother. Unfortunate circumstances, which do not need to be recalled, led to a tragic confrontation between Mother Elisabeth and an Apostolic Visitator who had been appointed to take over temporary leadership of the Order.

This was such a shock to Mother Elisabeth in her helpless condition that she seemed to suffer a slight stroke—after which she could neither move nor speak. Although she regained her speech and movement, she was ever afterward partially blind, and lame in one arm. She could sit up or get from her bed to a chair only with the aid of her Sisters. Although she never complained of this, the emotional strain had left her weaker than ever before. She had to accept the fact that she was no longer the independent Abbess of her Order.

Her faithful Sisters resented this more than she did herself. One of her daughters, Superior of a convent outside of Italy, came to see her loved Mother some weeks later. She wrote:

I saw her for the last time in February, 1956. She had lost the use of her legs and could no longer go about to look after her household, like the valiant woman in the Book of Wisdom. Now she was sitting upright in bed, her eyes bright and kind as ever. She welcomed me with her arms outstretched to embrace me, then put her hand on my head to give me her Blessing. Poor Mother! Her face was full of suffering.... For God's friends, only the bare cross remains at the end and the Chalice of sorrow and bitterness. All her life, Mother had followed in the foot-steps of Our Lord and, like Him, had suffered betrayal at the end. One year before she died, she was deposed as Abbess General—just as St. Francis of Assisi had been, before his death. Mother accepted it all as the adorable Will of God, but she felt it deeply.

Certain matters were adjusted for the good of the Order, but the new circumstances led to further trouble after Mother Elisabeth was there no longer.

Nevertheless, her work survived this crisis, as it did the later one. Perhaps because she continued to pour into it that mysterious "energy of suffering" which Teilhard de Chardin described in his remarkable little book about his crippled Sister, Marie-Marguerite. In the preface of this study, entitled *The Spiritual Energy of Suffering,* the noted scientist says: "While I, dedicated to the positive forces of the universe, was roaming continents and seas, you, immobile, stretched out, silently transformed in the depths of your soul the worst shadows of the world into light."

Surely this *energy* had gone out from Mother Elisabeth all through her life of illness and pain-offered-up. She expressed it in her talks to her Sisters, as recorded by them:

When persecution is pressing hard, it is then that I feel most the embrace of the Spouse for whom I desire always to suffer, the more the better, for I know the truth of St. Paul's words: We shall not be tried beyond our strength, the heavier the trial, the more abundant is the Grace....

Oh, never refuse Our Dear Lord anything. If he sends you trials, and He must, in order to try your fidelity, accept them, embrace them.

With the sweet experience of the Cross, we can love all humiliation, because we know that our Dear Lord desires to fold us in His loving embrace. Let it give you courage to be faithful unto death. What can be more beautiful than a life spent wholly for God—I know nothing more beautiful.

Mother Elisabeth was able to undertake a last project, which brought her great joy. She had long desired to make a foundation in America, her second homeland. It had been a great disappointment when the War blocked plans for a House in Minnesota. Now, through unusual coincidence, a country place had been offered to her, an hour from New York, in Darien, Connecticut. It had belonged to a Swedish evangelist who had come to New York at the very time when the young Elisabeth Hesselblad had migrated to the United States. Preaching in the Free Church Missions, he had met an American woman, also engaged in religious work. Together they had established an International Union Mission, with branches in Stockholm and New York. Their country house was a center for meetings and often a missionary rest home. They called it Vikingsborg, because it was situated at the head of a rocky cove, not unlike the Rock Garden, or *Skärgården*—the hundreds of islands around Stockholm.

The evangelist, was also an inventor and explorer and traveled to distant mission fields to build his work. After he died in 1917 his wife kept up the mission until her own death, in 1952. She had added a large music room, filled with trophies from many lands, in memory of her husband. Here she held weekly prayer meetings where many received help and, once, an almost miraculous healing took place.

When their children inherited Vikingsborg, it had outgrown its usefulness as a private home. But since it had been *dedicated to God's work,* they did not wish to sell it. They heard of Mother Elisabeth through the convent at Djursholm, and that it was her dearest dream to have a House in America. A member of the family traveled to Rome and was able to speak with Mother Elisabeth. She accepted the house without hesitation; with her ecumenical spirit, she appreciated that the place had

219

already been used for a Christian purpose. In her deep, commanding voice, she said: *"Vikingsborg will be a great work for God."*

After some delays, all details were arranged. Mother Elisabeth personally drew a plan for the transformation of the music room into a chapel. It was just a month after her death that four Sisters finally sailed from Italy to open the first Convent of St. Birgitta in the United States. It was her eighth foundation.

The months of 1956 passed slowly for the stricken Mother Elisabeth. On June 8, 1956, she celebrated the Golden Jubilee of her religious Profession, from her cell of pain. The Holy Father, Pius the XII, sent her a telegram of congratulation.

She had been moved to a tiny room and parlor off the second-floor stairway where she could receive Holy Communion from the convent chaplain, Father Boyer, who visited her regularly, though the office of *Unitas* had moved away. Anna Lenah Elgström was one of the last outsiders to have a short talk with her.

From Spain, where the memory of her visit and her personality was very much alive, came Father Leon, a young priest from Paredes de Nava, who had undertaken an official study of this historical town. He made a special trip to Rome early in 1957, to interview Mother Elisabeth, but found her too sick to see him. He spoke with Mother Richard and other Sisters and subsequently wrote of Mother Elisabeth: "A figure of the first magnitude in religious Rome.... On my visit to the Casa of Santa Brigida, I could sense already the breath of sanctity which she gave through her presence to this House and to the Order."

The Swedish priest, now Msgr. Henric von Essen, of the Catholic Church in Stockholm, relates how he first saw Mother Elisabeth in Rome at Eastertime, just after he had been ordained.

I had the great joy of saying Mass at the Birgitta Sisters' House. Every morning, I could say Mass in the large Chapel, or even, quite often, in the Room where St. Birgitta died. This was indeed a tremendous honor for a newly-ordained Swede. But I had one great disappointment. I had come down to Rome, having previously met all the dear Birgitta Sisters, who had been with Mother Elisabeth from the start, even the deceased Mother Katherine, and had looked forward keenly to meeting with Mother Elisabeth herself. But alas, now she was sick, lying in her bed, within the Convent enclosure, and could not receive any visits. It was a hard blow.... But one morning I was met with a gladdening message. After saying my Mass in Birgitta's Room, I was to go in to give Holy Communion to Mother Elisabeth!

There, in her sick-room, she had thought out a way of becoming acquainted with the new Swedish Priest—by letting him come to her bedside, with Holy Communion! And afterwards I was allowed to do this several times. We did not have any opportunity to talk or discuss, but I was able to come with Our Savior to His good and dedicated daughter. This, with all the personal and warm greetings and messages which were passed on to me every day when I came to the House of Birgitta, made up for the disappointment that I was not able to meet her, as I had so very much hoped to do.

During her last months, Mother Elisabeth was tended with great devotion by two of her Italian Sisters who were constantly by her side relieving each other, and one of them always sleeping in an adjoining room.

It was obvious that Mother Elisabeth was often in great pain, but she took little medicine, except for injections for her heart which were given regularly. She did not seem emaciatedly thin, although she was able to take only a few drops of milk or other liquid food.

She never felt sorry for herself, but spoke with joy, and anticipation, of the fact that she had not long to live.

"I am at the Station, waiting for the train," she used to say happily.

Speaking with the Sisters closest to her, it was touching to hear the little things they recalled, often with tears welling up in their eyes—small details in themselves insignificant, but showing the very human and loving side of Mother Elisabeth's nature, which was easily considered strong, because of her remarkable will and self-mastery, but less obvious in its gentler aspects.

Every morning, a Sister in the kitchen would send the convent cat up to Mother Elisabeth's room, with a small tidbit of meat or fish attached to his collar. She would then untie it and reward him for his visit; this clever cat amused her, and it reminded the Sisters of how she used to give them some little treat of candy or cookies or a refreshing drink if they were working overhard at some grueling task. She sometimes came to the laundry—no washing machines in those days—and gave a word of thanks and encouragement to those who were tired —or brought some story or surprise to relieve the monotony of sewing or mending.

Mother Elisabeth had no singing voice, but loved to hear her Sisters sing. She had a very good ear, and knew many songs by heart. In a weak voice, she used to hum: *Al Ciel', al Ciel' andro veder' un dio* (In Heaven, in Heaven, I'm going to see God one day).

Another song she loved was *Viva, Viva, Santissima Trinitá* (Hail, Hail Most Holy Trinity). An old Sister who was with Mother Elisabeth in those days often heard her half-whispering this line. Several months later, when a workman was preparing Mother Elisabeth's final resting place in the chapel wall, and sat down beside it to have his lunch, he suddenly started to hum this line. The Sister asked him how this happened. Had he ever heard Mother sing it? No, he answered; he had never heard it before. It just came to him as he worked there.

As her last days approached, there was no great change in Mother Elisabeth's condition. Her mind still seemed quite clear, although she could scarcely read because of her failing eyes. Two days before her departure, she had received Holy Communion, brought to her in her room by Father Boyer at 7 P.M., after he had presided at Benediction.

The evening before she died, she gave her blessing to the Sisters who were attending her, as she had many times. She looked up and murmured. "Go to heaven, with hands full"— she held up her hands in an earnest gesture—"full of love, virtues. . . ."

Later, the Sisters with her saw that her face was very ashen, and wanted to call Mother Richard.

"No—don't disturb *Mamina* (*Little Mother*)," she whispered, and seemed to go to sleep. An hour or so later, her breathing grew more labored. Mother Richard and two others arrived just as Mother Elisabeth's heartbeat seemed to falter; then, as if in final rest, she sighed deeply, and was gone into *the shadow of death.*

Soon all the Sisters were gathered around her bed, to give her their last homage of prayer and love. It was about four in the morning. A little later, the priest of their parish arrived to intone the prayers for a departing soul.

The report of Mother Elisabeth's death in the Swedish Catholic paper came directly from the *Casa di Santa Brigida:*

Her spiritual daughters in Rome inform us that for the last weeks she was very weak, and it did not seem as if her ailing heart could face the accelerated pace of spring. Her death was not altogether unexpected, but came, nevertheless, as a surprise because it had seemed as though she were a little better, during the last week. She died at four o'clock in the morning on the 24th of April, because of a heart collapse, and the end came so quickly that only a few Sisters were near her at the time. One could say that all the last weeks were a fight for life, but that the last hours were very quiet, very peaceful and without struggle —a few breaths, and her soul had gone to Her Lord, whom she had served so faithfully for all of her long life, and Who called her to Himself with the wonderful words of the Introit in today's Mass: "Come, ye blessed of My Father." After death, her face bore the most undescribably beautiful expression of nobility and rest.

For two days after her passing, Mother Elisabeth's body rested on the bed in her little reception room, surrounded by candles, and a growing wealth of flowers, and in the midst of her Daughters who prayed beside her.

Then her bier was moved to the Church where it remained another day and night. Here came a steady stream of grieving friends, who wished to see her once more, especially the poor of the district whom she had helped as a good mother in the hard times. And there were also many others to whom she had been a help and consolation in spiritual need; Sisters from other Convents, Priests and Prelates. . . .

223

Swedish newspapers honored Mother Elisabeth's memory with many articles and photographs. The account of her funeral in the *Svenska Dagbladet* was entitled: "Blue Cornflowers on Mother Elisabeth's Grave."

By our Rome Correspondent: The body of the Prioress of the Birgitta Convent in Rome, Mother Elisabeth, born Maria Elisabeth Hesselblad, in Foglavik, Västergötland, was escorted yesterday to its resting place in Verano Cemetery, in Rome. In the flower-filled Convent Church on the Piazza Farnese, the funeral Mass was said, while Sisters with white veils knelt around the simple wooden casket, with a cross of white flowers on its cover, together with a red and a yellow rose.

In the door of the Church, which was thrown wide-open on the sunlit square with its splashing fountains, the people of the district thronged in, those whom she had helped, the flower-sellers of the Campo dei Fiori, to listen to the Requiem Mass and to bring their last greetings. Many members of the Swedish Colony in Rome sat in the front pews. A great nephew, son of the brother, Dr. G. Hesselblad, represented the family of the deceased. The Vatican was represented by a pair of distinguished prelates from the State Secretariat. According to Catholic custom, no speech was made, neither in the Church nor at the grave, but the glances of those present were drawn to a burning heart which glowed in a stained glass window, and they took it for a symbol of her who had departed.

Between the lines of 29 Nuns, Mother Elisabeth's casket was carried out of the Convent which she had founded and where she had worked for so many decades. With lighted candles in their hands, her spiritual daughters accompanied her and some carried with them bouquets of flowers in the Swedish colors; yellow blossoms and blue cornflowers, followed her on her last journey, in remembrance of her homeland.

At the Verano Cemetery, Mother Elisabeth's nephew spoke a few words in Swedish, and according to the Nordic custom, threw a small bunch of flowers into the open grave—again the wild, blue cornflowers of the Swedish meadows.

A year after Mother Elisabeth's burial in Verano Cemetery, permission was obtained to place her body in the wall of the Church of St. Birgitta, near the altar, on the right-hand side, as one faces the beautiful crucifix in its azure-blue niche. On the opposite side of the wall, the burial place is seen from

224

the small, inner courtyard, within the enclosure of the Sisters' convent. Here, flowers are always kept, in a low bronze vase. . . .

So she is remembered in Rome in the House of St. Birgitta; near the Blessed Sacrament, on the one side, and on the other, with her Sisters in the intimacy of their sunlit cloister.

Epilogue

Look into the Future

THE development of the O.SS.S. has continued, and still continues, on every plane and in each country. India, in particular, has proved rich soil for the balanced plan of Mother Elisabeth, for convents combining the active life of service and the basic, contemplative practice of prayer.

In America, the Order has slowly gained its place as a convent offering Retreats and Days of Recollection, as well as taking in private guests for recreation and rest. Ecumenical meetings have often been held, and the convent welcomes guests of every faith as well as those of no particular beliefs— as indeed has been the policy of all of Mother Elisabeth's convents.

In Rome, Mother Richard was elected Abbess General in 1958. During this period various changes took place. A guest-house convent was established in Assisi, but this was subsequently given up. However, another one opened in this city of St. Francis, so beloved by Swedish travelers, in 1970.

The most surprising change took place at Vadstena, where certain Sisters wished to break away from the new branch of Rome to become an independent House, following the original cloistered Rule of the Order set up by St. Birgitta's daughter, St. Catherine. When this break was carried through, it caused much distress, and a number of Sisters left the Order entirely, at that time.

However, the Church authorities would not permit the House

226

of Vadstena to become completely independent. The Brigittine Convent of Uden, in Holland, was asked to accept the dependency of the house of Vadstena. This led to further difficulties. In 1963, the Dutch Sisters took over Mother Elisabeth's House at Vadstena, which she had founded in 1935. Recently a new wing and impressive chapel has been built.

In 1964, Mother Hilaria was elected Abbess General of the new branch of the Order, and harmony was restored to it. A third Swedish Vilohem and convent was opened in Falun, Dalarne, the very town where Mother Elisabeth had spent her youth.

In 1969, Mother Hilaria visited the five convents of St. Birgitta in Spain—the first time that a Brigittine from outside the country had been to see them since the journey of Mother Elisabeth in 1908–1909. The Spanish Sisters had frequently written to Rome, urging new contacts. After the Vatican Council, they had been encouraged to unite in a Federation, headed by a president, who could co-ordinate their different situations. Mother Hilaria was welcomed in Valladolid by Mother Inmaculada, the president, and was escorted to the convents in Paredes de Nava, Vitoria, Azcoitia, Lasarte, near San Sebastián. She stayed some days in each one, finding a vigorous life in these old, cloistered Houses, and an eagerness for future contacts with the Order in other lands.

On a visit to the American convent of Vikingsborg in 1969, Mother Hilaria went to Mexico, to find the convent founded from Spain in Mexico City. From here, two more convents had grown up, one in Puebla and another in Tacambaro. The convent at Tacambaro expressed a desire to be united with the new branch of the Order—sometimes called the Swedish branch with its center in Rome. In the summer of 1970, this desire was fulfilled with Vatican approval. Mother Hilaria assumed responsibility for this Mexican House of twenty-five Sisters. Some have gone to Lugano, others to the Vikingsborg Convent. They are now integrated as are the other Houses of the new branch, exchanging Sisters when desirable and maintaining close contact with the Mother House of St. Birgitta on the Piazza Farnese.

Here, for three years, a work of restoration and modernization has gone on. In consequence, the ancient House can now receive the flow of persons from Scandinavia who come in groups as well as individually to enjoy its peaceful and historic atmosphere. Among these are stipendiary students in Archaeology and Architecture of the Swedish Institute in Rome. The entire side of the House along the Via Monserrato has been changed, making its handsome gray marble steps the main entrance to the Guest House and giving easy access to the treasured rooms of St. Birgitta and St. Catherine.

At the same time, the crypt discovered under the church of St. Birgitta in 1966, has been transformed into a beautiful vaulted Chapel, now light and airy, large enough to hold some 80 to 100 seats. It was Mother Hilaria's concept, as a follower of Mother Elisabeth, and in her ecumenical spirit, to offer this Chapel as a place of worship for Swedish Lutherans and non-Catholics who come to this historic place. Details were worked out with Swedish authorities and the great culmination of these efforts took place on April 30, 1972, when the Chapel was consecrated and inaugurated by the Swedish Lutheran Bishop Sven Silén of Västerås and a group of Protestant Pastors, including a representative of the Lutheran Archbishop's *Curia* in Uppsala. It is now the Chapel of St. Catherine, where Protestant services may be held at a Catholic convent, in the heart of Rome!

During the year 1970, the 600th Anniversary of the founding of the Order, the State Historical Museum in Stockholm held a magnificent exhibition assembling many medieval art works representing Birgitta and her time. A small book was issued, handsomely illustrated and printed under the direction of Dr. Aron Andersson, noted historian and member of *Societas St. Birgittae.* To commemorate the 600th Anniversary of Birgitta's death, ceremonies are taking place in Vadstena and in Rome. A group of Pilgrims from the United States organized by the Guild of St. Birgitta and inspired by Margaret Sperry, Swedish-

American author, was invited to join with the *Societas St. Birgittae* in these celebrations.

The new life brought into the old Order of St. Birgitta continues to grow; its scope is international, but it is always rooted in its Swedish traditions and in the House of St. Birgitta in Rome.

Bibliography

I. UNPUBLISHED SOURCES (in the files of the House of St. Birgitta, Rome)

Diary of S. Reginalda, 1911–1920; 1923–1924.

Diary of S. Richard, 1920–1923; 1938–1945.

Letters by M. Elisabeth Hesselblad (donations to the House of St. Birgitta).

Letters to M. Elisabeth Hesselblad, from 1911.

Notes of M. Elisabeth Hesselblad, 1906–1925.

Eklund, Oskar. *The Most Extraordinary Woman in Rome.* Unpublished ms.

II. OTHER SOURCES

Adalsten, Karola. *Licht aus dem Norden.* Freiburg im Breisgau, 1951.

Chiminelli, Piero. *S. Brigida da Svezia. La Mistica del Norte.* Rome, 1930.

Flavigny, Comtesse de. *Sainte Brigitte de Suede, sa vie, ses revelations et son oeuvre.* Paris, 1892.

Graf, Ernest, O.S.B. *Blessed Richard Reynolds.*

Hesselblad, Eva., ed. *Maria Hesselblad.* Letters of M. Elisabeth to her family. Uppsala, 1965.

Jorgensen, Johannes. *Saint Bridget of Sweden.* 2 vols. Longmans, Green and Co., London-New York, 1954.

Lunden, Trygve, ed. *Den Heliga Birgitta Himmelska Uppenbarelser.* Vol. I–IV. Allram Malmö, 1957–1959.

Nyberg, Tore. *Birgittinische Klostergründungen des Mittelalters.* Leiden, 1965.

———. *De Birgittinska Ordensmannens Uppgift. Kyrkohistorisk Arsskrift,* 1968.

Unitas. Quarterly issued by the association Unitas, Rome.

Venerable Dona Marina de Escobar. Extracts from the writings of Venerable Fr. Luis de la Puente and Fr. Andres Pinto Ramirez, of the Society of Jesus. Valladolid, n.d.

Williamson, Benedict. *The Bridgettine Order.* London, 1922.